THE BATTLE AGAINST INJUSTICE

Is Justice Getting Punished?

THE BATTLE AGAINST INJUSTICE

Is Justice Getting Punished?

G. RAMA CHANDHRA REDDY

SERIALS PUBLICATIONS
NEW DELHI (INDIA)

First Published - 2010

ISBN: 978-81-8387-407-6

Published by

SERIALS PUBLICATIONS
4830/24, 1st Floor, Ansari Road
Darya Ganj, New Delhi-110002 (India)
Phone : 23245225. Fax : 91-11-23272135
E-mail: serials@satyam.net.in

CONTENTS

A.V.S. REDDY
State Election Commissioner

3rd Floor, Buddha Bhavan
M.G. Road, Secunderabad-500 003
Andhra Pradesh.
040-27535858 / 27544500 (Off)
040-27544580 (Fax)
Email: avsr_sec@yahoo.com
Website: www.apsec.gov.in

FOREWORD

Of late, it has been increasingly witnessed that various crimes are being committed with impunity, but those who perpetrate these crimes were left unpunished. This is because, in a series of high-profile cases, the criminals have not been brought to book and there is a widespread perception that the system has not delivered; since there is something wrong with the justice delivery system.

It has become a regular feature that witnesses generally turn hostile and clearly pointing to the role of money and muscle-power in a big way. It seems that the effects of money and influence extend far beyond the confines of witnesses. Frequently, the accused happen to be the kith and kin of politicians and people belonging to powerful lobby.

A combination of factors like poor investigation, shoddy prosecution, sheer incompetence, inefficiency, corrupt authorities and general insensitivity in the society have ensured that the criminals go scot-free.

An impression seems to have grown amongst the well connected that they can get away with everything and anything. In perspective, they appear to be right. It is difficult to recall an instance of any person from the power elite being convicted; in spite of scores of cases of corruption, rape, rioting and murder, went unpunished. By and large, police are the recipients alongside the bureaucracy and politicians of all hues. It, therefore, follows that the law makers and its enforcers are not feared or respected by the law breakers.

For a long time, India's judiciary has been respected for its mission, vision, independence, erudition, etc. The Supreme Court has delivered many a landmark judgment and has sometimes been a more powerful voice of the people than the legislative elite. But the entire system is so much overburdened that its nerves are so cramped, leading to breakdown of the system.

Cases have been pending for a decade or more before the courts, mainly because of constant adjournments, transfers, vacations and procedural rigmarole; thus delaying the justice rather than speeding up the process. What one gets is a mockery of justice, when one adds bribery, threats, false cases and hostile witnesses, etc., to the tally. Then, it is small wonder that these unscrupulous persons take the law into their hands.

A plethora of commissions and the resultant reports have made some practical suggestions for bringing in the much needed reform in Police administration. All the same, absence of pressure from people and the civil society has made it easier for politicians with vested and wasted interests to spoil any reform mooted in this regard. Those whose voices carry weight with the government have focused on all other issues ranging from privatization and economic reform, to foreign direct investment (FDI) and labour reform except on an urgent need for radical reform of the justice delivery system as also in administration. Many are of the opinion that only a social upheaval will bring orderliness into our polity, which could also address shortcomings vis-à-vis reforms in administrative and judicial systems.

Furthermore, most parts of the country are affected by the extremist violence. To a considerable measure, this growing spread of violent armed struggle is because of the perceived lack of a fair and equitable justice system. The answer to extremism is social, equitable and economic justice, not necessarily modernization of police forces in the country.

The 1984 riots against the Sikh community, the exodus of Pandits from the State of Jammu & Kashmir and their genocide, intrusion of migrants from Bangladesh in the north-eastern states; thus resulting in the sufferings of native inhabitants are some of the manifestations of the system, which is not being made accountable. In view of these developments, it is high time to address the foregoing concern areas of the administration in our quest for attaining good governance.

The Chief Justice of India (CJI), while addressing a Conference on "Alternative Dispute Resolution: Conciliation and Mediation," has recently warned that long periods of delay in disposing of cases would lead people to revolt and the legal system to crumble, as he made a strong plea for doubling the number of subordinate courts to 35,000. While India has developed in all other spheres, Courts are taking too much time to dispose of cases. He stressed the role of mediation and conciliation in justice delivery system. In China, only 20% cases go for trial and 80% are settled through mediation and conciliation. But in India, as the CJI believes not more than 5% of cases go for mediation. According to him, justice in India is less expensive; and therefore people are not going for mediation. The CJI is also not happy with the lawyers, citing their role in delaying cases. Even the oft quoted refrain from Justice V R Krishna Iyer that "Jail or Bail is the Hunch of the Bench" needs to be examined in detail, given the political and administrative interference while deciding the disposal of the cases. Unless positive measures are taken to increase the pace of case disposals, people will lose interest in and respect for the judiciary, which is billed as the third estate by the constitutional experts.

The book titled **"Battle against Injustice: Is Justice Getting Punished?"** authored by G Ramachandra Reddy touches all the aforementioned issues. In fact, he relates delivery of justice to the most of contemporary realities like Developments in Political & Legal Issues, Police Encounters-Instant Justice or Injustice, Advancement of Justice through the Process of

Accountability of State & Criminals, Advancing Justice by correcting wrong views on values and the YSR Phenomena, with telling effect.

All in all, the insights provided by the author in the book, with his vast experience in Police service, will add to the growing volume of Justice Delivery in India. I commend this painstaking work to the policy makers, who matter most in creating a salubrious atmosphere in all areas of Indian Administration. It is also hoped that this work will have similar value for policy people, academics, administrators and the judiciary alike due to its quality of narration and analysis in the present context of nation building.

16th December 2009 **(A.V.S. REDDY)**

Preface

Justice, according to Mr. V.R. Krishna Iyyar, Former Judge, Supreme Court, is the salt of the earth.

In this book I have attempted to relate delivery of justice with reference to

- Our defective or inadequate Constitutional Provisions.
- Abuse or blatant abuse of the legal scheme for political, parochial and corrupt ends.
- Near or total absence of accountability mechanism statutorily well defined for corruption, crimes and wrong doings. The accountability concept is the key to promotion of justice. True, fairness linked to justice as argued by Rawls is central. But fairness can be secured by proper accountability mechanism in the Indian context. Judiciary is the ultimate source of justice and if judiciary as an institution lacks accountability for its acts of corruption, inefficiency and misdemeanour, no justice is possible for realisation. Transparency and public scrutiny of public official, Minister and Judge also enhances the possibility of realisation of justice.
- **The biggest threat to Indian democracy is lack of accountability and transparency in governance.**
- Absence of fairness in decisions at the level of political and administrative executive and judiciary taken or not taken are in millions in day-to-day Governance.

- Spreading false view or fudging information by persons in responsible positions leads to unrest, crime and violence - the very anti-pode of justice. When violence engulfed in Andhra area after the announcement for separate State of Telangana, Hon'ble Minister for Finance Mr. Pranab Mukherjee said that nothing can proceed further without a resolution from the Andhra Pradesh Legislature. **The view of A.P. Legislature is recommendatory and not mandatory for** Parliament and Union Governmen to pass a bill and carve out a separate State. He is putting the cart before the horse.
- Related it to political developments and current events, the result of hasty and ill-thought out decisions.
- The use of force by police and security agencies and attempted to harmonize the use of such force and protection of Human Rights – the bedrock of justice system.
- Importance of action.

All laws - the civil, personal, criminal etc., are aimed at justice provided they are not arbitrary, discriminatory, provided further that they are enforced, interpreted honestly, speedily. The "rod of force" according to philosopher - statesman Bhismacharya is embedded in the laws of justice and without the use of force by State, public order maintenance is impossible. When I refer to the rod of force, I do not limit it to use of fire power by police and Army in the maintenance of public order, quelling insurgency, but extend it to incarceration in prison, death sentence and corporal punishments after due trial such as whipping or beating.

Accountability - Resignation of Union Home Minister

Since 2005 (The Indian Express News, dt. 08.04.2010) 1225 Security personnel lost their lives in the operations against Maoists. On 09.04.2010 Mr. Chidambaram sent in his resignation (a tokenism) owning "moral responsibility" for the botched Dantewada CRPF operation against Maoists. But there is no legal responsibility or Accountability of the police / para military leadership for failure that resulted in casualities in each of the several operations. Disciplinary action should follow prompt and severe to arrest atleast in future the irresponsible operations ordered by security and police leadership that cost unacceptable casualities. The buck of Accountability ended with the token resignation of Mr. Chidambaram and its rejection by the Prime Minister. This is called moral responsibility by a Minister in our Democracy which is totally inadequate.

I am happy that my views find support, though belatedly, in a speech delivered on the occassion of fourth R.N. Kao Memorial lecture by **Sri Mohammed Hamid Ansari, Vice President of India.** (The New Indian Express, dt. 21.01.2010). The relevant portion of this speech is as follows:

"It is hardly necessary to remind an Indian audience that ministerial responsibility to the legislature, and eventually to the electorate, is an essential element of democratic governance to which we are committed by the Constitution."

"How then is oversight and accountability ensured? The traditional answer and prevailing practice, of oversight by the concerned Minister and Prime Minister and general accountability of the latter to Parliament, was accepted as adequate in an earlier period but is now considered amorphous and does not meet the requirements of good governance in an open society".

Power Brokers

There is no accountability for the illegal wealth earned by professional power brokers which is a powerful institutions in society close to the seats of power. It is unlawful wealth. Anti-corruption law need amendment to make them accountable for their disproportionate wealth. It is true that power brokers can be booked if a conspiracy to defraud Government exchequer between public offical and power broker is proved. But to the best of my knowledge, we cannot book them for disproportionate assets which is a distinct and specific offence under anti-corruption law.

It is hoped that Accountability as envisaged by me strikes roots in our Democracy in the near future.

Tax Arrears

The Times of India, dt. 21.11.2009 discloses 2 lakh crores **Tax arrears** are to be realised – reason being that cases are contested in Special Courts, Tribunals etc., and where stay orders have been granted. How can a country be run if judicial intervention/delay like this happens? We have too many arm chair activists in the country. Social activists, RTI activists, forums for good governance identifying crime tainted etc. **We now need activists to challenge Court delays, stay orders, judgments, etc., if we want to save the country from financial ruin.** This large-scale lock-up of the Government revenue due to courts litigation will have serious impact on developmental and welfare schemes having an adverse bearing on **socio-economic justice.**

Judicial Leadership - More Courts

I have been writing in all these years on judiciary. I find ample support to my writings from Justice (Retd.) V.R.Krishna Iyer and Retd. Justice H. Suresh articles. Writing in *The Hindu* dt. 02.12.2009 Mr. Iyer Observed. "It is time we have an effective Executive which will call the bluff when judges invent alibi to explain away their incompetence and lack of integrity by asking for more number of courts". In a similar vein writing in *The New Indian Express,* dt. 03.12.2009 Justice H. Suresh observed "The Supreme Court just closed its eyes to judicial corruption and like ostrich buried its head in the sand".

Court judgements did not add sheen to the concept of justice. In interpreting Art. 21 (dealing with Preventive Detention affecting personal freedom) it is said that there is inconsistency. In A.K. Gopalan's case, it was held that freedom can be taken away by following the "procedure prescribed" by law. In latter judgements, the situation was slightly improved. The Supreme Court judgements, in respect of power of Parliament to effect Constitutional amendment (Art. 368) to curtail personal freedoms have not been unanimous and in support of Fundamental rights. Interpretation of Art. 356 (dismissal of duly elected State Government) has not advanced the cause of democratic and federal principles. In respect of compensation for the properties acquired by State, the same amorphous approach exist. The interpretation of law on reservation in public employment also suffer from vagaries. It is a matter of simple common sense that when a piece of private land is acquired by State from a marginal farmer, not a big landlord, due (market value) monitory compensation is paid or the person or his progenies are given public employment for every one or 2 acres so acquired. **These are simple common sense principles of justice which have no overtones of political party interests or which need no great depth of legal learning.**

More Powers

A wrong view is held by the political, intellectual and also judicial leadership that Chief Justice of Supreme Court suffers from "insufficiency of powers" to discipline erring Judges of higher judiciary. I do not entirely agree. The immediate cause is insufficiency of sincerity and professional honesty in invoking existing constitutional provisions of impeachment and the provisions of anti-corruption law. **Existing system though not ideal needs to be worked out before chasing for new powers.**

Public Institutions

It is not just the integrity of individuals but also that of public and social institutions that has come to be questioned. Take the case of C.B.I. as an institution losing credibility for professional integrity and impartiality. **Personal integrity, professional integrity, professional competence are three different aspects.** If a police official acquieces, compromises on account of influence and files dubious cases, closes good cases, makes unwanted arrests or does not arrest the genuine, he lacks "professional integrity" notwithstanding personal honesty. The institution of auditors colluding in the crimes of Rama Linga Raju of Satyam Infos is in public knowledge. The

University Grants Commission came under cloud for granting of recognition to 32 deemed Universities. The All India Council of Technical Education (a regulatory authority) has been accused of awarding recognition to sub-standard institutions and departments. Its Secretary Mr. Narayan Rao was caught red handed for demanding money to give recognition to an Engineering College in Hyderabad. The cricket control boards are hit by similar scandals. A whole lot of Indian institutions have betrayed the National cause. Mr. N. Ram of The Hindu, while interacting with IPS Probationers at the National Police Academy, Hyderabad on 02.05.2010 observed that corruption in the form of paid news is an awful phenomena in the Media. Press Council of India headed by Justice G.N. Ray also admitted the prevalance of this evil. In the last week of May 2010, Armed Forces Tribunal indicted Army leadership i fudging battle performance reports in 2001 Kargil War conflict. The aggrieved brigadier General Kishan Pal (Retd.) did not consider Kargil war a victory. The premier state institution of Army is in poor light both for discipline and professionalism. As a back as 2002 in an article published by me in the Hyderabad Edition of New Indian Express, I said that Kargil War is a victory without glory.

Institutionalisation of Incompetence

One of my colleague in the Tennis circuit a well read and also a winner of Gallantry Award (Retd. IGP CRPF) confirms my long held view that it is not only corruption that got institutionalised in governance but also incompetence. And this single large factor defeats justice to the last detail in the day-to-day life of common man.

Business of Profit

The wealth acquired through corrupt means by Chief Ministers, Ministers can be palmed off as though it is the result of profits of business enterprises of these Ministers, even at the cost of inflated profits reflected in Income Tax returns. Therefore you can never pin them down to an offence of "disproportionate assets" as defined in the Preventin of

Corruption Act 1988. The profits derived from business enterprise, even if they are dubious are "legal incomes", since such business is not legally prohibited. These incomes will explain the disproportionate assets. But those Ministers who do not have business to reflect legal incomes, but still have disproportionate assets can be easily fixed for the above offence. The Hon'ble Prime Minister of India came out with proposal to delink Ministerial responsibilities with business interests. Another Minister Mr. Salman Khurshid said that Business interests of Ministers can be entrusted to trusts as it happens in the USA as long as they hold Ministerial posts. Atleast since 1993 when I published my first book "Thoughts and Reflections on Law and Public Institutions" I urged for a legal ban on business of profit by all who hold constitutional posts that include Ministers. I am happy that my idea is getting acceptance in principle. However there is limitation because a Code of Conduct to Ministers is not enforceable in Courts. It lacks legal character. **Therefore it is wrong doing which goes against the grain of justice.**

The recent IPL cricket scandal touching a Union Minister reveal widespread and deepseated practice of "abuse of public office" by involvement in businesses and turning sports into business due to greed for riches by the political class. Politicians graduated in the art of "abuse of public office" and became millionaires. Subsequently they became Postgraduates and multi millionaires. Now they got Doctorates in "abuse of public office" and made themselves billionaires. "Abuse of public office" leads to wide variety of corrupt practices that include "sweat equity" valued 70 crores in favour of business women and friend of a Union Minister.

Civil Wrongs and Public Wrongs

Both are not one and the same. Justice Dinakaran is accused of civil wrongs.

- Civil wrongs are illegalised and remedies suggested in civil laws such as encroachments of Government lands.

- Public wrongs are not illegalised.

The "public wrongs" include favouritism based on party, caste, friendship and nepotism in decision taking by public authorities.

They also include

- Inaction (neglect of duties)
- Delays in administration
- Imperfect investigation that lead to accused escaping consequences of Law
- Similar imperfect Court trials
- Inaction to detect offences
- To prevent offences etc., etc.
- To protect VIP, VVIP and sensitive installations.

Compulsory voting and ineligibility to vote

These two issues were discussed by me. The former in the "preface" to the book "Threats to Indian Republic" and the latter in the "preface" to the book "Plain Speaking". All convicts, Bangladeshi illegal immigrants, criminals, terrorists, tax evaders, those defaulting on service charges such as payment of electricity, telephone bills, rent on Govt. accommodation etc., need disenfranchisement. Of course, slight change to the rules of Criminal jurisprudence is needed and it is the responsibility of judicial leadership. But these ideas did not attract national attention. But when Mr. Narendra Modi, Chief Minister, Gujarat contemplated legislation to make voting compulsory in local body elections, it is hailed as a path-breaking or historic idea by the Media mughals and intellectuals. The idea also got support from Mr. Lalu Prasad Yadav and Mr. Sriprakash Jaiswal, Union Minister. Mr. N. Gopala Swamy, former Chief Election Commissioner of India too lent his support. There is need to reconcile personal freedom of not voting with fundamental duty to vote.

Lack of legal provisoins, dubious legal provisions, gaps in law, particularly with reference to accountability makes justice a mockery.

Performance Appraisal of Bureaucracy etc

In all my writings for the last 15 to 20 years and more pointedly in Chapter 13 in the book "Challenges of Governance", I suggested (a) change/rationalisation of Annual Confidential Reports Format (b) appraisal by a Committee which is not totally dept. centric. *The Times of India,* dt. 24.12.2009 reported that there is a move where senior (Retd.) IAS Officers like Mr. Vittal are associated with such a Committee. Justice gets frustrated when undeserving Bureaucrats steal a march over the deserving by virtue of subjective assessment by immediate superior. Appraisal by a Committee checks caste ladden assessment and also corrects the timidity of departmental superior who is willing hurt but unable to do so as he lives in a glass house. On 26.05.2010 Armed Forces tribunal indicted Army leadership for fudging battle performance reports of a Brigadier in Kargil War. It is administrative injustice. Accountability for such wrong doings of the army leadership is urgently needed.

Bifurcation of Union Home Ministry

At P. 126 of the "Challenges of Governance" I suggested that veteran Police Officers like J.F. Riberio or K.P.S. Gill be made Union Ministers of State for Home to tackle terrorism which became a menace to the Nation. Media news (*The New Indian Express*) dt. 24.12.2009 suggest that Mr. Chidambaram has expressed the need for a separate Ministry to handle security issues of the State. At P.XV(Preface) to "Threats to Indian Republic" , I have argued for 'legal status' for complaints and compulsory registration. The Union Home Ministry is moving in that direction (*National Media news,* dt. 29.12.2009).

Capacity of Indian Establishment to handle Terrorism

The Times of India, dt 24.12.2009 quoted Mr. Chidambaram that luck came to the rescue of the Nation to prevent terrorist crimes like 26.11.2008 which means that he did not credit the Indian Establishment for this. In my book "Challenges of Governance" and "Plain Speaking" I said categorically that if

India is free from major terror attacks since 26.11.2008, it is largely because of the engagement and containment of terror in this part of the globe by the International Community led by U.S.A. where Pakistan was pressurised to undertake operations against terrorist groups inside its territory. It is now part of history how Pakistan is fighting terrorism to survive as a Nation. Therefore, more than luck, it is this scenario where Pakistan having been pinned down to fight its terrorist groups, is not able to sponsor major terrorist attacks on Indian soil. **At any rate Mr. Chidambaram's statement exposes the chinks in the armour of the establishment's ability to fight terrorism.**

The Importance of Knowledge

Knowledge according to Islamic Scholar Dr. Anwar Moazzam is superior to the blood of a martyr. At first I could not guess. On second thought, I agreed with him. Medical and scientific inventions like Penicillin etc., saved tens of millions of lives in the recent history. In that sense knowledge takes top billing.

This book "Battle against injustice" is a beginning. Volumes can be written on the main and sub topics of the concept of justice by enlightened intellectuals in the service of public cause.

I discern the guiding hand of providence in all my writings. I have raised in my writings issues of great importance. Only time and destiny will determine their rank in the realm of ideas. An idea when its time comes changes the course of history of Nations.

I am thankful to the respected and learned former Chief Justice Sri P. Chenna Kesava Reddy, the former Directors General of Police such as Sri M. Mahender Reddy, Sri KVV Subrahmanyam, Sri S. Chandrasekharan, Sri T. Suryanarayana Rao and above all Sri Mahmood Bin Muhammad, former Ambassador of India to Saudi Arabia and General (Retd.) K.V. Krishna Rao, former Governor, the state of J & K for the ungrudging and fulsome praise they gave to my writings.

Author
May 2010

PRELUDE / PROLOGUE

An Overview of Justice

Justice is not piecemeal or fractured concept such as division of territory of a kingdom or properties between the cousins or brothers during the times of epic Mahabharat but a broad and comprehensive one with a touch of relativity about it. More than justice in the division of territories, between the contesting cousins the **general wellbeing of the ruled** during those times does matter most in assessing the justice quotient for which of course we lack authoritative historical accounts.

- The condition of common man, special groups in society such as women, children, agriculturists, farm and factory workers, miners, weavers and other rural artisans etc. does count in making an assessment of justice.
- The nature and extent of religious, race, caste discrimination and prejudice; exploitation of human resources, talent and natural resources by the wealthy and governing classes is yet another indicator to judge justice.
- Crude and archaic social beliefs and practices of "Sati" (burning of bride on the funeral pyre of husband) prohibiting remarriage of young widows, prevalance of devadasi system, infanticide, female foeticide, unwanted and indiscriminate abortions, distress sales of girl child, human organs and trafficking in women as a business will have a telling effect on the status of social justice.

- Corruption, wide spread public and private wrongdoings, crime wave do not speak well about the quality of polity and governance and therefore needs to be factored into to judge the prevalence of Dharma/ Justice.
- Widespread poverty, illiteracy and disease are repugnant to the sense of justice that appeal to finer and sensible minds.
- Our religious texts taught compassion and care, kindness, truthfulness, non-violence as supreme forms of individual justice and at the same time identifying hatred, negative envy, pride and prejudice as negative form of justice.
- Religious duties of worshipping Gods, singing their praise, invoking their mercy, particularly the vedic Gods, Sun, Moon, Indra, Varuna, Vayu, Agni to perform their Dharma of showering bountiful rains etc., also cannot be divorced from justice as man is a part of Nature and a creation of God.
- Justice/Dharma also needs to be viewed from the viewpoint of balancing the nature and sustaining creations outside humanity. It is Dharma of carnivorous animals to kill their prey (violence) and condemnation of it will not strengthen the Law of Dharma.

The civilisation level of any country, society at any point of time needs to be judged not only from the point of civilized behavioiur of its people, materialistic prosperity of some sections of its society, development in literature, arts, crafts and technological advances but also from the criteria as to how the Rulers of the day strove and achieved advancement of justice to all sections of society or its defeat or retreat due to mal Governance of the State.

The epic 'Mahabharata' teaches: Dharma was four-footed (whole) and complete .... in (an earlier golden age) Krita Yuga .... After that dfharma declined by one foot (in each subsequent age) and adharma increased, with crime,untruth, and illusion.

Means and Ends

Justice or Dharma is subtle and its shades are different and the means employed to secure the ends are equally important. Some of the means employed to kill the mighty heros of hindu religious epic "Mahabharat" such as Bhisma, Drona, Karna, Duryodana, Jayadradha etc., are not considered ideal. Yet they were justified by Lord Krishna in the larger interests of upholding cosmic justice or correcting gross injustice inflicted on Pandavas. In his book "The Difficulty of Being Good" Mr. Gurucharan Das quotes Bhisma telling Yudhishthira about Kaushika (an ascetic without much learning) who was accosted one day by a group of robbers about a person who saw their crime. Kaushika had seen the witness person running into the forest and he knew that if he reveals, he may be responsible for the death of the witness. He must choose between the Dharma of Satya (telling truth) or Ahimsa (saving life). Kaushika choose the duty telling truth. The robbers caught the prey and killed him and for this Kaushika ends up in hell because he failed to understand that Dharma in this instance required him to tell lie to save the life of robber. One needs to be prudent. In our times, prohibition is an ideal. But since it generates revenues to the Government which can be spent on welfare measures, the ideal is abandoned. If one tells a lie to promote unity, good relations and peace, it may not offend justice.

Theories and Principles; Laws and Institutions

Theories and principles of justice are no doubt important. But more important is practice of justice by correcting or check of

- corruption
- inaction
- underperformance

It includes Court delays covering not only trials but also stay orders, review and revision petition disposals.

- Avoidance of wrong action.
- Exploitation by Governing and business classes.
- Absenteeism and misuse of time in work places.
- Wrong ideas
- Lack of Accountability
- Misuse of manpower in police and financial and other resources in Governance.

All the above represent a mammoth crime and wrongdoing in society. It is a setback to justice.

Duty/Actions – as principle of Dharma or Justice

Duties are not limited to the technical sense of the term - doing assigned job in a particular station in once's life–a job of teacher, doctor, police, military officer or civil servant, a judge or a minister etc.

According to Admiral Vishnu Bhagwat, "State officials are the custodians of Nation's ideals, of the belief it cherishes, of its permanent hopes, of the faith which makes the Nation, not a mere aggregation of individuals. They are unfaithful to their trust when by word and example, they promote a spirit that is complacent, evasive and acquisitive".

Niskamakarma - Dispassionate Action

Some western scholars viewed "selfless action" as unstained by sin as is the lotus leaf by the water of a tank. The impracticability of living in "Niskamakarma" has been expressed by Mr. Gurucharan Das in his book "The difficulty of being Good - The subtle art of Dharma". He made an analysis of traditional concepts or truths. Duty or action is one of them. He went on to quote Adam Smith that "to be self interested is to be "rational" and "prudent". Mr. Gurucharan Das went on to add "Nevertheless I did not dismiss Gita's insistent idea even though at times it seemed to me hopelessly idealistic". **According to me Niskamakarma needs to be our goal or ideal.**

The doctrine of "action" stands defined elaborately in GITA

- Desire driven action
- Giving up or renunciation of fruits of action
- Giving up action that is troublesome

For example one may perform acts of charity with a desire on the reward in next birth.

The three *Gunas* or characteristics of human nature are

- Satva
- Rajas
- Tamas

They are the causative factors for individual behaviour and action. Righteous action that covers the whole gamut of private and pubilc life is central to any scheme of justice. However right "faith" and right "knowledge" alone according to Gita it lead to right action.

According to me the "conscience" of sattavic (not tamosomic or rajasovic) persons that will also give guidance for right action. Think right for right action. The mindset matters most.

Religious philosophical thought on "action" as outlined in Gita is a guiding light for justice or is central to any scheme of principles of justice.

Action as Catalysts in Justice Delivery - A Philosophic discussion on Several Types of Actions:

I. Discriminatory Action

In some cases it is not unlawful and criminal. But it is all prevailing. Girl child in families is discriminated in subtle ways compared to a male. Though law confers equal property rights on women in practice (action) they are discriminated. Minorities, racial, religious etc., are subjected to discrimination in all societies. **An act of discrimination** by State or church or even society in the matter of religious faith and practices produces profound sense of indignity and injustice. Mr. Primakov, Former P.M., Russia in his book "A World

Challenged" by Terrorism referred to the discriminate practice of no entry into the Hindu religion temples to the untouchables in rural India which drove them to embrace Islam. Billy Graham and Dr. Margin Luther King Jr., two famous Christian Ministers of opposite side of colour divide in America, agreed that "11:00 A.M. on Sunday morning is the still most segregated hour in America". Islamic scholar claim the superiority of their creed in matters of religious practices that 11.00 A.M. Sunday segregation hour never comes. Whenever Muslims gather in mosques for prayers, Kings must bowdown next to peasants black next to whites and the rich next to poor.

Having a valid first class ticket, Gandhiji was thrown out the compartment by Railway officials in South Africa due to racial prejudice as he was not a white.

II. Selfless Action (Niskamakarma)

This benefits others who are all deserving of help or service. An act which produces good consequences covering a large section of population due to proper implementation of welfare schemes of Government, or an act of individuals and institutions that include industrial class promotes justice. Sri Satya Sai Trust, Puttaparthi funded drinking water supply scheme covering entire Anantapur district in Andhra Pradesh. There is also a super speciality hospital at Puttaparthy giving free medical assistance. Several Industrialists have funded and running hospitals etc., for the benefit of the sick. The great worth of intricate art of sculpture on temples, rock cut carving at Ajanta and Ellora, the great works of literature of ancient time, the inventions of yore in medicine do not bear the stamp of self interestedness. It is an activity for the excellence of the work according to me. Selfess Action includes performance of duties assigned in the present station in life to perfection without expectation of reward, recognition or some sort of gain and gratification of senses.

III. Selfless yet Unlawful and Criminal Action

- Some fake police encounters are undertaken without self interest of career advancement or for monetary consideration but in the larger societal interest. Yet they lack lawfulness in action. So Niskama Karma needs to be lawful apart from being selfless or disinterestedness.

- According to Mr. Fonseka, Former Army Chief, Sri Lanka, a section of LTTE leadership which was willing to surrender in 2009 was shot dead by the Sri Lankan Army at the instance of its Defence Secretary. This is yet another instance of unlawful action.
- Nazi officials during World War II also felt that they are discharging state duty in exterminating Jews and that there is no selfishness involved.
- Disproportionate use of force in ordinary law and order situations - unlawful.
- When Gandhiji was thrown out of first class Rail compartment in South Africa having a valid ticket, there is no selfishness, but there existed racial prejudice.

IV. Selfish and Wrongful Action

- Doing business of profit by a Minister or Chief Minister.
- **Usurping "powers", "positions" & "functions" etc**: Usurpring (not properties of others) "positions" fall under wrong action. In history, kith and kin overthrew lawful kings and ursurped thrones. Military rulers usurped the position of lawfully elected Presidents. In 1993, One M.L.A. in Andhra Pradesh usurped the position of Chief Minister by dethroning his father-in-law. In 2009, by manipulation, the Governor of Andhra Pradesh and the Congress High Command deprived Y.S. Jagan of the position of Chief Minister. Senior Police and Army officers usurp the "credit" of juniors and claim Gallantry and other awards. Judiciary usurped the "power" of executive. Senior officers and Ministers usurp the "functions" of juniors. *Late Smt. Indira Gandhi quoted her Grand Father on two kinds of persons- those who work and the second who take credit for the work of others. The later are in absolute majority in our Republic.*

- Spreading false views that corrupt an entire society needs to be placed in the above category. Example: Multi National drug companies (Allopathy medicine) through some Scientists condemn alternative medical disciplines such as Homeopathy, Ayurveda, Unani as useless though tens of millions of people use the later. **Such spread of false views have the effect of deceiving the society to think otherwise.**

V. Malafide Actions

Malafide actions falls into three or more categories. Some are unlawful and criminal and some are not. One category is where pecuinary loss is caused to public exchequer with corresponding gain to self or third party in the exercise of public power. This is an offence under The Prevention of Corruption Act, 1988. The others are where there is no pecuniary loss to the exchequer. They include distribution of party tickets from Parliament to Panchayat based on favouritism and similar distribution of party posts. Government appointments to the posts of Chairpersons of various Corporations and Board of Directors also fall in that category. In September 2009 Delhi Government released one Mr. Sharma, a murder case convict on parole on dubious grounds. This was opposed by Media and corrected by Judiciary as the decision was malafide. **Ill thought, arbitrary and capricious actions (not unlawful and criminal)**

Two District Grandalayas (Libraries) namely Warangal and Visakhapatnam purchased my books after due procedure. The books were supplied in the month of March, 2009. Meanwhile on certain allegation of fraud in purchases, the Minister's Secretariat issued orders to the Director, Public Libraries, Hyderabad to stop payments to the Authors / Publishers. I challenged the order in Writ Petition No.26557/2009 in the Hon'ble High Court of Andhra Pradesh on 03.12.2009. The challenge is that books were supplied on the order placed by lawful authorities and there exist contractual right for payment. If there is fraud, the Department can cause enquiries and suspend the concerned official or effect recovery of loss if any from such officials but not stop payment to Authors / Publishers. Meanwhile even before the matter is decided by Court and after getting notice from Court if the Minister gave exemption in my case and I received the payment in the month of January 2010. But other Publishers, who did not choose to challenge are yet to be paid for the books supplied. Therefore here the Minister concerned is acting arbitrary, capricious by though there is no proof of malafides in his action. In a case or two in a million malafide actions taken to Courts, Ministers can be held accountable. But in respect of arbitrary, capricious action (wrong action) which affect the principle of justice, there is no Accountability of the Minister as they are not criminalised by law. However all such decisions which are in millions hurts justice. But in a few cases where a person appoaches courts, injustice can be corrected.

VI. Rash and Negligent Actions

- Rash, thoughtless exercise of public power of using disproportionate force by police and security agencies. February 2nd week of 2010 witnessed a boy of 16 years being shot dead by BSF Personnel in the state of Jammu & Kashmir for simple reason of abusing the police. There is no selfishness. But it is a grave wrong action with potential to spread violence.
- Rash and negligient driving on roads though deprived of selfish element causes death and injury to lakhs of people.
- Neglect of duties (inaction) or under performance in natural calamities causes death and destruction.

VII. Corrupt Actions

According to Author Arundaty Roy, all democratic institutions-political, judicial and administrative etc., are purchasable. There is no justice unless we arrest this bribal culture. Democratic Governments in the country are available for purchase by National and Multi National Companies. According to me corruption is anti-pode of justice. Of course, it falls under illegal action.

VIII. Unrightful Action

Celibacy. I do not call it wrong action. It can be unrightful. This lead to ill effects / evil such as paedophile, committed not by ordinary mortals alone but by papacy in Europe. Pope in Rome was criticised for inaction on this crime. One unrightful action lead to another.

IX. Lawful and Rightful Actions

Dharma or justice needs to be both "lawful" and "rightful". A law may not be necessarily rightful. Gandhiji waged public movement against unrightful law which denied voting rights to the Indians settled in South Africa. A call to the cessation of Economic activity (Hartal) in British India was unlawful though it is a rightful action unaccompanied by any violence. In the same way civil disobedience a rightful act was also treated as unlawful. Actor turned Politician Kushabo justified premarital sex. Since it is not illegalised, it becomes legal. Yet it is considered as unrightful by the society at large. The problem of same Gotra marriage though not prohibited by the Hindu Marriage Act 1956 is condemned as unrightful. In the state of Haryana it lead to violence recently and also created social storm. So one need not view law alone as fountain of justice. Social, customs, traditions, religious practices in society lay claim to justce. In the same breath, it can be said that several wrongful acts were not declared illegal by the rulers of the day because law reflects largely the concerns and interests of ruling elite. Only actions which are both rightful and lawful lead to justice - the rest in injustice.

Except right and selfless action, the rest of the actions results not in service but disservice. Ill thought out, ill prepared and irresponsible action of sending 62 company of CRPF in the jungles of Chattisgarh on 06.04.2010 by the CRPF leadership resulted in infliction of 76 CRPF casualities by the Maoists.

One therefore needs to guard oneself against not only selfish actions but also the above mentioned criminal and wrongful actions to ensure justice.

Inaction and Underperformance

Inaction became an **easy option** in our administrative culture, 50% of the cases U/A 226 in various High Courts are for correction of inaction of public authorities. It was and is not only tolerated but romanticized. During 1945-46 communal riots in West Bengal, a complaint of abduction of Hindu Women by Muslim youth was cold shouldered by the then English Governor with the remark that it is a natural because Hindu Women are more beautiful. In all these years, I have highlighted in my writings, the wrong doing of inaction of public authorities. Not just inaction by a petty official but also by senior officials, judges, police officers, Army Generals, Ministers, Chief Ministers etc. After Madhu Khoda episode in Jharkhand State and of Gaali brothers in Karnataka, the Union Minister for Mines Mr. B.K. Hindique blamed Chief Ministers of States for "inaction" on illegal mining (The Hindu news dated 03.12.2009). Indictment is normal when a crime surfaces. But where is accountability for inaction and consequent loss of royalty revenues? Similarly inaction of public authorities/police officers on intelligence inputs on terrorist strikes, communal riots or sabotage as in the case of Kaiga Atomic Plant in Karnataka will have serious repercussions to the public peace and the Nation. **Serious inactions are far more dangerous than corruption, which need criminalisation and prosecution.** I can cite the cases of 1984 Anti Sikh riots, 1993 Babri Masjid demolition, 2002 Anti Muslim riots in Gujarat.

As the book goes to print, there is Media News (Times of India, dt. 12.02.2010). It is reported that many social sector schemes proposed by the Union Government have become a cropper as the money earmarked has not been spent. According to the Comptroller and Auditor General of India "A budgetary grant or appropriation not utilized indicate either poor budgeting or shortfall in performance or both". Media report suggests that while the Government is grappling with huge fiscal deficit and hence large borrowings to fund key social sector schemes, a staggering sum of 1 lakh crores in an year out of the money allotted to various Ministries remained unspent between 2005-06 and 2007-08. Unspent provisions of Rs. 100 crore each or more alone total Rs. 59,000 crore in these three years according to CAG. What is worse the CAG has pointed out that there is uncertainty even about whether all the amounts shown as spent in the Government accounts have actually been spent. In 2007-08 more than Rs. 51,000 crore was allotted under various flagship schemes in which the money is directly transferred to the Bank accounts of NGO's, autonomous bodies and District Authorities The CAG doubted whether these amounts have been spent or lying idle in their accounts. The unspent grants are an indicator of poor budgeting mechanism and failure of its monitoring tools which results in injustice due to unspent financial allocations.

There are communists whose literaray works aimed to benefit the lot of deprived and poor. There are modern day Maoists, Dalit movements, Revolutionary writers who want State power in favour of the hither to deprived classes. Are we to say that they are performing "Niskama Karma" or Karma which advances justice to a section of the populace which hitherto remained outside (in India) the power structure?

Therefore a larger debate on **action, inaction, selfless action, rightful action, selfish and criminal acttion** is called for the right education of the public at large and the governing classes, business classes in particular. World has changed a whole lot since the days of small republics in the days of Mahabharat. **The debate on action, selfless action, inaction, rightful action, unlawful action will continue to engage thinkers of all ages.**

Having attempted to understand "action" and also its different manifestations, it is useful to refer to some of the Constitutional provisions, the enforcement and interpretative process at which caused miscarriage of justice.

- **Art. 74(1):** deals with Council of Ministers to aid and "advise" the President. Art. 74 (2) states that the question whether any, and if so what, "advice" was tendered by Ministers to the President shall not be inquired into by Courts. Art. 75 (1): The Prime Minister will be appointed by the President and other Ministers appointed on the "advice" of Prime Minister. Art. 75 (2): The Ministers shall hold office during the "pleasure" of the President.

- The mode of appointment of Prime Minister becomes arbitrary if it is not spelt out in the language of the Article itself that a person who commands majority in Parliament should be called upon to be appointed as Prime Minister. We cannot leave such important matters to Courts to decide keeping in view the flouting of democratic practice of proved majority in Parliament by the President and more particularly in State Assemblies by the Governors as it happened recently in Andhra Pradesh. Secondly Ministers are appointed on the "advice" of Prime Minister or Chief Minister (in respect of Art. 164). What advice is tendered is not open or transparent. **That makes the Constitutional provision non-transparent and therefore undemocratic.** In the same way Art. 75 (2) speaks about Ministers holding office during the "pleasure" of the President. This word "pleasure" is too arbitrary to make it a democratic word. To make it democratic, viable criteria need to be spelt out in the Article such as *(a)* the Minister concerned is not crime or corruption tainted or convicted for these offences or *(b)* has failed to effectively perform duties allotted or *(c)* is guilty of a public or private wrongdoing. In the absence of definitive criteria, removing a Minister at the "pleasure" of President which effectively means pleasure of Prime Minister dictated by party leadership becomes undemocratic and unjust. **Such lack of viable criteria in Ministry formation gives advantage to crime tainted, rich and moneyed classes.**
- Art. 355, 356 - dealing with proclamation of emergency and imposition of President's rule in a State - grossly unused.

- Art. 164 - dealing with appointment of a Chief Minister and Ministers by the Governor - grossly unused.
- Art. 200, 254, 255 - dealing with the powers of Central Government to approve State legislative bills on public order and Terrorism - misused.
- Art. 156 - dealing with appointment of Governor - No criteria or objectivity in appointments.
- Art. 361 - dealing with immunity from Accountability for the actions of the Governor - unjust.
- Art. 151 - powers of Comptroller and Auditor General of India - his recommendations are not acted upon by the Government.
- Art. 292 - Parliament's power to control finances - failure to exercise such power leads to injustice.
- Art. 84, 102, 173, 191 - dealing with qualification and disqualification required for MP, MLA. - Anachronic provisions.
- Art. 309 – 312 - All India Services - Misused or unused for wrong ends.
- Art. 32, 226 - dealing with Writ powers of Higher judiciary -abused occasionally.
- Art. 368 - dealing with amending powers of Constitution by Parliament - invariably abused by the Executive.
- Art. 124, 127 - dealing with appointment of Judges of Higher judiciary-lacking transparency and objectivity.
- Art. 105 (2) - dealing with Members of Parliament accepting bribes in transacting Parliamentary business- exempted from criminal prosecutions.
- Art. 3 - now a burning topic regarding carving out new States.

Most of these Constitutional provisions make Accountability and Transparency of Governance that include Judicial Governance a casualty. This makes our Democracy ritualistic in the sense of holding periodic elections to political institutions from Parliament to village panchayat. Neither poverty levels are brought down nor is the economy as strong as it is in China. There is lack of justice.

I have given a few instances. They are illustrative though not exhaustive.

RULE OF LAW: Rule of Law is not mere law as is generally understood. Rule of Law is life blood of justice

According to Prof. Dicey, Rule of Law is a principle of fair play and equity. In my book "Challenges of Governance" I have discussed this principle in a separate chapter. Rule of Law is higher than law or even a Constitutional provision. The latter needs to conform to Rule of Law viz., principle of equity and fair play. It is not just laws and Constitutional provisions which need to conform to Rule of Law in a true Democracy, but also all decisions taken by the political, administrative or even judicial functionaries **I give a few examples for better understanding of the concept.**

- There is threat to Rule of Law when one public functionary sits in judgment of his own action or organisation doing the same.
- Hitherto police investigated either by itself or through CID (a branch of police) cases of suspicious deaths that include cases of custodial deaths, deaths in police encounters. This goes against the grain of Rule of Law. An independent legal forum such as an enquiry by a Magistrate will conform to the principle of Rule of Law.
- The Government viz. political Executive have power of withdrawal of criminal prosecutions (Sec. 321 Cr.P.C. 1973) pending in Courts. During 1980s two Chief Ministers (Mr. Jagannath Mishra of Bihar and Nandini Satpathi of Orissa) faced criminal prosecutions for corruption. When they were returned to power, they withdrew criminal prosecutions against themselves from Courts record. Though the matter was challenged in Supreme Court, the main issue got

skirted for a decision. Here there is violation of Rule of Law. One is sitting in judgment in one's own case. Therefore such withdrawals though permissible legally, will conform to Rule of Law only when a decision is taken by Chief Ministers other than the accused Chief Ministers.

- There is threat to Rule of Law
  (i) Where there are no proper checks and balances in the judicial appointments, particularly higher judiciary. Where it becomes judicial centric - such as a committee of Judges of Supreme Court (to the exclusion of political Executive or any other body or a commission which has fair representation for outsiders) making appointments.
  (ii) Where lower judicial appointments are not regulated by independent body like UPSC and where they are centralised in High Courts. Absence of any law on the pattern of **All India Services Act 1950** to regulate recruitment to lower judiciary makes such appointment arbitrary.
  (iii) Where an enquiry into substantive charges of corruption against a judge becomes judicial centric and which bars other legally established agencies of enquiry and investigation.

This Rule of Law breathes life into the concept of justice and strengthens the root of Democracy.

These examples are illustrative and by no means exhaustive.

Shadow Boxing with non-existing Legal Provisions

There is a whole lot of shadow boxing with legal provisions - their application and interpretation included. I give a couple of examples.

Sec. 129 Cr.P.C. 1973: It deals about dispersal of "Unlawful Assemblies" of 5 or more persons and use of "as little force" and cause "as little injury" to person and property. But the above legal provision has not covered the following public order situations such as

- "Armed riotous mobs" with deliberate purpose of unleashing violence.
- "Armed gun battles" between police/security forces and outlaws that include Terrorists.
- "Subversive Gatherings" or groups of armed people who blaze their guns and blast landmines and procure and prepare guns and landmines.
- "Mass uprisings" against atrocity perpetrated by person or a group in society or even committed by police and security agencies.
- Situations: Where intelligence inputs suggest that terrorists are planning to strike targets. Are we to wait for them to strike or preempt such a strike timely and decisively?

An unlawful assembly dispersal is totally different from handling of the above situations.

Unfortunately, the same legal yardstick (Sec. 129) is applied uniformly in their handling.

In the same way, recourse to use of force in "self defence" U/s. 97, 103 IPC 1860 is also indefensible by public authorities (security and police, forest official, customs officials etc.). Sec. 97 mentions about "right of private defence" against person and property by "every person". This "every person" cannot be construed and include "public authority". True right of private defence is available to private persons and public authorities as interpreted by Courts. But "Public Authority" is not spelt out in legal provision of self defence from Sec. 96 to 106 IPC 1860. There is error in judicial interpretation.

What is not **statutorily** spelt out cannot be overstretched by interpretative process. So Sec. 129 Cr.P.C. and Secs. 97 to 103 IPC 1860 need to the best of my knowledge appropriate amendments in handling public order and terrorist conditions, instead of leaving them to shadow boxing by police and judicial leadership.

Fasts now occurring in Andhra Pradesh for and against separate Telangana State is self mortification of flesh. It cannot be legally a suicide. Yet mechanically, Sec. 309 IPC 1860 (attempt to commit suicide) is applied by police and accepted by judiciary. Therefore this shadow boxing of law needs to end.

The recent judgment of a court sentencing accused in Bhopal gas tragedy for 2 years of imprisonment U/s. 304 A IPC (Rash & Negligent Act) caused public outcry for leniency of punishment. When there is no legal definition for an offence of the magnitude of the tragedy and prescribing deterrent punishment of life imprisonment, the police and courts have to be content with shadowboxing or misapplication of inadequate legal provision such as Sec. 304 A IPC.

It is unfortunate that police and security agencies are condemned to work with **dubious legal provisions** such as Sec. 129, 174, 176, Cr. P.C. 1973 and Sec. 94 to 106 IPC 1860 in handling the terrorists and outlaws particularly in respect of "gun battles". Even more unfortunate is that custodian of the Constitution, laws, rule of law viz., the Supreme Court of India in its long history of 60 years has not rightly judged these dubious legal provisions or pointed out their short comings. **Guidelines issued by Courts are no substitute for precise legal provision. There is miscarriage of justice under criminal law.**

Soft laws, softer enforcement, softest interpretation of criminal, civil, company, tax laws bred not justice they intend to promote but legal injustice. Some of the well meaning socio-economic legislation are bogged down in corruption defeating justice. Prevention and punishment of criminals under all laws is important aspect of justice which the Indian state failed miserably to correct.

The Constitution - What it means?

Reservationists, libertarians, corruption and crime tainted have a good go or field day in the Constitutional stakes. The legal fraternity that includes Judges and lawyers are also happy as it throws up a lot of work and creates more number of Judges posts. In the same way Governing classes whose record for frequent and widespread violation of citizens rights through their inaction, wrong and malafide action, corrupt and high handed or arbitrary action are also happy in the sweep stakes of the Constitution, the legal framework and the existing public institutions. All are happy with the prevailing *status quo,* protected or undisturbed by the Constitutional scheme. For the patriot, the honest and the efficient Indian, the Constitution promises nothing. Of course welfarism politics took care of the needy poor or even deprived the poor of initiative to work or develop skills in various trades and crafts. For the poor (some 300 million) the Constitution is not appealing. **The awareness and awakening of civil society, launching possible public struggles can make possible, a new Constitution where Accountability and transparency are firmly rooted in legal provisions to make the Constitution to adopt the Democratic spirit and temperament of the times.**

We adopt Constitution, frame laws, create institutions to advance justice. But all this result in monstrous injustice to society - all in the name of justice primarily because of misuse of Constitutional and legal provisions by persons incharge of the institutions and their ability to get away without Accountability. Justice is denied to the common man, honest citizen in day-to-day life.

The preamble to the Constitution mentions India as a soverign socialist secular democratic republic and to secure to all its citizens justice, social, economic and political, liberty of thought, expression, belief, faith and worship, equality in status and opportunity, fraternity. The Directive Principles (Arts. 36 to 52) enjoin the state to follow certain principles of policy which *interalia* include State's duty to protect environment, forests and wild life, protection of monuments and places and objects of National importance, promotion of internal peace and security. Neither the preamble of the Constitution, nor the Directive Principles cast duty on the State to protect the lives, liberties and properties of its 90% of peace loving, crime free citizens. This is not a stated goal of the State. **More than security of environment, forests, wild life, monuments etc., human security gets top billing.** It is common knowledge that State (its Public Authorities) have endangered thousands of lives of innocent by neglect or design or by both where communal forces, terrorists and Maoists caused blood shed. Unless this basic duty of the State evades enshrinement as a right or a Directive Principle and public authorities held Accountable, I am certain that blood letting will continue unabated. **National issues like terrorism, crime and corruption are trivialized by the Rulers in the last two decades**. The State is a delinquent in the discharge of its duties.

Author
May 2010

1

Delivery of Justice

Justice is said to be king of kings. The incarnations of Supreme God, it is said, also take birth on planet earth to correct injustices or to uphold "Dharma" meaning justice.

Justice is one of the Constitutional values along with Democracy, Secularism and Social Justice.

The idea of delivery of justice has begun rather than culminate with my effort. Our knowledge of justice is as vague as it is vast. One should be able to distinguish between the ethical and political conception of justice where the rights, powers, privileges, dignity of the Governing classes need to be subordinated to the welfare of the Governed.

Philosopher – King

Sage Socrates identified knowledge with virtue and vice with ignorance. Knowledge refined is wisdom (Gnan). Are all knowledgeable people virtuous and the illiterate wicked? The question defies precise answer. A just man according to Socrates is one who knows what is just or right. He traced justice to both man made laws and the Divine law which guided or continues to guide mankind. I see meanings in the above reference of Socrates to law. **For according to me, we do not have man made laws that regulate charity, kindness, love and caring, impartiality, efficiency, in human conduct**

and working. But these values are prevalent in their limited way because of the guiding hand of God. **And there is no guarantee that man made laws are fool proof in justice delivery.** Plato made threefold analysis of human soul into

- Rational
- Spiritual
- Sensual or appetitive faculties

From the interrelationship of these elements, Plato drew definition of particular virtues.

- Courage - was the subordination of the spirited to the rational faculty.
- Temperance - the subjection of the appetitive to rational.
- Justice was described as a regulative virtue, which produces general harmony in character and good order in conduct.

A just man according to Plato is like a well ordered city. The unjust is likened to Anarchy. If we go by his thesis, violence which stalks India on an unprecedented scale unceasingly represents an unjust State.

Knowledge has several disciplines

- Scriptures - theology
- Law
- Literature
- Inventions in medicine and surgery
- Invention in Agricultural and domestic tools
- Dance and Drama
- Divine Music
- Art and Sculpture etc., etc.
- Scientific inventions of the last 3 centuries

History of mankind has not proven that justice and right action are the prerogative of knowledgeable. The knowledgeable are not free from corruption and other crimes nor are they free from Favouritism and Nepotism.

I had occassion to read **Mr. Amartya Sen's** book "The idea of justice". He is an Author per excellence. Mr. Sen gave an interview to The Times of India, dt. 27.07.2009 outlining the contours of justice which is a very serious subject of study by the rulers and laymen alike Mr. Sen noted manifest injustices as follows:

- Slavery
- Subjugation of women
- Wide spread hunger and deprivation
- Lack of schooling
- Absence of available and affordable health.

In our country according to him we need to concentrate on removing injustices that are identified and removable. **There needs to be a systematic assessment of how to reduce injustices in the world.**

The subject is indeed vast and complex. Injustices, inequality abound in all spheres as evil is a part of creation. Some persons, a part of society are continuously visited with injustices, defeat, disease, ill fame, poverty, while others are visited with success and glory, justice, health, riches and fame etc. This can be only explained from an understanding of the religious doctrine of **cause and effect**. One's own good and bad deeds of the past lives hold a mirror to the current situation.

But that does not mean that governments and institutions, various organisations in society should adopt hands off policy. We create institutions, post persons to man them, reform the institutions, make additions to their numbers, enact laws etc., in order to mitigate injustices. But injustice like evil cannot be eliminated. **Only effort can be made to mitigate it.**

Every ruler, the ancient, the medieval, the modern seek state power in the name of justice; though they end up serving justice to themselves, friends, sycophants, and political followers as well as those who support their wrong doings in the power structure. **Even Maoists and Terrorists see justice in their cause**. Mindless violence is justified for people's justice.

Sri Amartya Sen's book "The idea of Justice" dwelt on various abstract theories of justice. Based on these and improving on them he constructed his own theory of justice. Mr. Sen is a winner of Nobel Prize in Economics. Mr. Sen calls Economics as a "dismal science" with cheerless readership.

While writing the book which concerns mainly political and moral philosophy, Mr. Sen exhibited a wide range of scholarship on the subject of justice.

The improvement he wrought on the subject of justice lies in advancing the enlightened tradition of **reducing injustices** rather manifest injustices which were pursued in different ways by Adam Smith, Condorcet, Wollstonecraft, Bentham, Mill and Marx.

Fairness and Justice

Mr. Sen extensively quotes political philosopher John Rawls on the subject of justice. **Rawls focused on fairness as justice.** And fairness extends to establishment of just institutions as well as the right behavioural pattern or right conduct and action of men who operate these institutions. Fairness as justice which is central to the thought of John Rawls envisages according to me action free from bias, from arbitrary and authoritarian decisions. While there is no fundamental disagreement with Rawls' views, Mr. Sen quotes a few examples of how justice is answered beyond the pale of **state institutions.** He cites American civil war that lead to the **abolition of slavery** which he terms as manifest injustice. Slavery was legally abolished. But segregation still exists for which affirmitive action by the state is needed. There are also according to me in the contemporary political situation, instances of how justice is sought and some times achieved by political agitation and also through revolutionary movements. The Maoist movement in India indirectly impacted several socio-economic measures that benefited the lives of marginalized sections. The left parties (Communists) are in the thick of political agitation for land distribution, removal of unauthorized occupation of Govt. lands by vested interests and also in opposing the allotment of land to industrialists by

Govt. for Special Economic Zones. Their fight is against injustice perpetrated by Democratically elected Governments, by neglect or design or both.

Democracy Synonymous with Justice

Mr. Sen recognized the innate relationship between Democracy and Justice in which justice needs to be judged "not only by the **institutions** that exist but the extent to which the voices from different sections of society can be actually heard". He differs from Mr. Rawls when he states "that success of Democracy is not a matter of having perfect institutional structure but also depends on actual behavioural patterns and the working of social and political interaction". There is no chance of trusting the virtuosity of the institution. He did not elaborate on the working of social and political interaction. He probably had in view, when he spoke about not trusting the virtuosity of institutions, the situations and times when institutions get moribund as we see in India.

Mr. Sen feels that Democracy can be seen as Government by discussion (quoting John Stuart Mill) and not a mere well fought election. But I must add that even in the fiercely fought periodic elections in the cause of democracy, injustices lurk in different shades and colours. Electoral irregularities, electoral frauds, corruption open the doors to injustice. So Mr. Stuart Mill's views find partial remedy to the subject. Democracy is a form of Government that is supposed to promote justice. But the means chosen to attain Democracy are turning out to be corrupt and violent. Not only in India but also in Iran, Indonesia, Afghanistan and some East European countries political parties are responsible for this situation. The champions of the political ideal of Democracy are aiming to promote justice-political, economic and social. But they end up by resorting to unjust practices / crimes all of which complete the chain of injustice in the conduct of election process that ushers the rulers to the seat of state power. So the path to the democratic state power is fraught with perils of several crimes and injustices. **Electoral malpractices, corruption, violence are the antipodes of justice.**

Impact of Public Reasoning

Another improvement which he suggested is that **public reasoning** is central to the idea of justice and goes on to quote reasoned philosophical dialogue in Bhagavad-Gita between Lord Krishna and warrior Arjuna on the merits of war where several Gurus (Teachers) and kith and kin are pitted against him. This fits into his theory of justice viz., deontology versus consequentialism, Arjuna represents consequentialist, while Lord Krishna represents deontologist. Mr. Sen also quoted Moghal Emperor Akbar (16th Century A.D) who emphasized public reasoning in the conduct of state affairs. Akbar's efforts helped to reduce injustices in social practices which prevailed in India such as (a) child marriage (b) young widows not allowed to marry.

Enhancement of Justice

Mr. Sen mentions about reform of institutional structure at global level such as reform of **patent law** to make drugs for AIDS etc., available easy and cheap. This according to Mr. Sen falls under the scheme of **enhancement of justice.** In the same vein, it can be argued that U.N. the Apex International body requires a thorough reform. Even according to Mr. Obama, U.S. President, U.N. requires fundamental Reform as several of its resolutions do not breath justice to the countries outside the powerful and chosen group of U.S., West Europe countries. In the same way world trade agreements need to breath justice to all the participating nations.

Mr. Sen also mentioned about non - parochialism as an attribute of justice. In the Indian conditions one can safely conclude that **partiality** based on nepotism, castiesm, party, hurt the cause of justice immensely.

Neeti and Nyaya

In support of his view point on justice Mr. Sen fell back on Sanskrit literature which gave expression to **Neeti** and **Nyaya** both of which are two sides of the same coin. Neeti represents organisational propriety, rules and procedures while Nyaya represents comprehensive concept of attaining justice (an abstract term indeed). "The central recognition he argues, is not just a matter of judging institutions and rules but judging societies themselves".

According to me in the context of Indian criminal justice system, where Court trial of criminal cases or even in the enforcement of Preventive Detention laws, **rules of procedural fairness** advanced justice to the criminals while denying the same to the society.

Impact of World Events

Mr. Sen pointed out how global concerns such as economic recession in the U.S.A. and West, global terrorism affect the lives of other nations and the concept of justice.

"First, what happens in this country, and how its institutions operate, cannot but have effects, sometimes huge consequences, on the rest of the world. This is obvious enough when we consider the operation of world terrorism or attempts to overcome their activities, or events such as the US-led invasion in Iraq, but the influences that go beyond national borders are altogether omnipresent in the world in which we live."

International Peace Treaties, Extradition Treaties, Economic Treaties etc.

These treaties according to me need critical review as to whether they ushered in justice to all Nations and its people. For example, the **Treaty of Versailles** was considered unjust and it lead to rearmament and out break of world war II shattering world peace. Therefore one needs to look at the prevailing situations / conditions in various epochs in societies and take corrective and constructive steps to preserve peace and justice.

However in his book of more than 400 pages Mr. Sen did not touch on specific laws, Constitutional provisions, or other institutional infirmities, various situations and conditions in which justice is denied or compromised in the Indian context in the last 60 years of our Republic.

So I pick up from where he left and attempt to state how political, judicial, administrative powers, the exercise there of kept the scales of justice unbalanced.

Justice is a splendid ideal. It is sought often not only by democratic ideal but also by communist ideal. Communist ideal emphasises economic justice. Democratic ideal stresses both political and economic justice. **There is no absolute justice**. One needs to bridge the gap between justice and injustice.

Exercise of Public Power

Realisation of justice primarily according to me is an enormous **exercise of public power** for which the laws of a Sovereign Nation and the institutional infrastructure needs to be sound and just. And at the same time the persons who implement the laws, man the institutions need to be persons of high degree of rectitude and efficiency in order to ensure justice in a given society. Of course the institutional mechanism as David Gauthior pointed out needs to have proper checks and balances. But I add that they need to work in a transparent way and persons incharge of them being made accountable for non-performance, wrong doing and corruption. The problem of right institutions and right person to head them is a challenging problem in the Indian context and realisation of justice is becoming increasingly difficult.

Constitutional Justice

Justice is not an abstract concept to be discovered or rediscovered from the writings of the Philosophers of yore or from the musty legal parchments. It is as much a living, a dynamic concept that operates in every one's every day life. **For attaining justice, people adopt a Constitution, the rulers frame laws, the laws create institutions and the rulers appoint individuals drawn from various streams of service to man these institutions.** With all this, justice remains elusive sometimes becomes a mirage. The preamble to the Constitution of India speaks about ushering in justice social, political and economic to its citizens. And justice is not a mere ideal expressed in Constitutional texts. **Constitution will only reflect the spirit of time at which it was made.** But to realise the ideal, there needs to be down to earth **clinical analysis** (periodic) of the working of the legal provisions, institutions and individuals manning them. **Constitution of India while eloquently expressing about ushering in justice social, economic and political, has also permitted enactment of special legal provisions to secure justice to socially and educationally backward classes which at this point of time became controversial to deliver justice to all sections of society.**

Inequality in Devolution of Power

When the Constitution was written, the powers of the three organs of State viz., the Legislature, Judiciary, the Executive were defined. It happens that judiciary is given more powers. It is also true that there is unequal distribution of power among the various functionaries of the Executive. For example, the President of the Republic, Governors in States do not have real powers. Then again in a federal set up or Quasi Federal, like India, the Centre enjoys more powers at the expense of states. **Consequently, it can be said that justice is diluted on account of unequal devolution of power.** This analogy extends to other political institutions such as the local bodies which are clamouring for decentralisation of power. Power includes financial powers too. **For justice to be meaningful, local bodies need more powers that include financial powers.**

50% Reservation to women in political institutions of village Panchayats

Media reported on 28.08.2009 about the Union Cabinet decision to reserve 50% of seats to women in village Panchayats by amending the relevant provisions of Indian Constitution. Hither to there existed 33% reservation. It is sought to be increased. None bothered to know and report whether this 33% reservation helped women in general and **helped the cause of Good Governance of Panchayats in particular.** In the absence of such a data, I am afraid that the move is an electoral gimmick. I am not against empowerment of women based on merit but not on the strength of numbers. Numbers in gender, numbers in castes and communities are counted and considered for electoral advantages. Neither merit nor integrity and character is weighed. A more equitable principle of **economic criteria** for reservation in political institutions, public employment is not taken into account by the political leaders. So realisation of justice through the principle of merit and honesty as well as through **economic criteria** will place the principle of justice on a more solid foundation.

Each Constitutional provision, amendments, legal provisions need critical study, analysis in its operation before pronouncing judgement whether it meted justice or injustice to society - not exclusive justice to the political, administrative, judicial establishment or the criminal segment of society or the vested interests and commercial interests of companies, international companies included. For all of us know how Governments favour multinational companies through various concessions all at the cost of Indian Tax payers' money and which is a gross injustice. Therefore all laws criminal, civil, industrial, company laws etc., need critical examination by authors on the topic of justice if last word on justice in Indian society is to be pronounced.

And justice is a concept which needs scanning and monitoring in every governmental legislative initiatives, inactions and more particularly in their wrong actions periodically on yearly basis. Every decision under the laws taken by Administrator, Minister, Judge carries in its bosom the principles of justice or injustice and the decisions are in millions in a year. **Only a fraction of them are challenged before High Court / Supreme Court as arbitrary, whimsical, partial or corrupt.**

Even emperors like Asoka, Akbar made all attempts to render justice and also exhorted their officials to do so. Finally we seek God's intervention for rendering justice. In the Ninth Major Rock Edict, explaining the great value of Dharma / Justice, Emperor Ashoka said "The ceremony includes regard for slaves and servants, respect for teachers, restrained behaviour towards living beings and donations to Sramanas and Brahmanas". He exhorted his officials to follow his example on energetic action in the cause of Dharma. In the 14th year of his reign, he created a cadre called "Dharma Mahamatra", charged with the duty of inculcating Dharma, redressing wrongs and organising charitable gifts. When Ashoka mentioned about regard for servants, I am reminded about the way they are even now abused and ill treated in Indian Society. When he mentioned about restrained behaviour towards living being, I am reminded about how our farmers overwork the cattle, the bulls used for tilling and also neglect their upkeep and food in the last 5 decades. So justice means, Justice in the treatment and looking after servants, and living beings like animal kind. Our poachers, bandits like late Veerappan killed any number of elephants for the sake of ivory and tigers etc., for their skins and body parts which have high market abroad. This is all considered as unjust human behaviour though it is resorted to by a few people or gangs of criminals.

Justice in the Cause of Good

Good and bad in creation should be equally balanced. But the Media (print & electronic) highlights the latter. Good is rarely reported. **Probably Media is handicapped by lack of daily, monthly statistics of good deeds.** While for crimes, wrong doings etc., you have ready reckoner from police Crime Records Bureau and from the Law Courts. But if this culture of reporting good is cultivated by the Media by making a beginning, it is not difficult for Investigative Reporters, Journalists, Columnists to make out a case for good. **And that would be doing justice to the cause of good.** There are hundreds of TV channels devoted to news, crime stories, fun and frolic, music, sports. But channels which report and promote good are scarce.

At least since the days of Roman Empire predating Christian Era, there existed a legal definition of crimes and punishments. All wrong doings are not defined as crime. But all crimes are wrong doings. Good doings - the opposite of wrong doings were not attempted to be legally defined to be suitably recognised and rewarded by the State. May be such good doings bear fruit by way of superior next birth. This is a different religious / theological debate. However, I urge for a legal right for recognition and reward for good deeds or right actions well performed.

Universality of Justice

Dharma / Justice is a Universal Law as I understand religious thought right. Yama Dharma Raja (God of Death) is said to be supervisor of this Universal Law. He is credited to be impartial and non discriminatory in the strict enforcement of this Universal Law.

Politics should be based on Justice

Politics needs to be secular. But politics is not just all about being secular. **It needs to be universal.** Universality can be added to politics only through the universal principles of justice, and that is what a politician does not care for. A politician thinks that he should not be concerned with it because, if he is a true politician, he must look inwards towards the interest of his own people. So, every politician, as part of a system and not through his own fault, has two faces - an inward-looking face and an outward-looking face - and there is such a paradox between the two faces.

It is the duty of a politician to be loyal to the cause of his people. This is all right, that is fine and good. Even if the dictates of justice require a politician to favour the cause of another country - rather than his own country - the loyalty of the politician is still fixed only in that single direction.

This is another aspect of secularism that is so disturbing, and which stands in the way and obstructs the cause of peace.

You may have, many a time, heard American Presidents declare with the loudest of voices, heard all over the world, 'Now, we are going to usher in a new era of World Order' - A 'New Era or World Order?' Loud words, but what is the world order?

Is it a total domination of a few countries over the rest of the world? Is it an 'Order' of enforced peace whereby weak nations will have no choice but to follow the dictates of powerful people - follow their dictates down to the very tunes they play?

New definitions of justice are made here and there, and they are always variable because they are not based on absolute religious principles. Justice changes its definition in Kuwait - in its application to the situation of the Gulf crisis. It changes its definition in application to the situation of Palestine. It changes its definition in relation to the situation in the South American and Central American states. It changes its definition in application to East European politics.

It goes on changing its definition from time to time and it is amazing how this jugglery goes on in the name of honour, in the name of justice and in the name of world peace, and no one raises a voice against this.

It is a hollow game! We are just like puppets whose strings are being pulled by unseen faces behind political facades. When shall we awaken to the realities of life, and how shall we change the face of politics so that it becomes universal - and there are no two faces to politics, just one? Unless we achieve this purpose - this noble goal - it is impossible to establish any 'World Order' in the world.

Specifics

In all my books I have quoted specific Constitutional and Legal provisions which are not in conformity with the rules of justice. I quote a few examples

- Art. 356 - which was grossly abused by Central Government with **allegation of injustice** by democratically elected state governments.

Art. 356

"**Provisions in case of failure of constitutional machinery in States.**—(1) If the President, on receipt of a report from the Governor of a State or otherwise, is satisfied that a situation has arisen in which the Government of the State cannot be carried on in accordance with the provisions of this Constitution, the President may by Proclamation—"

(a) Assume to himself all or any of the functions of the Government of the State and all or any of the powers vested in or exercisable by the Governor or any body or authority in the State other than the Legislature of the State.

(b) Declare that the powers of the Legislature of the State shall be exercisable by or under the authority of Parliament.

(c) Make such incidental and consequential provisions as appear to the President to be necessary or desirable for giving effect to the objects of the proclamation, including provisions for suspending in whole or in part the operation of any provisions of this Constitution relating to any body or authority in the state.

This Article was in the news again at the dawn of October 2007. The context is different. It is not in the context of Supreme Court sitting in judgement over the executive decision of proclamation of President's Rule in a State. **The Supreme Court threatened recommending imposition of President's Rule in Tamilnadu for disobeying its orders declaring bandhs and strikes as illegal.** The Supreme Court also issued warning as to why the law of contempt of court should not invoked against the Government of Tamilnadu.

Granting without admitting that judicial order declaring a particular action of government as illegal, the consequences that flow from it are material. The consequences of an illegality are imprisonment in jail, a sentence of fine or even disqualification from public life. That may be an acceptable proposition as in the case of High Court of Bombay which in 1990s imposed a fine of Rs.20 lakhs on BJP & Shiva Sena combine for observing bandhs. But in the case of Tamilnadu the consequences held out are more frightful viz., recommendation for imposition of President's Rule cutting short the life of democratically elected State Governments.

And which Authority should judge the rightfulness or justice in such an action of the Supreme Court? **It is in this context that the present stand of judiciary needs to be examined.**

Bandh is a cessation of business activity including that of administrative business. It also hinders free movement of public. Nevertheless all bandhs or strikes if not accompanied by violence or coercion do not violate any law enacted by Parliament or a State Legislature. They are also not against the democratic values as opined by Philosophers on Political Science. A large section of political class, media lend support to such a view. Article 19 of the Constitution guarantees freedom of expression and a bandh or a strike is an extension of the freedom of expression of dissent. However, the opinion of Indian judiciary is different.

It is useful to study **Article 356** of the Constitution of India. **It has three aspects.** The **first** aspect is recommendatory authority. This authority stipulates two sources. One is the Governor of the State and the second is "otherwise". This second source is not clearly spelt out neither in the text of the above Article nor probably in judicial pronouncements. Obviously therefore, a citizen who invokes Article 356 before the Apex Court may also come under the word "otherwise". The **second** aspect is the action taking Authority. It is the Union Council of Ministers which decides on the recommendations of the Governor. When the recommendations of the Union Council of Ministers are approved by the President of the Republic, a proclamation is issued imposing President's Rule. On this second aspect legally there is not much of ambiguity though there exists political acrimony. The **third** aspect which is not much debated in the intellectual and legal circles is that the phrase **"Government cannot be carried on in accordance with the provisions of the Constitution".** The proper understanding of the above phrase in Article 356 in legal circles to the best of my knowledge is not complete. The phrase "Constitutional breakdown" does not figure in the above Article. But it is only a judicial innovation.

It is in the context of the phrase **"the Government of the State cannot be carried on in accordance with the provisions**

of the Constitution" one needs to assess the impact of Article 356 and the direction in which it is moving in judicial interpretations, debates in the legal and intellectual circles. There are nearly 400 Articles in the Constitution. Any recommendatory authority such as a Governor of a State, a political party, a citizen invoking the above Article before the Apex Court have to first state the specific Article or Articles violated by the elected State Government in order to make out a case for action under Art. 356 of the Constitution. To the best of my knowledge not more than 3 to 4 Articles were utilised for invocation of Article 356 even where an element of bias has been attributed. It is not enough that Article 356 is invoked in situations **of political instability and failure of public order.** These two situations largely resulted in misuse of Article 356 by the Governors of the State. It is precisely for this reason that the recommendatory authority whether it is the Governor or the other sources have to state their case precisely as to the nature of Article or Articles of Constitution that the Government of the State has failed to adhere. It is true that the VIIth Schedule of the Constitution of India listed "public order" as a State subject and as I said already the issue of public order is lending itself to gross abuse. Therefore, if the Supreme Court also becomes a recommendatory party for invocation of President's Rule in the State of Tamilnadu, it becomes necessary to state what Constitutional provisions have not been adhered to by the Government of Tamilnadu.

Having said that, I must point out that the Constitutional provisions are very weak. The provisions have not been enacted to address fundamental public isuses that Constitutional Authorities in a State such as a C.M. or a Minister do not stand charged for serious crime or corruption charges (crime free Council of Ministers). Constitutional provision should also reflect on the **secular agenda** of the Constitutional functionaries in the State. In our Constitution there are no enforceable provisions or Articles in this regard. Article 356 becomes more relevant for dismissal of State Governments in the above situations where **secular agenda** is not adhered to or when the Constitutional Authorities are facing serious **criminal and corruption charges.** These are some of the glaring gaps in the constitution.

The present activism of judiciary recommending President's Rule in the State of Tamilnadu can be traced to Article 142 of the Constitution of India which is reproduced hereunder:

"Enforcement of decrees and orders of Supreme Court and orders as to discovery, etc.—(1) The Supreme Court in the exercise of its jurisdiction may pass such decree or make such order as is necessary for doing complete justice in any cause or matter pending before it, and any decree so passed or order so made shall be enforceable throughout the territory of India in such manner as may be prescribed by or under any law made by Parliament and , until provision in that behalf is so made, in such manner as the President may by order prescribe. (2) Subject to the provisions of any law made in this behalf by Parliament, the Supreme Court shall, as respects the whole of the territory of India, have all and every power to make any order for the purpose of securing

(a) The attendance of any person,
(b) The discovery or production of any documents or
(c) The investigation or punishment of any contempt of itself".

A plain reading of the above Article does not lend support to judicial **legislative activism.** Granting without admitting that judiciary has indirect legislative power, the moot point that needs to be debated is the nature of consequences that follow in case of judicial orders on bandhs and strikes are not implemented. According to me the nature of consequence may be limited to Contempt law and not extended to a recommendation for imposition of President's Rule cutting short the life of democratically elected State Legislatures. **There are no explicit constitutional provisions which spell out the legislative power of Apex Court unlike Articles 123, 213 which give such power to the President and Governors to promulgate ordinances.**

As regards the larger question whether bandh or a strike is illegal, it needs to be debated in the context of International Law, UN Conventions or Resolutions, precedents in Law practises of other democracies. **The question is too large to be left to the decision of Indian Judiciary.**

There is no thought or debate in the legal and intellectual circles on key Constitutional provisions and their implication. I express my views on some of them.

Articles 243 (A), 243 (P) deal with elections to Panchayats and Municipalities and reservations of seats to SCs/STs. Article 226 to 235 deal with High Courts etc. Articles 251 to 254 deal with inconsistency and repugnancy of State laws with the Central laws. In case of inconsistency, to the extent of such inconsistency or repugnancy, they will be void. In any case, such repugnancy has to be decided by judiciary and these Articles and judicial decisions have to be cited as reasons for invoking Article 356. Articles 265 to 300 deal with taxes, property, contracts, suits etc. In particular, Articles 266 to 267, deal with consolidated fund of India and the States as well as "public account". Clause (3) of article 266 states that no monies out of the consolidated fund shall be appropriated except in accordance with law for the purpose and the manner provided in the Constitution. Article 274 requires prior approval of the President to bills affecting taxation in which States are interested. Article 293 refers to restricted borrowing by the States. Articles 301 to 304 deal with trade and commerce among the States. Articles 309 to 320 deal with service conditions of the Unions and States, constitution of Service Commissions, conditions of service etc. Article 323 (A) deals with constitution of tribunals, Article 320 deals with elections. **Some of these articles mandated State Governments certain dos and donts.** If there are not adhered to, it can be said that administration of the State cannot be carried on in "accordance with the provisions of the constitution". There is no Article in the constitution which states that **government formation** in a particular State needs to be by a leader of single party or a combination of such parties enjoying majority in the Assembly. Therefore, invocation of Article 356 by abuse of power on the ground that no single party is able to form a government in a particular State is misplaced and this certainly is not the vision of the framers of the Constitution. Article 352 mentions about "war" or "external aggression" or "armed rebellion" as a ground for invoking President's rule. Art.355 authorises central govt. to protect states from "internal disturbances". Such protection does not mean imposition of Presedent's rule under Art. 356. "Internal disturbances", "armed rebellion" are grounds under Art. 352 which speaks about proclamation of **Emergency** in the country or any part of its territory. But Central Government is fighting shy of proclamation of emergency and short circuiting dismissal of State Government by resorting to Art. 356.

The distinguishing feature of "public order" a phrase mentioned in the 7th schedule of the Constitution and "insurgency" or "armed rebellion" are:

- In public order conditions the adversary is not armed with modern weapons, ammunitions and explosives which the army possess.
- The adversary is not trained in the battle combat skills as a group to fight the state.

It is time to substitute the phrase "public order" with "insurgency" or "armed rebellion" in order to curtail misuse of Art. 356 by the Central Government.

- **Art. 105 (2)** - which when interpreted by Supreme Court does not allow corruption cases to be filed against a Member of Parliament who accepted bribes while transacting parliamentary business. A bribe giver is held as an offender while a taker as innocent - discriminatory.
- **Art. 164** - which allows back door entry to the seats of power to those who were defeated in the normal election contest is unjust.
- **Sec. 8 (3) and 8(4)** of the Representative of People's Act 1951 - which is discriminatory.
- **Sec. 321 Cr.P.C. 1973** - abuse of public power in withdrawing criminal prosecution leading to injustice to the society.

- **Sec. 434 Cr.P.C. 1973 -** Abuse of "public power" in releasing life convicts.
- The Lok Ayukta Legislations intended to fight corruption in Public life - which have not included a Chief Minister in its purview and which in several state legislations have not criminalised the offences leading to prosecution - discriminatory and violates justice.
- **The Prevention of Corruption Act 1988** provisions and the **single directive system** which exempted the All India Service Officers from being enquired into for corruption allegation without Government permission - discriminatory.
- The **Judicial rulings** which similarly exempted Judges of Supreme Court, High Court from being enquired into for corruption charges by State investigative agencies - discriminatory and arbitrary leads to injustice.
- The recent amendment to Land Acquisition Law for Special Economic Zones (SEZ) when Government acquires land of farmers at the price fixed by it but not the market value and hands it over to Industrialist for setting up industries, it was attacked that there is no **demonstrable public purpose** in such laws. Even judicial ruling disapproved it. There is injustice.
- The Indian Express dt. 26.08.2009 reported about A.P. Government tightening the legal provision by prescribing life imprisonment for **acid attacks** on women but not against men. This discrimination is unjust.
- **Art. 20** of the Constitution of India gives right to silence to a person accused of an offence. Recently one High Court stayed **lie detector test** to be conducted on Rama Linga Raju of Satyam Computers responsible for defrauding share holders to the tune of Rs. 10000 crores. So every judicial decision not mere legal

provision also needs to be examined by Authors on the subject of justice to judge whether such and similar decisions will advance the cause of fair criminal investigations in which crores of depositors money is involved. There are lakhs of judicial decisions of lower courts, which are challenged as unjust and taken in Appeal. But when Supreme Court gives a final verdict, there is no other Appeal. **Such judgments of Apex Courts have to be evaluated by Authors for fairness and justice.**

- **Laws (Art. 15, 16 of the Constitutions) in India provide reservation in public employment based on social and educational backwardness of caste and communities.** The reservations were made for 10 years initially. It is renewed every 10 years. The benefits are enjoyed by the **creamy layers**. Those who got into public employment on reservations initially are able to educate their children well as against those who are excluded, and these children and their children are getting into public employment from one generation to the next. So this creamy layer which enjoyed reservation benefits for 2 generations needs to make way in favour of non creamy layer - those families which did not reap the benefits. **The same logic holds good for reservations to State Assemblies, Parliament and other political institutions.** There is another example. The Forward Castes are also hit in the process. At any given time there will be 60% poor or lower middle class in these forward castes. It is just to empower them to public employment. For this uniform **economic criteria** to all castes and communities for the purpose of public employment accomplish justice in a large measure. In the same way State economic support for students now available to SC, ST, BCs need to be extended to economically poor among Forward Castes so as to put justice on an even keel.

Governor's Decision that Cause Injustice
Art. 164

In the wake of political crisis in A.P. after the death of YSR, Andhra Jyothi, Telugu Newspaper on 27.09.2009 reported about change of Governor - a more pliable Gentleman. I think I have discussed the issue long time back in my book "Fault Lines in Indian Democracy". We beat our breasts for fixed tenure of a petty police officer. What about fixed tenure to an important Constitutional Authority who can appoint a Chief Minister? No one is concerned. Where are our Constitutional provisions guiding our Democracy? Who has to convene the CLP? Is it the Governor or the Speaker of the Assembly and what is the time frame in the specific situation like the present? All these questions cry for an answer because of incomprehensive language in Art. 164.

In the A.P. episode of 2009, where in Mr. K. Rosaiah was sworn in, there is a tricky terrain of lack of popular mandate and majority in Legislature. Is the swearing in of Mr. K. Rosaiah incompatible with call of justice? It is alleged that the Governor acted at the behest of the party leadership. Y.S. Jagan did not have the handicap of Dr. Jayalalitha in 2001, when she was invited by the then Governor, Fatima Beevi to be sworn in as Chief Minister even though the former stood convicted for 2 years on Corruption charges and was disqualified under R.P. Act 1951. But Jaya had popular mandate, her party AIADMK having been returned to power in Tamil Nadu. **So popular mandate and Constitutional or legal provisions do not always sail together.** We also had instances of Lalu Prasad Yadav and others who staked eligibility to hold Constitutional posts notwithstanding their being convicted. There were also instances when Mr. Bangaru Laxman had to quit the party post of President BJP, not on conviction but on the expose of Tehalka.com for receiving Rs. 2 lakhs which was caught on camera. Mr. George Fernandes had to quit ministerial post on Media exposure etc. Mr. Natwar Singh was sacked as Minister on the whiff of a scandal of oil coupons received by his kith and kin from Iraq. So there is **jungle justice** resulting from in our legal scheme in respect of Ministerial responsibility or

Accountability which finds expression in different types of justices in different situations and applicable to different persons.

So justice is not abstract philosophy. It needs realisation in the just legislation by the State, fair administration by Constitutional Authorities, bureaucracy, its interpretation by judiciary and finally a review of all these annually by Ruling Establishment.

Land Ceiling Laws of 1971 - Economic Justice

Across the country land ceiling laws came into existence since 1960. The severest one was the A.P. Land Ceiling Act 1971. It limited land holding to 10 acres of wet land and 30 acres of dry land. Extra land was acquired without compensation or grossly inadequate compensation. **Is there any meaning to justice in this legislation?** I am not against land being distributed to landless. But give compensation at market value to the land owners before acquiring their lands. While Government lavishes lakhs of crores on Industrialists by way negative action of waiver of bank bad debts and inaction of not realising taxes to be paid by them and also by wrong action of allowing several concessions to the industrial units, it deprives a poor farmer owning land of 10 acres due compensation. Is there any justice? Then Government have lakhs of acres of land of its own. Did it contemplate to develop arid land and then distribute them to landless, instead of acquiring lands of land owners who sacrificed their energy and effort in developing their lands from one generation to another? On the top of it, the Government did not even entertain the idea of giving one job to a family in public employment to all those whose surplus lands are acquired under the land ceiling laws. **In the absence of all these, I consider the 1971 land ceiling laws as totally unjust.** I do agree to the populist sentiment involved in the land ceiling laws. It gives land to landless in villages. Second it humbles the land owner before the landless. It socially empowers the landless vis-à-vis the land owning. Nevertheless populist sentiment required for electoral advantages (Vote Bank) need to have the element of justice in its bosom.

In the same way, the Land Acquisition Act of 1894, being invoked to favour Industrialist (Special Economic Zones) was attacked as unjust to farmers. Government acquiring farmers lands at the price fixed by it and giving them to Industrialists for **no demonstrable public purpose** was attacked as gross violation of the concept of Justice (economic). Industrialist can purchase lands at market value and if Government is capitalistic in its orientation, it can allow other concessions in taxes and services to the Industrialists but not hit the farmer below the belt.

Banking Law

Take the instance of secrecy in banking laws - regarding non disclosure of names of bank loan defaulters publicly. It is totally unjust. It favours the industrialists. Indians have reportedly deposited 1456 billions worth U.S. dollars in Tax havens abroad. (76 lakh crores, 7 times the extent of National annual budget) Particularly in Swiss Banks. Our banking laws, economic convensions are so loose that it is not easy to repatriate the money, much difficult to send the offender to jails. **Unless this money resulting from the loot of Nations wealth is brought back and offenders jailed, there is no justice whatsoever.** The problem has been there since long. No Government in India is keen to act on this because political class is involved. When media or other international agencies bring out the issue into public domain, Government Ministers say that they will look into it or indulge in evasive replies. Merely asking Swiss Banking authorities to furnish wealth stashed in its Banks by India (called as fishing expedition) serves no purpose. **There is pressure on Switzerland by USA and West European countries to abandon banking secrecy.** India's approach is passive which has the effect of scuttling justice. In United States of America President Obama made it an election issue in the year 2008. But in our country it will not be an issue to be included in election manifestos. The Indian political establishment zealously protects such wrong doings of tax evaders and violation of other financial laws. **1% of global population is reportedly holding 57% of the**

wealth of the world. Economic justice heavily titled in favour of rich.

Poor Government services or lack of services, particularly medicare etc., result in injustice.

Government Schemes

Justice needs to be grounded in the implementation of schemes, flagship schemes of Government. Government gives land for "Weaker Sections" Housing Societies. In the course of implementation of schemes, they are converted to housing society for well-to-do – all due to corruption and political influence which goes unchecked. There is injustice. Just take the case of **white cards** to poor in Andhra Pradesh, which allow the beneficiary to draw cheap food provisions. There are lakhs of ineligible well to do families enjoying the benefits. Where is justice in the scheme? Take the case of occupation of land by land grabbers. Water bodies (irrigation or water supplying tanks in and around Hyderabad city) were occupied by land grabbers due to Government's neglect or design or both. Is it not injustice to nature and the general public?

Delays in Court Trials

Pendency of Crimes and Complaints

The Times of India news which interviewed Mr. Sen quoted facts and figures. Of course justice cannot be measured by the figures alone.

- 30 million PT cases in courts.
- 75,000 complaints yearly before NHRC.
- 27,000 cases of violence against dalits and any number of cases of crimes against women in 2006.

Of course all crimes are unjust. When one has grievance of injustice, crime is resorted to. These crimes, or even wrong doing of exploitation, coercion etc., are in tens of millions each year.

Apart from crimes, wrong doings, there will be millions of unjust decisions in Administration which are challenged as arbitrary in Courts etc. Even decisions of Courts, Tribunals are challenged as illegal and arbitrary in appellate Courts. All litigations arise out of injustice real and perceived and some consumers of justice are not satisfied even with court verdicts.

Justice delayed is said even by our Judges as justice denied. Some 3 million cases are reported pending trial.

Yet another area of injustice is unmerited acquittal of criminals by Courts. It is another case study for the champions of justice. They are also in millions in numbers. Each case needs to be studied and analysed.

Interim order of Courts such as granting bail etc., also needs study so as to know whether it advanced tne cause of justice to victim and the public at large not justice to criminals alone. Such delay in murder case disposals or unmerited acquittals of accused degenerates sometimes into what is called "retributive justice" viz., retaliation by victim's kith and kin resulting in counter murder of accused.

The strength of Courts lies in simplifying Court procedures, disciplining defence lawyers, avoiding lengthy judgments, putting extra effort by increasing work hours, rejecting frivolous petitions, revisions etc., all forming part of cutting down Court delays.

Detailed Reasons for Court Delays

(1) Frequent adjournments in trial of cases. Both Bench and Bar are responsible. Judges do not have control over the trials as much as the Bar has.

(2) 50% of petitions in High Courts are from factory workers, pavement dwellers and other ordinary people. Article 226 is invoked. The litigants approach the High Court after their grievances are not addressed or wrongly addressed by the Govt. authorities (Article in the Indian Express by V. Krishna Ananth, Advocate High Court, Chennai).

(3) Government's failure in proper governance leads to litigation vide Art. 226 of the Constitution.

(4) Government's failure to implement Court orders leads to filing contempt petition doubling litigation.

(5) Government is a big litigant in appeals to superior courts, when it loses its case in lower courts. It is prestige for Government. It also acts at the behest of vested interests. Thirdly monetary concern matters little as litigation is prolonged at public expense.

(6) No proper guidelines evolved by High Courts in disposing of writ petitions. Government Pleaders, Advocate Generals taking their own time to file counters and High Courts allowing them all. In simple matters 6 months to 1 year time is taken for disposal of a petition U/A 226,where a strong judge aided by definitive, well drafted court procedures can give relief in 3 months.

(7) Non accountability of **public official** for delayed or wrong decisions which are taken to Courts for settlement when even after the case goes against Government. Accountability is important so as to reduce the cause of grievance. When a Court holds that there existed a right on petition before it which the public official failed to recognise and address due to corruption or other causes and which lead to court litigation, the public official and Ministers need to be held accountable first for failure to take right decision and second for the consequence of contributing to litigation. A legal right available to the petitioner is denied by public official.

(8) Law officers, who recommend filing appeals or who fail to properly guide Govt. while filing counters to petitions in High Courts, need to be held accountable, if the case handled by them is lost and also for tendering wrong advice to Govt. (a) to concede a point in the petition against Govt. (b) to defer going in appeal as a matter of routine and prestige.

(9) Govt. and Supreme Court need to set their house in order before asking for more courts.

Any way late R.K. Jain, Supreme Court Advocate and Scholar has written enough on judicial / court reforms. His writings need to be looked into. His views on the subject are as follows:

(a) Absence of judicial restraint leading to the "Jurisdictional Hunger'.The Apex court is not restricting itself to significant questions of Constitution and ordinary law. The Apex court is meant to lay down the law for the entire country for the purpose of bringing uniformity in case law on Constitutional and legal issues. It should not deal with every single case which comes before it because the counsel chooses to file it. It is dealing with cases that even the High Courts would throw out.

(b) It opens up litigation virtually abinitio. In A.R. Antulay's case it overruled its own judgement. No decision of the Supreme Court is final by its own reasoning.

(c) The Supreme Court goes through every detail of the case, its hearings stretched over years to give final judgement that adds nothing to the existing body of law and interpretations.

(d) In the U.S. the Supreme Court sits en masse (full strength of 9 Judges), picks up roughly 200 out of 5000 cases, discharging the rest as not involving significant questions of law thereby mitigating the problem of pendency.

(e) The Supreme Court takes upon itself newer responsibilities never intended by the Constitution. While the PIL is a momentous development, the Supreme Court is not able to deliver Justice by providing relief to the voiceless suffering millions.

(f) Worse than the rampaging jurisdiction of the court, is the erosion of Indian Jurisprudence into an incoherent mass of confusion, each Bench pronouncing judgements according to its predilections with a **conflicting body of case law,** at times bad law opening up-lacking harmony and uniformity while multiplying avenues of litigation leading to misapplication of case law to the millions of cases thereby hurting the rights of victims.

(g) The Supreme Court is said to be lacking modern managerial techniques for auditing pendency in the lower courts and guiding their disposals.

(h) The court allows unending arguments with the Bar refusing to accept any measures of discipline.

(i) Leadership failure of the apex court contributed to the collapse of credibility of lower levels.

(j) The Supreme Court failed to evolve uniform and sound principles of evidence by taking a re-look at the concept of 'proof beyond reasonable doubt' etc.

(k) Failed to prioritize the work of the lower courts with focus on prompt trial and disposal of crime with anti-national objective, extremist crimes, crime relating to communal riots, Mafia crimes, other grave offences like murder, dacoity, corruption, fiscal offences which threaten national unity and economy. (This is my view)

For the last 2 decades, there is a misdirected effort to create any number of Courts, Tribunals etc. Fast track, family courts, Consumer forums etc. The Govt. needs to review their work output to begin with for their continuance, before undertaking the creation of more courts. In that way in a period of time there may be demand from political class for more number of MLAs, MPs, Ministers posts in the country. We have to cry halt to these numbers game. We need to focus on tapping the **human resources of talent and integrity** and streamline procedures, enforce accountability.

Justice to the Accused in a Crime – Fair Trial

The constitutional, legal safeguards to accused citizens involvings fairness to the accused implies (a) the right to reasonable notice of the nature of the charges against him, (b) the right to have the case against him presented fairly to the court, (c) the right to be heard and to lead evidence, (d) the right to confront the witnesses against him, (e) the right not to incriminate himself, (f) the right to be produced before a magistrate within 24 hours, (g) the right to reasonable bail,

(h) the right to be defended by a lawyer, (i) the right to a speedy and public trial, (j) the right to be tried by an unbiased judge, (k) the right not to be convicted for an act which was not an offence when it was done, (l) the right not to be tried twice for the same act. **Sec.304 Cr.P.C. provides State legal assistance while victims have no such assistance.**

Court Punishments and Justice

"Equality in justice is a primary condition of attaining justice; yet no one could even pretend to believe that it is obtained under the present system. **That is true not only of criminal, but in civil cases also.** There is one law for the rich and another for the poor whenever the preparation of defence is an item of importance in the case. Nor is that all. In the personal relations of life, as in divorce, for instance, lack of means generally implies lack of access to the courts. Often, also, in civil cases the inability of a poor person to employ a counsel, still more to employ really skilful counsel, is a fatal bar to their obtaining justice. Another area of inequality is notable. If a poor person steals conviction follows rapidly; if a rich person steals, he is usually bound over on the plea of nervous trouble. If a taxi-driver is proved to have been drunk while in charge of a car, he pays the penalty; but it is notorious that magistrates do not like to convict the rich young man in a similar position, since he will usually appeal and often get his conviction reversed on appeal. What is disorderly conduct in resisting the police in White chapel is not seldom regarded as an ebullience of high spirits in Mayfair. If directors of a company in high social position pay no attention to the affairs of the company, they are not held responsible when it is compulsorily liquidated; but if a petty official is confused in his accounts, charges of embezzlement are difficult to avoid. Clearly, we need to remedy such a state of affairs."

"In part, of course, we cannot remedy it by legislation, since, in part, the temper which is responsible for the position will change only as the social atmosphere changes. A magistrate who sees guilt in a poor thief, but nervous disease in a rich one, will continue to make the distinction until differences of economic status are negligible; a judge who does not believe that distinguished directors of public companies ought to be responsible for a **negligence they are paid to prevent,** will only find them responsible when there is a genuine relation between income and service. Wherever, in this aspect, differences in the administration of law are dependent, not upon the law itself but upon the **social results of the inequality of wealth**, only a movement towards the equality of wealth can obliterate those differences. The situation here is only a particular aspect of a much more generic problem. Things seem wicked in the poor which are not wicked in the rich; the rulers of civilisation were horrified when Bolsheviks murdered Aristocrats, but they were not horrified when Aristocrats murdered Bolsheviks. The atmosphere I am seeing to describe was perhaps best shown in the Franks murder trial in Chicago when it seemed to be assumed by the public opinion of America that the sons of millionaires would not, despite their guilt, be sentenced to death by the Courts. The temper, in fact, which permits the English peer a special trial by the House of Lords will only disappear with the abolition of the privileges typified by the House of Lords." (H.J. Laski)

The Numbers Game and Justice

Every Head of **public institution** who is expected to do justice to his job demands more public funds and numbers if he wants to be effective to do justice. And it is believed by the political masters of the day.

In the third week of August 2009, Print and Electronic Media quoted the Prime Minister of India about creation of some 60 to 70 more Special Courts to try C.B.I. cases (Central Bureau of Investigation) in a drive to fight corruption. **But he did not address the main problems:**

1. Plugging loopholes in the existing Anti Corruption Law (The P.C. Act 1988) as suggested by me in all my writings.
2. Similar action in respect of Lok Ayukta Legislation meant to fight corruption in public life.

3. Failure to enact Lokpal legislation covering the corruption of political, judicial, senior bureaucracy and senior army leadership.
4. Failure on the administrative side to punish the corrupt by way of removal from service, by denial of important postings etc.
5. Withdrawal of single directive system (Executive instructions of Govt.) which did not permit causing enquiry (not to speak of filing FIR) against top All India Service Officers.
6. Granting functional and financial autonomy to the anti-corruption units with least interference by political executive.

Again the Prime Minister convened a conference in the same week of Director C.B.I. and all Directors of State anti-corruption units at New Delhi and exhorted them to catch **big fish.** How can these anti-corruption units catch big fish particularly when Government did not answer the points at 5 and 6 raised above: As Prof. H.J. Laski said public are deceived by State, Parties, Media because of lack of machinery of co-ordinated information. I will give one instance of how public is deceived by the Government etc. Public policies regarding infrastructure developments are not in public domain sufficiently in advance. Secrecy surrounds them unless there are media leaks. Consequently realtors, contractors, political class purchase lands in and around cities at cheap prices. Poor Agriculturists who sell the lands cheap suffer. Justice is denied to them. The Media, the intelligentia according to me need to raise the above issue to enlighten the general public. Else they will be failing in their role as the watch dogs of Democracy.

Creation of more Courts, belief in numbers (not the actual performance output of public official that includes a Judge, the full potential of work he can deliver) is taken into consideration by the Prime Minister. It is unfortunate. In the same way, there is also a demand from judicial class for more Courts and more Judges. **We believe in the adage of more the merrier.** More funds are also demanded everywhere, by every department for better or excellent performance of public duty. And for their claim to gain acceptance, they quote figures of population - judge, population - police ratio from West and other countries. I have in all my writings argued against this false view. **When one corrects false views, a great battle in society and Government is won.** An increase in number of Judges, Police needs to be linked to the following :

- A rise in the number of criminal gangs.
- Rise in crimes, grave crimes.
- Rise in number of casual offenders.
- Police ineffectiveness in prevention and investigation.
- Judicial inefficiency in trials, convictions, liberal grant of bail, other interim matters.
- Political interference in investigations, appointment of police officers, prosecutors etc.
- Ability of Govt. and judiciary to discipline Lawyer community.

Having more competent judges, not more number of judges, is the solution to the persisting problem. (V.R. Krishna Iyer, The Hindu, 02.12.2009)

My writings on judiciary in all these years got adequate support. Former judge of Mumbai High Court Sri M.N. Suresh, writing in the New Indian Express dated 03.12.2009, observed that no action either to dismiss or prosecute Justice Ramaswamy was taken though charges of criminal misappropriation were proved. No action against Justice Bhattacharjee was taken for receiving $80,000 as royalty from a suspect Middle East publisher. He went on to suggest amendment to the Constitution to provide for dismissal on proven charges of corruption, the need for independent complaint mechanism and independent Tribunal for investigation and action that includes prosecution. Justice Suresh further castigated the present Union Law Minister for succumbing to judicial lobby in not passing a good law on judicial accountability. Independence/ Autonomy of public authorities that include judicial authorities is now viewed in a negative sense of independence to indulge in wrong doing, inaction and corruption. This is really a pathetic situation in the administration of the country.

Crime growth need not be necessarily related to the growth of population. *Perse* general public are peaceable and not prone to crime. **Failure of governance overall including judicial governance gives rise to crime rate.** More particularly failure of criminal justice system in which the government, police, judiciary are all partners is a factor that needs consideration. Even when these different branches work at cross purposes, criminal justice fails and gives rise to crimes, criminal gangs, terrorist gangs. Now take the instance of left wing extremists (Maoists or terrorist crimes). How is Maoist violence and terrorism related to population growth? So failure of governance, of criminal justice system, faulty govt. policies gave raise to these twin big threats to the Nation. I will give one more instance to the reader for a proper understanding. Now corruption is an offence (crime). How is general population growth connected to this crime? It is the exclusive domain of the establishment - political, administrative and judiciary. Corrupt acts (crimes) are in a million in a month in the country, though a few are detected and exposed. As the strength of establishment raises, crime of corruption also rises unless Govt. takes stern measures to fight it. So we need to dispel wrong ideas / false views. **And unless the Media Intelligentsia, my kith and kin, don this role, they will be doing not service but disservice to the Nation.**

In all this *hullabaloo* about numbers and justice, we tend to forget misuse and over use of police personnel etc. In July 2009, it hit headlines, when a Constable of Hyderabad was deputed to Delhi to work at the house of one police official working in Hyderabad and that Constable meeting with death on way back. The Govt. undertook scrutiny of such misuse by police officers and attempted to check. But the effort is a tip of an iceberg. Such a misuse of police men by political class is more pronounced. Ministers, MPs, MLAs, lower level political functionaries are all given indiscriminate and disproportionate security cover only to be grossly misused. The Govt. did not raise its little finger to correct this. Is there justice in the unequal treatment of police when compared to political class in this matter?

We Misuse / Overuse Personnel and at the same time Clamour for More Numbers

In the month of April 2009, I was passing through Road No. 2, Banjara Hills. Mr. Jaya Prakash Narain, President Lok Satta Party was about to leave his residence / office for filing nomination papers as MLA. There were about 20 to 30 party workers, peaceful indeed. There was a small band. But there were nearly 10 Constables to cover the gathering. Similarly, on my way to Tennis Court, I see a large number of Police personnel at the R.R. District Collector Office though the Police Station Saifabad is 100 yards away. For every whiff of a protest, a small gathering, procession, a large number of police men are pressed into action. Similarly large religious festivals are served with thousands of policemen. There is no rationalisation in drawing men for the so called bandobast duties. We need to accept responsibility to handle them with smaller number, even if there are discordant notes.

Then, when we talk of justice through numbers, and more funds, we need to know why justice to public is not met. A depleted public exchequer cannot meet contingencies like war. Is it not injustice in the long run to the Nation? Recently there was news item about a systematic attempt by North Eastern State Governments **diverting 10% of public funds to militant groups.** It is anti-National. The fact is admitted by Govt. Is there justice in pumping in funds which are poorly audited and which lack any measure of Accountability of the authorities responsible for such diversion?

And above all a periodic review (5 or 10 years) needs to be done to evaluate police and judicial services that accrued to the community due to increased number of judges, number of police ranks. The relevance of population rise is an easy comfort mode for authorities to demand increase of numbers. For the first they are accountable but for the alternative of population rise there is no accountability.

Population - School, Population - Hospital Ratio has Relevance

Opportunity

Is a powerful force for realisation of justice. Every nation, society, organsiation at all times work / strive to progress towards the goal of justice. The opportunity of education open to women since the last 3 or 4 decades advanced the cause of justice to women.

The Govt. of India provided opportunities to the hitherto disadvantaged sections of Hindu society (socially and educationally backward classes) by providing reservation in political institutions and public employment. It was initially made for 10 years and continued since then. And it needs review and revision in favour of non - creamy layers. At the same time more equitable principle of social justice is adoption of **economic criteria** covering all sections of society including religious minorities for such reservations for 2 to 3 decades and finally putting a full stop to all such reservations.

Capability and Merit

Capability and merit lost their sheen before reservation in public employment(Quotas). 50% of public employment falls under reserved category. Public employment in India is about 25 million. Meritorious, however great, can only contest for 50% of the 25 million posts. When capability is discounted to the extent of 50% justice is faltering. Even among the reserved group, creamy layers of the group cornered the benefits. The children of those who entered Govt. serivce in 1950 and 60's have better education than the ones who have not got into Govt. service at that time. These children score a point over the later category and continue to dominate the 50% quota. **There is injustice here though there are opportunities.** Capability and merit were in a way frustrated by the reservation policies of Government.

The legal system is not found but made. It should be therefore suffused with justice. The legal system should throw open political, judicial, administrative office to

capability/merit. To this end the following need observance :

- Reservations in public employment and political positions based on socio-educational backwardness need to stop.
- Alternatively the creamy layer of the socio-educationally backward segments of society need to be removed from the enjoyment of the benefits.
- Possible substitution of the present reservation policy in public employment with economic criteria.
- The best course for equitable justice in the field of social justice in public employment is to give state support to education to the disadvantaged classes, so that they get opportunity to compete with advantaged sections.
- Abolition of the vulture of "Spoils System" in public employment.

Patronage

The 'Spoils System' which prevailed in public employment in U.S.A with each change of party coming to power in the previous centuries, has not died down at least in India. Each Chief Minister of a State is a monarch of all that he surveys? Appointment of

- Advisers to Government
- To various commissions that include the recent RTI Act of 2005
- To various Temple Trust Boards
- To various Market Yard Committees
- Grandhalayas (Libraries)
- To PSC Chairmanship & Membership
- To posts of Govt. Advocates at various Courts etc., etc.

Run into a few thousand in number in each state. There is no criteria. There is no transparency in appointment. All this makes our Democracy a mockery of justice in public employment or employment run on state funds. **Equality of opportunity based on tested criteria of merit is absent in the spoils systems. Justice is lost.**

Legal Provision of Capital Punishment in Laws - is it unjust?

There are a few theories about **justice** in the above legal provision.

Retributive Theory

According to this theory, the basic purpose of punishment is to avenge the wrongdoing. If an offence has been committed, the offender must be punished, punishment is an end in itself.

Deterrence Theory

As per this theory, the aim of punishing an offender is to deter him and other possible offenders from committing similar acts in future, thereby securing peace and stability in the society. **Punishment inflicted on an individual criminal becomes a source of security for the society in general.** An unpunished crime not only leaves the perpetrator of that particular crime free to commit further offences, it also encourages others with similar intentions and motives. So the offender must be punished.

Reformist Theory

"A man is not born a criminal. It is the society that makes him so". Reformists believe that the purpose of punishment is to reform the offender and finally integrate him into the society again. According to this theory, punishment should be such that it helps him realize his guilt and arouses a genuine feeling for change.

I have expressed my views on the subject . I choose to reiterate certain points. On 28.02.2008 Lok Sabha TV featured interview by TV Journalist Mrinal Pandey with former President of India, Sri A.P.J. Abdul Kalam. He was questioned for his views on this subject. Mr. Kalam expressed his views **against capital punishment** for the following reasons.

- That several countries abolished capital punishment.
- That convicts are poor and used by others to commit murders.

I respect him as the nation too respects. He is an example of honesty, character in personal and public life in the present day. But I differ with his view. His view has the following flaws. One, the countries which abolished capital punishment do not have the seriousness of crimes and variety of terrorism we have. Second, murders are of various kind. **For ordinary murders, no capital punishment is needed.** But the same logic cannot be carried forward to other offences like the "rarest of the rare" or terrorists or for contract killers etc. A middle path is needed. Third, the alternative prison term (if death sentence is not awarded) is 14 years. If it is 30 to 40 years death sentence can be abolished. Fourthly, that murder convicts are exploited by rich is not sound logic. The terrorists who strike and cause hundreds of deaths are also poor. They are exploited by terrorist groups, national and international. Some times Nations sponsor terrorists. So it is not possible to exonerate them because they are poor or because they are monetarily, ideologically, religiously exploited.

So the last word whether capital punishment is just or unjust needs to be pronounced in the prevalent climate of crime and Terrorism in a particular country.

Does Justice to Prisoners Cause Injustice to Voiceless Victims?

Art. 72, 161, Sec. 432, 433, 433A Cr.P.C. 1973 speak about powers of public authorities like President, Governor, the Govt. of the day to grant

- Pardons
- Suspend
- Remit or commute sentences

to those sentenced to death or life imprisonment and lesser periods of prison sentences. Thus there are two schemes. One is the Constitutional scheme and the other is the legal scheme.

I have discussed this subject in a separate chapter titled "Reformation of the convict" which was incorporated in some of my books. I have discussed both the legal and Constitutional provisions and also the Court judgments covering these provisions. Judicial decisions are contained in

- Maruram Vs. Union of India (1980 SC 2147)
- Bhageerath's Case (1985 Cr. Law Journal 11/79-SC)
- Ashok Kumar's Case
- Keher Singh's Case (1989 Cr. LJ 941 SC)

Of all these judgments, the minority judgment of Justice Murtaja Fazal Ali in Maruram's case is sound and meets the principle of criminal justice as applicable to both the accused and society at large.

Sec. 433 Cr. P.C. is a crucial section. The appropriate Govt. can commute a sentence of imprisonment for life for "imprisonment for a term not exceeding 14 years" which means 14 years is the minimum jail term. But over the years, political Executive and judicial decisions watered down the above provision. The Indian Prisoners Act permits remission of prison term for good behaviour in prison. Then the period spent by convict as an undertrial is set off against the prison sentence awarded. Allowing the set of period to be deducted from the jail term awarded is a judicial decision. So legal provision, judicial and political Executive decision in commutation of sentences made possible for the life convict to come out of jail in 7 to 8 years thus making criminal justice a mockery. Justice Murtaja Fazal Ali observation is worth quoting.

"Thus it seems to me that while considering the problem of penology, we should not overlook the plight of victimology and suffering of the people who die, suffer or are maimed at the hands of criminals."

In A.P. on the eve of Gandhi Jayanti, 2009, 940 life convicts were released from jail by way of commutation of sentences. Some have spent 7 years or even less. I must state that commutation of prison sentence is a state policy, which promotes peace and tranquility in society but not a routine affair when occasions like Independence day or Gandhi Jayanti are used or misused for the purpose. Suppose if in Kashmir the separatists arrive at an amicable settlement with Govt., the separatist convict's prison sentences can be commuted. Similarly, if Maoists lay down arms and join the mainstream their prison sentences can be commuted. Commutations of prison sentences or withdrawal of prosecution (Sections 433 & 321 Cr. P.C.) need to be related to public policy and not otherwise. To the best of my knowledge Court' decisions on executive power of commutations is limited to Art. 14 of the Constitution as to whether there has been reasonableness in the procedure adopted for releasing the convicts. **The Courts have not tested the public policy behind the exercise of executive power in commutation of prison sentences.**

Late YSR was at this game since he assumed office as Chief Minister. He attempted to commute the prison sentence of one G. Venkata Reddy who was the husband of one Congress MLA in Kurnool district. It was not approved by High Court at that time if I remember well. This game of commutation of prison sentence has also the backing of civil rights groups. Mr. Gaddar expressed support and demanded release of Maoist prisoners. So political parties, civil liberty groups are vying with each other for justice in favour of life convicts. **But the victims who are in millions, the peaceable society at large, some billion in population is a mute spectator to the rape of justice in advocating justice to criminals and convicts.**

Natural Justice

This is yet another kind of justice traceable in the judicial interpretative process to Art. 14 and 16 of the Constitution of India. (Union of India Vs. Tulsiram Patel 1985 Supplmt (2) SCR 131 at 232). Simply put state action should be free from discrimination and arbitraries. These principle of natural justice are applicable not only to legislative enactments and state action but also to Tribunals, Authorities or a body of men not coming within the definition of State in Art. 12 . These principles of natural justice expanded the frontiers of unending of administrative litigation. Fairness and impartiality of administrative decision are central to the principles of natural justice. To take deterrent disciplinary action against public official for inefficiency or even corruption and wrong action became difficult for Government in view of the expanded meaning of the principles of natural justice. An order of detention by the District Collector and Magistrate of an unsocial and goonda elements, a Mafia member, smugglers under the laws of preventive detention are also vulnerable to these principles of natural justice. Therefore criminals, anti social elements, delinquent and defaulters in administration got benefited at the cost of good in society.

It creates rights that law has not recognised. This is because of the interpretative process of Art. 14 and 16 of the Constitution of India. Under sections 169, 170, 173 Cr. P.C. 1973, the police submit "charge sheets" in successful investigation against accused. In case of unsuccessful investigation, they send report (Final report) to the Judicial Magistrate dropping further action into the case. Though there is no right U/s 173 Cr.P.C. to give notice to the informant / complainant providing him of an opportunity of being heard his part of the story against police dropping investigation, the Supreme Court in Bhagavant Singh's case laid down that such a notice is necessary. The complainant has now a right of being heard by a Magistrate before he decides on the police action of dropping investigation.

Monetory Compensation Under Various Laws Such as

1. Consumer Protection Act
2. Motor Vehicles Act 1988 (Sec 168, 173 regarding Quantum of compensation)
3. Workmen's Compensation Act 1923
4. Railways Act 1989
5. Land Acquisition Act 1894 (Sec. 4, 22, 24)- determination of market value for compensation
6. Arbitration and Conciliation Act 1996 (Justice in monetary claims).

are all governed by the provisions of Art. 14, 16 in which the frontier of the principles of Natural Justice are advanced and decided by Courts of Law. There is no right for a particular amount. But the Courts apply the principles of Natural Justice to determine the quantum of amount when contested.

The principles of "Natural Justice" cover distribution of State largesse under Art. 299 of the Constitution - the tendering process in Government contracts.

Several administrative decisions of the Government, Quasi Judicial Authorities, Universities which are in tens of million and when challenged as arbitrary, malafide are governed and determined by Courts on the principles of Natural Justice. Seniority in Government service, interse seniority as between two sources of recruitment are also tested on the principles of Natural Justice.

Even while implementing the mandate of a legal provision, it is necessary to observe the principles of Natural Justice viz., that the decision of public authority is reasonable and that an opportunity of being heard is given to the aggrieved.

Consequence of Neglect of Action in Public Duties (intentional and unintentional) – Results in Injustice

It causes enormous injustice in communal or caste riots in India. It also happens in natural calamities. Loss of life and property are involved.

Extra Legal Justice or Instant Justice – Unjust

In the Indian scenario of tackling a person responsible for atrocity, crime Lords and Terrorists, police shoot them down in a stage managed armed encounter. It is said to meet instant justice to the victim in particular and society in general as society gets rid off the bigger evil. Again to correct this instant justice meted out by police, judiciary gets into action on public complants, to call the police to accountability for such extra legal killings as it happened in Gujarat in 2004.

In sum every legislative provision touching criminal, civil, family, consumer, labour laws etc., etc., their implementation needs to be reviewed periodically every 5 years as to whether

they worked justice to its consumers. Only a fraction of these cases are taken to Courts of Law for correction of wrongs, violation of rights.

Justice to Workers

"From the standpoint of politics, the problems of industry have two aspects of importance. There is, first of all, the problem of safeguarding, throughout its operations, what are called the natural rights of men. An industrial system must satisfy the principles of justice; it must give to the worker a secure and adequate livelihood, reasonable conditions of work, and a full opportunity to share in the making of the conditions upon which happiness in work will depend. He must not feel that his life is at the hazard of another man's will. The broad characteristic of modern industry is the absolute separation of management from labour. The area of consultation is narrowed down to the conditions attaching to the price to be paid for labour and the physical conditions of its employment. The worker has no right to express his ideas upon methods of production. He has no organised opportunity for suggestion. Even when he has demands to make, or grievances to put forward, their formulation usually involves a test of power in which the thing of import is not the moral quality of the demand or the grievance, but the strategic condition of the parties to the industrial relation. Nor, finally, has the worker any claim upon the product of his work. Once his price has been paid he is insignificant in relation to it. **He is, in a full sense, that animate tool which to Aristotle was the essence of the slave." (H.J. Laski)**

Justice to Unorganised Labour

Mr. Dipankar Gupta in his latest book "The Caged Phoenix" (that is India) brought out interesting facts about the economic growth trajectory of India. Small scale sector industry (SSI) and unorganised business sectors employ some millions of workers. There exist some 7 times higher units than the registered. They are not strictly governed by labour laws. They employ labour through a contractor to evade responsibility.

The wages are poor and hours of work long. Many times there is no record of wages. All this misses scrutiny because of corrupt bureaucracy. **This makes millions of labour force vulnerable to injustices of various kind.** In unorganised and unregistered business, small scale industrial sector, there will be no trade unions or they are defanged. According to Mr. Gupta these unorganised industries profit not so much by improving productivity as by simply depending on cheap labour. **For the purpose of my writings on the subjects of justice, his view is relevant to state that there is exploitation of labour and that exploitation is injustice.**

Military Rule

The doctrine of military necessity, (military coup d Etat) where democratically elected governments are overthrown and military rule established is often witnessed in our neighbouring Pakistan. Is that not violation of political justice? Under the cloak of democratic institutions, President Musharaff jailed Judges of Supreme Court. Not withstanding their frail Court decision, jailing Judges without due trial is unjust to the core. David Henry Thoreau observed "where a State / Nation unjustly imprisons a person, the right place for such person is the prison". **So injustices under military guided Democracies are carried to absurd proportions.**

Human Rights

It is patently unjust to focus, to agitate on the rights of criminals and terrorists forgetting the **rights of Community**. The big moral appeal of human rights has been used for a variety of purposes, from resisting torture, arbitrary incarceration and racial discrimination to demanding an end to hunger and starvation, and to medical neglect across the globe. The substantial history includes the invoking of 'inalienable rights' in the American Declaration of Independence and similar affirmations in the French declaration of 'the rights of man' in the eighteenth century, but also the relatively recent adoption by the United Nations of the Universal Declaration of Human Rights in 1948. All Human Rights do not have definitive legal anchor in the laws framed by the soverign nations. **In an overall context, maintenance of good human rights record in its multi dimensional angle is a reflection of the prevalence of justice.**

Public Contracts

Mr. Sen focused in his book the importance of freedom and opportunities in the realisation of justice. It is no doubt true. But in the Indian conditions opportunity minus wealth, political and administrative connections have their limitations. Public contract works worth lakhs of crores are cornered by rich and powerful in politics and society. One need to have economic muscle even to make initial monetory deposit to tender for public contracts. In the above sense economic disparities act as hindrance to the realisation of economic justice even if one is an Engineering graduate and competent to execute the works.

Tax Laws

Graduated income Taxes which lighten the burden upon small incomes by its transference to the swollen revenues of the rich and famous so characteristic of our present times will help to reduce the gap in unjust tax law provisions. Wealth Tax receipts are reported to be less than the cost of collection. Only a tiny fraction of country's wealth is subjected to tax. In India only 30 million people pay Income Tax.

Unfair Accusations

It has become a National trait to accuse and injure the sentiments of others. Mr. Justice D.V. Shylendra Kumar of Karnataka High Court wrote an epic Article in the Indian Express on 19, 20.08.2009 against the view of Chief Justice of India that judges are not willing to declare their assets for public disclosure. Unable to find holes in Mr. Kumar's character, integrity and impartiality, the Chief Justice, Supreme Court stated that Mr. Kumar is in the habit of seeking publicity. Nobody is willing for right action. If some one suggests, he becomes an object of hate and character assassination. Among some 300 judges of Superior judiciary, none supported the right action viz., that judges should not hesitate to make their assets public. Where is justice then? There is double injustice. One is reluctant to disclose. The second is counter attacking the person who wants right action.

Social institution of Caste

The social institution of caste in India is a breeding ground of social injustice. Access of lower castes in rural areas to village temples, common wells is denied. Untouchability still exists notwithstanding legal prohibition. **This is another aspect of justice quotient.** Discrimination is injustice.

Religion

In the religious institutions such as Hindu temples, Matts, Churches, Mosques, there are media reports, enquiry reports on the acts of corruption, malpractices of pilfering gold and other precious metals by the staff, occupation of temple lands by realtors, land grabbers in collusion with temple staff and political class. **All this makes no sense of justice.** Unless we run our religious institution honestly, efficiently, there is no justice to the genuine religious/spiritual piligrims who are in tens of millions.

Political Parties

The political institution of **party** in India is a big monolith, immune to any reform. Not Democratic. No periodic elections to the post of "office bearers". All nominations. No definitive criteria for giving ticket to contest for a seat for Assembly or Parliament, no democratic way of choosing a Chief Minister by a ballot vote in Assembly, a Prime Minister in Parliament. Only nominated persons will be voted to seats of power. There is no transparency for party fund collection and expenditure. Certainly not any trace of accountability for money collected from undesirable sources and spent on wasteful items, programs etc. All this makes political justice a mockery. **Lack of transparency in party functioning is injustice to democracy. Political parties are the wheels of Democracy.**

The political parties are abetting communal discord for their selfish pursuit of power. They are abetting caste and communal identities and fostering violence not only at the time of electoral contest by the subtle way they draw muscle men into the field but also by unleashing open violence on the streets for various causes. This is a set back to peace and also to justice. There is a vested interest in the poverty levels of the masses in the practice of politics. Below poverty line groups voting rights are vulnerable for exploitation by the political leaders. **Political leaders discover gold banks in the vote banks of the targeted groups. The vote banks crown them to seats of power and thereafter these political leaders become super rich by exploitation of their office.**

The N.R.E.G. Act (National Rural Employment Guarantee Act)

This sort of legislations normally meant to relieve specific drought situations cannot be made a permanent feature of our lives. **Otherwise people get addicted to Government's benevolence**. The Indian Express recently reported about a Minister in A.P. admitting to heavy corruption in the implementation of the Act. Second it needs to build State / National assets such as permanent irrigation tanks / ponds etc. It cannot be a work for the sake of unproductive work. Third the work force can be deployed to reclaim arid government lands fit to be cultivable. Only in such conditions, the Act becomes meaningful. **It has one unintended benefit. It helps to reduce migration of rural unemployed to town and metros.**

The N.R.E.G. Act is dishonest in its conception with an eye on Vote Bank and corruption is the name of game in its implementation.

Advantages

- It gave legal right to work for 100 days in a year.
- Assets created benefitting the poorest (work on individual land holding not on the land of community - double benefit accrual)

- It is said to have increased the bargaining powers of rural landless for increased wage.

Disadvantages

- Failed to create community / National assets.
- Failed to develop **skilled** working community from among the rural landless.
- Farm labour became dear.
- The bargaining power of landless vis-à-vis a landlord, zamindar is acceptable. But such a power vis-à-vis another marginal farmer owning 10 or 20 acres of land is not sound logic.
- Working hours are reportedly minimum - less than 6 hours.
- Corruption has set in at the expense of National Exchequer depleting its strength.

  Instead of the present system where payments are made for developing ones own assets, it is better that vocational training centres are set up in each Divisional Head Quarters of a District where training is imparted to motor mechanics, drivers, and in various crafts and trades. This will make available a large pool of skilled workers in a period of 5 years. **Millions of unemployed rural youth will become self employed.** At present a driver with 5 years experience is getting a salary of 7 to 10 thousand which is almost on par with a teacher of a High School. So all this needs to be looked into before sqandering of public money with vote bank legislations such as the present one.
- Public assets need to be built on this surplus labour.

  So long as the disadvantages are not removed by amending the law, I do not see merit in it and to that extent it lacks fairness and justice.

Wildlife Laws

I was going through news papers, dt. 28.07.2009 and TV news of 27.07.2009. In Warangal, a wild bear was trapped and done to death by villagers as it was destroying crop and also attacked villagers in the past. In Tarimela village, Anantapur district one Cheetah was surrounded and killed by villagers. It is reported that criminal cases will be filed against villagers. I have no time to go through this Wild Life Preservation Act. What else will the villagers do except to kill the man eaters or wild animals? Should they not protect their crop or themselves? In defending their crop and person, they can kill the animal. What is the great sanctity of animal life under the above circumstances? It is one thing if professional hunters, poachers, smugglers of ivory and skin go to forest and kill animals. It is different if animals which poach into the habitats of human dwelling and get killed by villagers. **I do not see any merit into this legal provision of prosecution where villagers kill wild animals, when they or their crops are threatened.** This is not a just legal provision. One can observe some hundreds of unjust legal provisions. **The domestic violence law against women was criticized by no less an authority than the Chief Justice of India, as it was leading to misuse and harassment of the family of male members. So injustice is built into some laws all in the name of justice.**

Injustice in Wild Allegations - TVs News, dt. 28.07.2009

Omar Abdullah, Chief Minister, Jammu & Kashmir was allegedly involved in a sex scandal of 2006. Muzzaffar Baig, PDP (Opposite party) leader alleges that Omar was involved. The CBI which investigated the case says that Omar is not involved. Allegations, counter allegations even in A.P. politics are very common. Both in and outside Assembly. **It is high time that defamatory allegations (character assassination) if not proved need to be penalised to the extent of disqualifying the person concerned for 5 to 10 years from public life so that irresponsible public statements are not made..**

Man made laws need to conform to Dharma or justice. Now take a simple example of defamation law in Indian Penal Code 1860. This requires that the defamed person needs to prove the charge against the Media (Newspaper). This evidentiary rule of accused (Media) being innocent till proved beyond all doubt etc., is not just. Media is an institution.

Individuals cannot fight it. So the rule of justice requires that the rule of evidence needs to change and that the burden to prove the allegations reported when challenged need to be proved by Media on a lighter principle of prima facie evidence. (Preponderence of probability).

Law and Regulation Vs Popular Perceptions as to what is Reasonable or Just

It happens that law or rules covers certain unreasonable or unjust provisions. For example two ministers in UPA government at the centre were having 5 star lifestyles. Staying in 5 star or 7 star hotels in New Delhi by paying public funds of Rs 1 lakh per day(for want of suitable government accommodation, TV News, dt. 08.09.2009). Rules permitted this financial extravaganza. But it was perceived as unreasonable. And when media exposed it, they coolly left the 5 star hotels. In the same way law may not cover all wrong doings by way of prohibition of them. But what is not prohibited by law need not be admissible for public perception or justice. Here justice and conscience come into play. Now take the **business empires** of Ministers or CMs or their kith or kin. Law did not prohibit a C M or Minister to set up industries, business propositions etc. But it is condemned by all right thinking people as it is against public interest. **Public interest is central to principle of justice.**

Non Violent Mafia

There is mafia in bureaucracy, polity, media, games and sports where intolerance, jealousy is the name of the game. The mafia has not spared the cultural arena like cinema, where it is monopolised for the benefit of few, barring entry to new aspirants. **The mafia subverts justice.**

Non-violent Protests, Agitations Protect Justice

Protests, agitations, mass mobilisation civil / disobedience such as refusal to pay taxes, hartal (call to cessation of business activity), the chief weapons of non - violence which Mahatma Gandhi, advocated have positive results to correct the course of injustice. In public life there are hundreds and thousands of non-violent acts which achieved the desired results. On the eve of 2009 election in India, Jagdish Tytler, alleged to be involved in the massacre of Sikhs in Delhi during 1984, was denied a party ticket to contest Delhi Parliamentary seat by Congress Party due to protest and non-violent agitation launched by sikh groups.

Bloated Ego, Jealousy, Prejudice

When one fails to give due credit to the deserving in various fields of effort and achievement due to extraneous factors such as dislike, prejudice, jealously, insolence, there is denial of justice. When our Democratic institutions such as Political Executive, Bureaucracy, Judiciary fail to standby the victim, the aggrieved, whose rights are violated, can we say that justice is secure? More often, in a vast majority of millions of cases, the above institutions stood by the offender, violator of law.

Poverty, chronic poverty, wide spread ill health, lack of opportunity for education and inability of state to correct them causes injustice.

Communal Riots

Where the state fails to act (preventive action) to protect lives of people in communal/race riots, there is gross injustice. Subsequent action to prosecute accused is a different one where you cannot restore lost lives. A state loses legitimacy if it fails to protect its citizens.

Equality in Resource Sharing

As described by me, public employment (some 25 million in strength) is an **intangible state resource** Quotas or reservation in public employment if relatable to economic criteria, is perfectly just up to a certain period. But if we cast quotas in the world of caste and religion, the justice quotient is lost. The Economically Backward Classes among forward communities are discriminated against. In the same way, if quotas are perpetuated or cornered by the **creamy layers** of the quota group, it works injustice. These are all the various variables in assessment of justice. **So there is inequality in sharing this in tangible state resource**. Consequently injustice is caused to those who are outside quotas system. This also results in economic disparities as between those who enjoyed the **intangible state resource** and those who were excluded. It defeats the premise of Karl Marx "From each according to his ability to each accordig to his need"

Profligate Financial Practices

President Obama proclaimed his interest to protect consumers from predatory companies. The collapse **Lehman Brothers** and the Govt. bail outs that followed is a reminder. The lobbyists, law makers and "turf - protecting regulators" stand by companies. The latest in Indian financial markets is the collapse of Satyam Infos with Rs. 10000 crores loss to depositors. **Such frauds in Indian companies are in thousands.** Financial bail out of such companies works double injustice to share holders and to public exchequer.

Executive Delays Cause Injustice

It is reported in Media that there are 26 mercy petitions before the President of India for well over a decade and this delay causes injustice to convicts sentenced to death. It is likely to cause **death row syndrome** in the convict which is avoidable by prompt execution or commutation of it into life imprisonment. **Therefore, it is not judicial delay but also delay at the level of political executive, administration, etc. that cause injustice.**

The Role of Intellectual in Correction of Injustice / Constructive Criticism

Role of intellectuals, Authors, groups in Civil Society, Community of Lawyers who influence decisions through writings, public campaigns, filing public interest litigations in Supreme Court and High Courts is immense

The Issue of

- Public declaration of Assets and liabilities of Judges of Supreme Court and High Court.

- The prevention of elevation of D.P. Dinakaran, Chief Justice, Karnataka High Court as of Judge Supreme Court (facing corruption allegation).

were made possible not by Government of the day or the powerful public institution of Supreme Court as it is by the intellectuals and the concerned leaders in the community of lawyers. **It represents a gain to the principle of justice.** Even so, its success is limited as disclosure of assets is voluntary and is not legally binding with penalty or punishment for non-disclosure or suppressing material facts in disclosures. The path towards realisation of justice is halting and half hearted.

Therefore there needs to be separate law for making assets public or RTI Act 2005 needs a separate provision to that effect. In an All India Conference of Central Administrative Tribunals on 01.11.2009, Mr. Prithvi Raj Chavhan, Unicn Minister of State for Personnel expressed the desire to make RTI Act "proactive". **That was my argument for the last 4 years and it represents a gain to the principle of justice if amendment is carried out.**

It is not that the disclosure of Assets by a Judge, Bureaucrat is the be all and end all of transparency, the avowed object of any legislation on the subject. For this the legislation on the subject need to cover (1) proactive disclosure of information relating to (a) assets (b) various functions discharged (c) failed to discharge, the constraints for non-discharge. It should also prescribe. as already mentioned. penalties and punishments that include jail term for deliberate neglect to disclose. Pro-active functioning of information commissioners is also needed where they inspect periodically office / offices, examine complaints received, identify complaints where information is not disclosed and report against the authorities for penalties and punishments. All these issues cannot be left to concerned citizens who are one in one million and who do not have wherewithal to fight litigation / petitioning the public authorities.

The intellectuals, civil society groups need to be reminded that Transparency is a means to an end - the end is Accountability for failures, corruption etc.

I give one example of non - accountability of All India Service officer for corruption though The Prevention of Corruption Act 1988 did not give them any special exemption. The Executive instructions called the **Single Directive System** require prior permission of Government to commence enquiry into corruption charges against Joint Secretary level official and above which enquiry is rarely permitted even if sought. Therefore concerned citizens will be less enthusiastic and do not risk to seek permission for enquiry against the powerful institution of All India Service Officers. Accountability is defeated. In the same way the Supreme Court laid down decisions that no enquiry against Judges can be taken up by legally constituted organisation like CBI etc., without its prior permission. This also defeated Accountability. **Therefore these prior permissions have to go.** There needs to be "pro-active approach" to detect corruption and enquire by the leadership of Government and judiciary. We need to have institutions like **Lok Ayukta** to pro-actively detect corruption. Then only Accountability for corruption becomes meaningful. **The above two instances placed Judges and Senior Bureaucrats above the principle of Accountability for corruption.**

So these larger issues of Accountability need to attract the attention of civil / society groups and intellectuals in order to make the fight for cleanliness in public life and in Government or judicial services meaningful and thereby **advance the causes of justice.**

In November 2009, Media, rights groups, civil society in general challenged the decision of Shiela Dikshit, Chief Minister Delhi to release Mr. Manu Sharma, a life convict on parole for two months on unverified or false plea of attending to his mother's illness. Mr. Sharma was sent back to jail and miscarriage of justice was halted. I recall the role of Media and civil society in highlighting several unsolved high profile murder cases, which finally bestired the investigating agencies to detect them. When justice through the **agencies of the state** that include judiciary remain a mirage, **non state actors** like Media, intellectuals or even the Mafia comes into picture to settle disputes and render a modicum of justice. **Maoists also Claim their movement is meant for justice.**

Role of Selfless and Public Spirited Person in Promoting Justice or Correcting Injustice

Though Gandhiji did not exercise **State power,** he fought for Human Rights, Woman and Dalit rights, against unjust laws that offend Human rights and thereby protected "political freedoms" and social justice both in South Africa and India. Vinobha Bhave launched **Bhoodan movement** which helped distribution of land to lakh of landless. Jaya Prakash Narain fought against deprival of political freedom during the emergency days. **They fought for liberty and equality, the twin pillars of justice.** These instances are illustrative and not exhaustive. In a different way revolutionary left wing movements (Maoism) replaced abject submission, public invisibility of Dalits etc., with the public visibility and assertiveness which brought cheer and a measure of self respect to their lives marked by a deep felt sense of injustice.

We create public institutions (through Constitution and laws) from Panchayat to Parliament, Magistrate's Court to Supreme Court, Tribunals, Judicial Forums, Commission etc. Even outside these legal institutions, there exist common Panchayats (elders in village) which arbitrate on matters of justice. Sometimes in the Indian context, Mafia a non-state actor also arbitrates to secure justice where legal systems have gone corrupt or inefficient. Puranic, historical, present day wars were fought in the name of justice. French and Russian revolutions were inspired by the principles of liberty, equality, peace and justice. Insurrection, armed rebellion, military takeovers - all take place in the name of justice. The immediate provocation for 1857 revolt (Sepoy mutiny in India) was perceived injustice to use greased cartridges that offended religious sentiments.

We have to take into account every facet of Executive, Police and Judicial action to judge justice. When police refuse to register a cognizable crime, or arrest an offender, delays or subverts investigations, when a judge grants liberal bail, when he acquits a case unmeritoriously, there is injustice. For each case there are layers and layers of action and each action of public authorities needs to be judged as fair or unfair on its merits. Withdrawals of prosecutions with bad motives, not consenting for enquiry into corruption charges against senior officers by Political Executive have the ramification of breach of justice. Injustice lurks in larges areas of public functions. **There needs to be enforceable right against injustices to mitigate their impact.**

Higher judiciary, apart from being Courts of Appeal in criminal trials and judgments of lower courts, also possess powers to ensure life and liberty of citizens against Executive lapses or excesses (through its writ jurisdiction). This is intended to ensure justice to citizens.

Protection of Rights

Rights protection is a central theme of any theory of justice-those rights recognised by law and improved through judicial innovations. The protection of Human Rights Act 1993 is an addition pursuant to which an elaborate mechanism of a National Human Rights Commission and States Human Rights Commission were created. These Human Right Commissions do not have powers of investigation and prosecution of persons responsible for violation of Human rights. Even before the Human Rights Act of 1993, rights are enforced through judicial process (Art 32, 226 of the Constitution). But access to this process was beyond the reach of common man. This answered a fraction of criminal justice. Mr. Amartya Sen described illiteracy, malnutrition, lack of healthcare as "unfreedoms". I add widespread and deep seated malaice of Corruption to the list of "unfreedoms". Removal of these unfreedoms through concerted effort of Good Governance result in realisation of "Positive rights". To buttress my view point, I quote a report of Mr. Mahboob-ul-Haq of Human Development Centre.

"It is a cruel injustice when the economy is continually raped by corrupt official and politicians, by drug mafia and various other mafias by loan defaulters, by those who misappropriate State patronage - and they are creating new, unethical norms which destroy the very fabric of society". Corruption and inaction offend Human Rights and this is written about by me for the past 10 years.

Summing Up

Constitutional and Legal Provisions

Political justice or Political Empowerment: Reservations of seats in Parliament, State Assemblies are provided for the SCs, STs. (Art.330 - 332 of the Indian Constitution) It necessarily follows that they are correspondingly represented in the council of Ministers.

This is positive advancement of **political justice**. But there is a negative aspect to it where the Constitutional Provisions (Art. 356, 75, 164) are misused in the formation or dismissal of Council of Ministers at the Union and State level for which there are a number of instances in the last 40 to 50 years. **Political justice precludes such a misuse**. In the same way political justice precludes suppression of political freedoms and liberties as it happens commonly and particularly when it happened in mid 1970's when emergency was proclaimed. All these negative features of political justice or injustices stand corrected sometimes with the intervention of judiciary. Dissolving of State Assemblies, withholding assent to Legislative bills by the Governor or the President contrary to public perception, are all issues falling under **political justice.**

Social Justice or Empowerment: Art. 16.4 - makes provision for reservations in public employment which is nearly 25 million strong in India.

Art. 31 A. has the effect of forfeiting right to private property. Art. 31 B created 9th schedule and is nicknamed as the Constitutional dustbin for dubious socio-economic legislations placing them above "judicial review". The 93rd amendment to the Constitution sought to provide reservations in unaided Educational institutions. In public perception, this abuse of existing Constitutional provision, inserting new ones through amendment have not met the requirements of justice– in its politico-social connotation.

Economic Justice: Art. 46: The state shall promote educational and economic interests of weaker sections of the people and in particular, of the SCs and STs and protect them from all forms of social injustice and other forms of exploitation.

Art. 335: The claims of the members of SCs and STs shall be taken into consideration, consistent with the maintenance of efficiency in administration, in the making of appointments to services and posts in connection with the officials of the Union and States. And for this purpose, there are SC, ST Commission and Committees to oversee the enforcement of the above provisions.

To promote educational interest there already exist.

- State economic support to students of SC, ST and BC communities.
- Hostels and Social Welfare Institutions providing for lodging, boarding facilities, free supply of books etc.
- Special hostels where special tutors teach once in a week in A.P. State.
- Regional workshops for career guidance and make them aware of opportunities.
- Study circles to enhance competitive spirit in All India and other services (A.P. Study Circle for instance) where free boarding, lodging etc., is also available.

Economic Support

For non-students, loans are arranged to SCs, STs to purchase agricultural lands. Economic support is given to agricultural operations such as to dig borwells. Land ceiling laws are passed to distribute acquired surplus land to landless SC, ST, BCs. Government land of various denominations is distributed to landless for agriculture and for housing sites. Money is given under "social defence" scheme for those who suffer indignities at the hands of upper castes. Monetary aid is given to those who suffer "Atrocity". There is provision for rehabilitation of bonded labour. Mid-day meal scheme benefits millions of children. Sarva Siksha Abhiyan covers education of needy. Residential schools exist for orphans. Indiramma and Rajiv urban housing schemes are being implemented. There are special schemes for minority upliftment. There are several schemes, flagship scheme like National Rural Employment Guarantee scheme to benefit the rural unemployed.

For the benefit or welfare of BCs there are also

- Washer men Co-op. Societies Federations.
- Nayee Brahman Co-op. Societies Federations.

which are provided finances etc.

However the non-changing format of political reservations and reservations in public employment resulted in skewed form of justice - the creamy layers of this section of society monopolised the benefits to the detriment of non-creamy layers.

Added to the above, is corruption and leakage in socio-economic welfare schemes that almost defeats justice - it intends to promote.

Justice has three prominent names as discussed above. But there are other shades of justice.

- Civil Justice
- Criminal Justice
- Administrative Justice
- Gender Justice
- Exgratia Justice
- Natural Justice
- Retributive Justice
- Revolutionary Justice

Justice under Civil Laws

This is a very vast and vexed subject into which intellectuals need to do research by interacting with victims, Revenue Authorities, judicial statistics and civil rights groups, "injustices" under civil law will be in millions in an year. According to me justice under civil law is even more pathetic then under criminal law. In my book "Archaic Criminal Laws, Enforcement, Interpretation" I made an attempt to do justice to the job of analysing criminal justice. However, I did not undertake such an exercise with respect to civil law. I however give one instance from personal experience. My son Uday Kumar took a sub-contract in civil works from M/s. Yeturi Construction Company, Hyderabad. From out of sale proceeds of my house, a gave some money to him. Since there were dispute in the settlement of final bill, the matter went to an Arbitrator. Justice Iyyangar is a reputed judge. He gave Award of Rs. 35 to 45 lakhs in my son's favour. The company did not settle the bill. The matter was taken to City Civil Court judge. It was pending for well over 3 years. Civil cases do not require prolonged trial of examination of witnesses etc. And the High courts have absolute powers under Art. 235 to control subordinate courts, unlike Governments failing to exercise such control over senior bureaucrats, because of judicial intervention. Cannot the learned Judges of High Court, monitor, review, inspect pending cases and pullup or take disciplinary action against subordinate judicial officials? The alibis of more courts, finances will not carry any credibility with victims of injustice. More than number of Judges or finance, it is the Court procedures, the mindset of judicial leadership that needs a change. The lawyers community's strangle hold on judicial officers need to be freed for any measure of improvement in speedy disposal of cases. It is such type of gross delays that paved way for Mafia (non-state actors) to interfere in civil disputes. If judicial leadership is sensitised to justice delivery to common man, 50% of the problem is addressed. When the mining cases of Reddy Brothers (Gali brothers) of Karnataka was suspended by A.P. Govt., the High Court moved with breakneck speed to dispose of the writ petition. By occupying the post of judge and putting on black robes one need not get sensitised to justice - a noble and magnificent concept which only a few people possess.

Criminal Justice

In my book "Archaic Criminal Laws, Enforcement, Interpretation" I have detailed how our legal scheme of framing laws, enforcement and interpretation bred injustices to millions of victims and citizens. Court ruling on the Constitutional provision of liberty and freedom that include Art. 22 (dealing in the preventive detention) lead to erosion of stability and security to society and to the peaceful citizens. The provision of death sentence (Sec. 302 IPC) lacks teeth. Law makers cannot prescribe death sentence to gravest of grave offences that include murder. Only judiciary has discretion in that matter (rarest of rare cases). Life imprisonment provision lacks clarity as to the length of prison term. Its spirit was eaten away by Sec. 433, 433A Cr. P.C. 1973 and Art. 72, 161 of the Constitution whereby political executive can commute life imprisonment by "abuse of power" to less than 10 years and murderers get out of jail after 8 to 10 years of prison term. Sec. 321 Cr. P.C. permits withdrawal of prosecution from court record and by abuse of the said power justice is rendered mockery. Courts can suspend prison terms given by them under Sec. 389 Cr.P.C. U/s. 482 Cr. P.C. and Art. 226 of the Constitution, criminal investigation or even prosecutions can be quashed by High Courts. Abuse of power by judiciary in sentencing policy lead to lenient sentences. Loose principles of evidence allowed by judicial interpretation such as "proof beyond all reasonable doubt", "benefit of doubt", "presumption of innocence" till conviction or even after an appeal against conviction is filed have defeated criminal justice to the last detail. The doctrine of bail to accused as evolved by Courts caused hurt to justice to victims as it was too liberal. Not according permission by the Central Government to anti-Terrorism bills of the State, not executing death sentence awarded to Terrorist by delaying mercy petition for over a decade etc., resulted in **politicisation Terrorism** and defeat of criminal justice. Delays in criminal trials is evidenced by the latest case of one Ruchika, molested by a DGP ranked official in Haryana. It is said that case took more than 10 years to conclude. **Sabotage of enquiries, investigation by Government agencies by way of closure of genuine and foisting false cases, or weakening of evidence is a subversion of Rule of law and therefore need criminalisation to minimize damage to criminal justice.**

Laws, Rules

Some of our rules are arbitrary denying justice in day to day life of common man. I discussed it at some length in the preface to my book "Fault lines in Indian Democracy". Suffice it to give one instance here. There is no transparency in conducting Autopsy on dead body (a victim of murder). The doctor's opinion many times is tained for various reasons. It leads to acquittal of the case in Court or leads to police closing investigation. **There is miscarriage of criminal justice**. The rules do not provide for presence of kith and kin at the time of autopsy. **I wonder how this affects Truth**. I go to the extent of videographing of entire autopsy. **Secrecy breeds dishonest view of autopsy.** In the year 2008-2009, one Moddu Seenu, prime accused and an undertrial prisoner who shot dead Paritala Ravi, Ex-Minister and notorious factionist of Anantapur district was found dead in a cell in jail at Anantapur under suspicious circumstances. One co-cell mate admitted to have killed him. Other circumstances contradict such a theory. It is said that he was done to death by means other than clubbing in jail (place other than the cell in which he was locked) and brought to the cell. It is alleged that Moddu Seenu was threatening to expose political bigwigs ruling the State and who used him to kill Paritala Ravi, the entire investigation took a different turn. **Moddu Seenu's parents and wife demanded and agitated for being present at the time of autopsy to know the nature of wounds etc. It was denied.** The nature of wounds may give clues as to whether they support prosecution theory. Therefore such rules need removal and more transparency lent to autopsy in high profile murder cases so as to secure criminal justice.

Mr. Amartyasen referred to **Neeti and Nyaya** concepts of ancient India. Neeti meaning the **institutional structure** such as laws, rules, enforcing and interpreting agencies etc., to realise Nyaya (justice). Present day "Neeti" largely allowed the powerful criminals, criminal gangs, tainted governing classes, the rich and mighty in society to escape accountability for their crimes thereby denying "Nyaya" to tens of millions of victims. The importance of right institutions and right working of them is underscore by Sri Sen for realisation of justice.

Revolutionary Justice

In 1990's bloody revolts by the people in some East Europea Nations that include Rumania resulted in overthrowing undemocratic regimes.

Restitutive Justice

Victims of wrong doing by public authorities need compensation. The public authorities need to be held accountable and punished. Companies which are in lakhs (small and big) and which cheat on depositors money should be compelled to compensate the depositors by way of auction of the company properties.

Retributive Justice

An offender needs to be punished punihsment is an end by itself. Where one in present life escapes the consequences of crime or wrong doing the said person need to under go punishment (according to our religious beliefs) in the next birth.

Gender Justice

It is a hot subject of Indian politics. I think women got right to vote in the early part of 20th century and not before. Now they want adequate or equal representation in political institutions particularly in Parliament and State Assemblies proportionate to their numbers.

Ex-gratia Justice

Present day Governments are extending justice to all those who died in accidents and natural calamities.

Protecting Justice

True justice can be "advanced" in India by Govt. schemes, flagship schemes of public welfare if properly implemented. But "protection" aspect of justice also needs to be focused.

Justice can be protected when "public power" is not abused not just in millions of decisions taken by the political, administrative executive and the judiciary, but also when you choose right persons to administrative, judicial, political and constitutional posts that include Ministers, Governors and the President of the Republic who are free from the taint of crimes, corruption and other wrong doing.

As the book goes to print the Times of India English daily Newspaper, Dt. 18.02.2010 front paged Supreme Court's ruling that "High Court can order CBI enquiry" with reference to police firing in Midnapore, West Bengal where some 14 Trinamol Congress persons lost their lives. The Supreme Court was hearing the petition of West Bengal Government challenging High Court's order for CBI probe. There were similar High Court Order:

- Bombay High Court ordered CBI probe in October, 2009 into custodial death of Altash Shaik.
- Orissa High Court ordered CB probe in January 2010 into foreign exchange derivatives contracts sold by some Indian Banks in 2007-08 indicating it could expose a large financial scam affecting economy.

The Court orders or interventions U/A. 32, 226 are intended to **prevent injustice in sensitive cases** according to the Attorney General Mr. G. Vahanavati in the context of "higher principles of Constitutional Law"

It is therefore relevant to quote Art. 32 and 226 of the Constitution.

Article 32. Remedies for Enforcement of rights conferred by this part -

1. The right to move the Supreme Court by appropriate proceedings for the enforcement of the rights conferred by this part is guaranteed.
2. The Supreme Court shall have power to issue directions or orders or writs, including Writs in the nature of habeas corpus, mandamus, prohibition, quo warranto and certiorari, whichever may be appropriate, for the enforcement of any of the rights conferred by this part.

Art. 226

{226. Power of High Courts to issue certain Writs. (1) Notwithstanding anything in Article 32 {***}, every High Court shall have power, throughout the territories in relation to which it exercises jurisdiction, to issue to any person or authority including an appropriate cases, any Government, within those territories, directions, orders or Writs, including [writs in the nature of habeas corpus, mandamus, prohibition, quo warraanto and certiorari, or any of them, for the enforcement of any of the rights conferred by Part III and for any other purpose].

From a reading of the above Articles of the Constitution the following position emerges.

The Supreme Court can give writs, order, decrees for the enforcement of Fundamental Rights, while High Courts can give not only in respect of Fundamental Rights but also for "any other purpose". The phrase any other purpose has very wide amplitude and it was also criticized for misuse by Courts in Tax and fiscal laws. There was an attempt to amend Art. 226 in 1960's when Mr. M.C. Setal Vad was the Chairman Law Commission. However it is also necessary where abuse of office by political and administrative Executives became rampant as the Indian Republic gets older by years.

It is this legal phrase 'any other purpose' that according to my limited knowledge gave rise to public interest litigation, where any person whose Fundamental rights are not directly affected can approach Courts for relief in the interest of public cause. At any rate by ordering such inquiry through CBI, the Courts are upholding not only Fundamental Rights but also the Constitutional value of Justice mentioned about in the preamble of the Constitution,

The phrase "for other purposes" has wide amplitude lending itself for loose interpretation if not misuse for personal gain. The High Court of A.P. in view of the prevailing public order in Osmania University was questioning the type of police forces deployed, force used etc. These are purely Executive decisions and certainly is not the role of judiciary. It lead to a

M.I.M. member of the State Assembly to criticize both Human Rights Commission and judiciary in the Assembly debates. At best judiciary can direct State Government to cause "judicial enquiry" into use of disproportionate force by police.

Justice is bizarre even in judgments of Courts Mr. Justice V.R. Krishna Iyyer, Justice O.C. Reddy former Judges of Supreme Court wrote Books and Articles on the subject. Though I have not read the Book of O.C. Reddy, I cite a few instances from my understanding of the judiciary.

- Supreme Court took away the power of appointment of Judges of High Court and Supreme Court by excluding Executive from a role.
- Supreme Court ruled that prior permission of the Chief Justice is needed by investigating agencies if they want to investigate cases of corruption against Judges etc.
- Supreme Court ruled that 60% of Judges posts in High Court are to be from Bar while 40% from Bench. This ratio of recruitment to higher judiciary is not regulated by any Act of Parliament like the All India Services Act 1950. The members of Bench felt that it is unjust. They say that 60% for Bench and 40% for Bar is a just measure.

Court judgments, atleast 50% of them are a part of the problem and not solution to the problems of injustice.

I have argued for a right against injustice. The source of injustice to being with are inaction, indiscrete or ilthoughtout action, high handed and arbitrary, malafide, illegal acts that include the acts of Corruption by persons exercising public power under legal and Constitutional provision. The list can be enlarged by including misguided actions of Terrorists who do not care for the loss of innocent lives which any rational person will term it as an act of injustice. Some of the above actions converge into each other. When such action lack proper Accountability they continue to visit the common man causing injustice. Accountability has various facets of which prison sentence is severest.

We do not use Art. 309 of the Constitution against scores of incompetent, corrupt and crime tainted Army Generals, Judges, All India Service Officers etc., while NDA Govt. misused the said Article to dismiss Admiral Vishnu Bhagavat an honest and professional soldier. There is double injustice. Constitutional provisions became handy to perpetuate administrative injustice.

According to Lord Atkin justice is not a cloistered virtue and its delivery should be allowed to suffer criticism. Every public official be it a Minister, a Judge, a Civil servant is singly and collectively responsible to address people's grievances, prevent injustices, violation of Human Rights as enshrined in various legislations.

Justice no doubt is important to the principle of democracy and its practice. But the idea of justice predates the present democratic model. It is at the heart of human relations, welfare and prosperity of society. It is central to any form of government whether it is Democracy, theocracy or monarchy absolute or Constitutional. But the prerequisites for justice are a)Integrity in public life that eliminates corruption b) efficiency that cuts down delays, inaction. c) impartiality or fairness in action that also cuts down arbitrariness or ill thought out decisions. d) transparency in decision making process. e) Accountability for lacking (a) to (d).

2

Developments in Political, Social and Legal Issues

Law needs to reflect justice to the greatest numbers - several laws reflect justice to vested interests in society and governing Establishment. Any legal provision needs to reflect the will of the majority.

It is known that all civilised nations are governed by Constitution and laws. America is said to be a nation of laws and immigrants. Sound laws and systems are a prerequisite to people's welfare. That is the significance of law. But the subject of law is a complex one. It engaged the minds of great philosophers and thinkers since the time of Plato, Montesquieu, Bacario, Jeremy Bentham who at various times and circumstances attempted the definition of laws. Laws do not lend themselves for an easy definition and understanding. For otherwise we do not need an elaborate network of framers of law and equally elaborate layers of judicial class to interpret them to lend proper meaning. This also may be with reference to subjects other than law. If students or readers can understand the subjects by a mere reading of books, an elaborate system of various faculties in Universities becomes superfluous. The subject of use of force by police in a vast and populous country like India, resurfaced recently in a judgment, dt. 06.02.2009 of the High Court of A.P. The judgment dealt with the subject of police encounters / gun battles with Terrorists and analysed various Constitutional and legal provisions. This judgment of a full bench, on appeal by the state police organizations, was stayed by the Supreme Court. This subject is not new to either High Court or Supreme Court of India. It was there for well over decades cropping up from time to time with conflicting views and judgments leading to no finality in legal position. I had an occasion to go through some of the judgments on the subject and more particularly the various legal provisions having an effect on Court judgments. I have written about 35 pages on the subject. It forms a separate chapter in the book. I have also drafted an article of 3 pages and sent it to National Newspapers for publication. It took me 3 months to draw conclusions which according to my judgment are right. Considering the fact that Indian Superior judiciary took several years, indeed a decade to solve this legal problem or still remain unsolved for want of right guidelines, I think my effort for the past three months is not too long a period. I am a lay person, albeit an Author but without the assistance of luminaries of law profession which assistance is available abundantly to our judges in the Court room while hearing the cases.

Crime and Violence

The road to the corridors of power is not always a peaceful march. This is true of democratic Governments of 20th and 21st centuries. Nazis came to power in Germany through ballot box. Revolutionaries seized state power in Russia (Bolshevik Revolution). Oliver Cromwell in Britain abolished Parliament and seized power. Military Generals at various times deposed elected Governments and seized power. Hezbullah – a terrorist group in Lebanon has considerable strength in Parliament. Maoists who believe in violence as creed won elections in 2008 in Nepal. In 2009 E.U. Parliamentary election, 2 ultra British Nationalists were elected sending alarm bells across Britain. Fundamentalists in religion are represented in Parliament and other power structures in several countries. In Pakistan terrorist groups are in league with Army, ISI and Foreign Policy Establishment. Taliban ruled Afghanistan briefly.

Dominance of Political Class and Commercialization of Sports

Political class who annexed power are now annexing economic power - industrial enterprises, businesses, contracts etc. They are also annexing sports bodies from cricket to other games. There is money there. Also prestige and glamour. It gives their lives the much desired lustre. And corruption is taking roots in sports and games. One Retd. IGP CRPF (a well meaning person) tells me that Rs. 30 lakhs was demanded for selection of a Cricketer to IPL. Hundreds of thousands of crores of public money is spent on sports and games, with a full fledged Ministry and several other authorities at various levels. Several functionaries / authorities are not "public servants" who can be booked for corruption related offences. Therefore, there is no accountability for misuse of funds or corruption. In some of the sports organizations which attract women, sex stories are not uncommon. **Sports & games became a big business.** In Andhra Pradesh Olympic Association is the Cockpit of fight between two political heavy weight members of Parliament. Sports and games associations became personal fiefdom of ambitious politicians. **Politician is gradually getting emptied of public service and drifting into business.** They are running their own businesses or they are partners of business / industrial class.

Ranking Civilisational Levels

Very often we find Nations being ranked by various agencies in terms of levels of corruption. Corruption is one of the several thousands of defined crimes. It would be better if the civilization level is assessed and reported on the basis of overall crime rate, violent crime more particularly. Another relevant factor is whether a Nation is tolerant and Secular in order to rank its civilisation grading. **For example scandinavion Nations of Europe are rated as relatively tolerant and secular and where crime rate is also low.**

Castes

In India we have many social castes. But we also need to put up with various castes in the ruling establishment. The Political, Bureaucracy, Judiciary, Teachers, Doctors etc., etc. We also need to take into account the higher castes and lower castes. The All India Servcices are the upper castes. So also Judges of High Court and Supreme Court. Every caste is trying to preserve, protect and advance its identity, interests and trying to subordinate the lower. Caste system is becoming rigid year by year.

Audit / Review / Revision

We always hear about these words in Bureaucracy and in Judicial circles while hearing cases etc. The State institutions such as Political Executive, Judiciary, Police, Bureaucracy all are expected to fight crime, evil and injustice. But if they fail should we not review the working of these institutions in every 10 year period and totally reform them on the mere strength of statistics and public pulse?

Political Parties

There is a mad rush for retired Bureaucrats to join politics- this party or the other. Recently some I.A.S. Officers joined PRP in A.P. and contested Elections. But they lost. I believe they spent a lot of money. There are others in other parties either as contestants or as spokespersons. **There is no political neutrality.** Being a retired official, one does not cease to be public servant as long as one draws pension from Govt. Exchequer. A better option for these gentlemen All India Service Officers is to forego their pension and fight election and be spokespersons.

Learning

It is not bookish or voluminous study or even assimilation or even transmission of knowledge alone to the society. Learning involves a) learning to help the needy in different situations, b) learning to serve, c) to respect and support parents, elders, relations and deserving friends, d) learning to control one's tongue, pride, prejudice, e) learning to be law abiding including payment of all taxes, f) learning to be hard working and honest, g) learning to know your bodily functions, to keep them healthy, h) learning to know what to eat and drink, i) learning to keep proper company, j) learning to know the universal law of cause and effect, j) learning to be kind to animals, k) guarding your mind against evil thought, l) guarding your tongue against irresponsible, defamatory talk, m) to be un-hypocritical viz., be true to your own conscience "To thine own self be true" a phrase used by William Shakespeare in HAMLET. Buddha said that a learned man who does not practice Dharma is like a beautiful flower without scent.

Doing is learning. The students of sculpture, weaving, painting, masonry etc., are all in the process of learning. Learning is not by books alone. Musicians, singers and players of instrumental music do not fall back on books for the genius of composition or playing of the musical instruments. Even farming practices are drawn from human experience. Learning according to Philosopher John Dewey is learning to think through the application of real problems.

When you win a battle against incorrect ideas, you are a learner, rather learned. You have buried ignorance. Your judgment of men and matters tends to be right. You are enlightened.

Democracy

It is not periodic elections replacing one set of politicians with other. It has to be judged on

- How civil liberties are protected
- Functioning of various Government departments, corruption and red tape free.
- Accountability for crimes, wrong doing of **establishment**. Crimes of ordinary people is not difficult to be brought to accountability. **But accountability of establishment is not easy.**
- Poverty levels

- Status of crime
- Status of special groups that include women.
- Participatory decision making at various levels in Bureaucracy and political establishment.
- The health of **Parliamentary process** that includes State Assemblies–defections, trust votes, impeachment of judges, debates and discussions, passing legislative Bills, working of Parliamentary Standing Committees as watch dog of public spending etc., need attention to judge the health of Parliamentary process.
- The electoral processes–how fair and peaceful they are. We are witnessing turbulence in Iran on the allegation of fraud in the counting process.
- Police excesses and atrocities.
- Judicial functioning.

Change / Reform

There will be change in policies in tackling terrorism such as imposing ban on Terrorist groups or lifting such ban. Having strict laws or not to have are all policy shifts in Governance. But any change proposed or not proposed should be in the national interest and not party interests.

Change is a buzz word of the day. Mr. Barack Obama cashed in on this word "Change", Mr. Chiranjeevi failed.

Reform or change is everlasting. **Buddhism** represented marked change in religious beliefs with its emphasis on character. While **Islam** emphasized five times prayers every day. There is no idol worship. **Marxism** represented change. Its political face is minority or Party dictatorship. Its economic profile is the state control of the means of production. **Democracy** represented change in political thought. Secularism, social justice are also facets of the ongoing change. From 1960 to 80s, public sector was a focussed area, while in 1990s economic liberalization ushered in change in economic activity in India.

The subject of reform or change permeates the books authored by me.

Change / Reform is an inevitable process. When people are disillusioned with the laws, systems, and their functioning, change is demanded. Any policy or legislative initiatives should have National interests at heart and not party interests.

- There is clamour for Tax Reform foremost among them is the comprehensive Goods and Service Tax (GST). It is expected to stabilize Indirect Tax revenues. If the proposed change works well. (say in a period of 10 years) it can continue or we can revert back to old system or evolve a new.
- From 1960 to 90s, we had primary of public sector. Since 1990, the focus shifted to privatization or private public sector participation.
- Educational Reforms are on cards. Reform of Examination system was articulated by Krishna Kumar, Director NCERT.
- Postal Reform. Since the system failed, new private courier services have come up. Public and private sectors are operating in postal service.
- Police Reforms - Too vast a subject - appointments, promotions to various ranks (not all India services alone) matching the competing claims for promotion between All India Services (IPS) and the state services, improving efficiency, integrity, political neutrality and accountability for the absence of those need to engage our attention.

Judicial Accountability– Change

In his book "A Grammar of Politics", H.J. Laski 20th century Philosopher of political thought observed, "The men who are to make justice in courts, the way in which they perform their function, the method by which they are to be chosen, the terms according to which they hold their office, are at the heart of political philosophy. We know how a Nation-State dispenses justice, we know with some exactness the moral character to which it can pretend. So the following factors are relevant.

Apart from faulty selection and promotion process, lack of accountability for judicial corruption, wrong doings, delays are said to be at the heart of failure not criminal justice alone but justice in its entire gamut. The construction placed by judicial pronouncements, took away whatever little teeth that Government put into legislative enactments. Judicial pronouncements it is said destroyed the effectiveness of laws.

I have read a news item recently about change/reform in respect of judiciary with particular reference to accountability of judicial actions. It was articulated by Mr. Veerappa Moily, now Hon'ble Minister for Law and Justice. it is a welcome change if he succeeds in his attempt. **But change need not be excessive or superfluous.**

The Hindu Newspaper, dt. 27.6.2009 quoted Mr. Veerappa Moily, Union Law Minister about legal reform to make higher Judiciary Accountable. He mentioned (1) legislation to make declaration of assets and liabilities of judges mandatory (2) another legislation with a provision of punishment short of impeachment. I am afraid all these attempts will not become propaganda material for party's interests. When one talks about provision of punishment short of impeachment, it makes me wonder what exactly the punishment proposed. **Impeachment is a process for removal of Judges from service and removal from service is itself a punishment.** We need not find alibis for the failure of the collective responsibilities of the Members of Parliament with regard to Judge's impeachment. **Impeachment is a means to the end - the end is removal of Judges for proved misbehaviour or incapacity.** Good behaviour is a condition precedent for continuation in service. And we cannot contemplate shorter punishments of censure or postponement of increments of Judges just as we do for Bureaucrats. **So the second bill according to me is a suspect legislation.** The same Newspaper quoting Mr. Moily reported that on an average 15 years is taken to dispose of a case by Courts. **Art 124 - 217 of the Constitution can be amended to include inefficiency along with incapacity so that proved cases of inefficiency in trials etc., are also a subject matter of impeachment. Existing Constitutional Provisions**

need to be effectively worked out. Amendment to the said articles should also include simple majority in Parliament to remove a Judge. These are some of the crucial changes / reforms needed. Judicial function is a soft one unlike the functions of Army or even police which are arduous and risky.

Before coming to the core aspect of judicial accountability, let me touch upon the accountability of criminals (accused of an offence) who will be in millions. The accountability for crime perpetrated by individual citizen or groups, terrorists, Maoists is negligible. Not even 33% of those accused of grave offences get convicted and undergo prison sentence. 2/3rd are let off on the principle of "presumption of innocence" of accused. Millions of accused escape accountability for crimes. And this evidentiary rule of "Presumption of innocence" is not anchored in any legal provision. **It is a judicial innovation in the evolution of criminal jurisprudential principles in the interpretative process of the legal/constitutional provisions.** Therefore, for non-accountability of criminal class for their crimes, these jurisprudential principles are responsible and they were evolved by judiciary. **Judiciary therefore, by its interpretation indirectly aided defeat of accountability of those millions accused and charge sheeted for an "offence" simple or grave. So, the evidentiary principle of "presumption of innocence" of accused and the Democratic principles of accountability for law and people, are conflicting each other.** The Nation has to choose the accountability principle.

The discretion of short sentencing after convicting an accused, further discretion of Appeal Courts to reduce the period of short sentence made under the relevant provisions of Cr. P.C. 1973, power of quashing criminal prosecutions U/s 482 of the Cr. P.C., Article 226 of the Constitution, liberal grant of bails, proof beyond doubt, benefit of doubt, quality of witness whether one is interested or hostile or trustworthy, evidences of police officer, solitary witness, Mensrea (mental state of accused), confession of accused, extra judicial confession and the entire edifice of law of evidence rests in the hands of judges. Evidence is clay. The judge is pot maker. What the judge considers is evidence. Judicial ruling on all these penal, procedural, and evidence law go in favour of the community of offenders of law. They are the main beneficiaries to escape accountability for crimes. Of course the community of 1 million strong defence advocates are collateral beneficiaries. Law makers heavily trusted our judges. Hope that they repose the same faith in police for right action.

Now, let me come to the judicial accountability proper. Intellectuals, some giants among them, legal eagles, all talk about - NJC (National Judicial Commission), etc. to enforce judicial accountability. I have no reservation about it provided it is not judiciary centric. But the intellectuals failed to zero in on the Target much less hit bull's eye. We move in circles making one wrong move after another, yet clamouring for change without undoing the first wrong move.

Point 1: Judicial rulings thwarted taking cognizance of an "offence" of bribery by the judges of High Court or Supreme Court either under Sec.154 Cr PC by Police or u/s190 IPC by the JFCM having jurisdiction. The rulings required that permission of Chief Justice is necessary for taking cognizance of an "offence". This is a slap on the face of Law as well as Rule of Law. **An act of bribery is not part of public duty or received in the purported discharge of duty. So much so these rulings place judiciary above law and the Constitution.** **Suggestion**: These wrong decisions of judiciary need correction by way of appeal to a larger bench to begin with. That by itself represents positive change.

Point 2: "In House" or domestic enquiry into charge of corruption. This system has no legal anchor. No provision of law provided for this. And it offends Rule of Law of Prof. Dicey's view viz., that no person or institution be a judge of its own wrongful actions. Secondly even where there are proved charges in in-house enquiry, there is reservation to refer them to FIR by judiciary or the Govt. or both. After all the proved charges are arrived at not after enquiry by petty police official but by the Supreme Court Committee of Judges. **Suggestion:- All proved charges need to be referred to FIR.** Reversal of wrong decisions/judgments itself represents a welcome change indeed.

Point 3: Government's inaction to act and impeach through Parliament in cases where evidence is gathered (Mr. Justice Ramaswamy case). **Suggestion: reversing inaction is itself a change.**

Point 4: Judiciary is assuming under Art. 141, powers of legislation which do not exist in it . A judicial ruling may be binding on all the lower courts, but is not relevant for taking cognizance of an offence. Law is different from case law. Like Art. 226 and 32 getting abused by judiciary and needed review by Parliament, Art.141 also needs review and amendment. Under the Constitution, apart from Parliament and State Assemblies, the President of the Republic and the Governors of states have power to legislate through ordinances. **The Supreme Court of India has no such power. It is not a third house of legislature as observed by Pandit Nehru.**

There is nothing infallible about court judgments that include Supreme Court judgments. Mr. Justice O.C.Reddy (retd. SC Judge) wrote a book I believe, on incorrect Supreme Court judgments. I had a glance of **Supreme Court cases, June 7, 2009.** In Civil Appeal No. 1741 of 2009, decided on 20.3.2009 (State of Bihar vs Narayan Singh), the Supreme Court while dealing with regularization of illegal appointments to Government Service, lamented as to how court judgments have gone wrong perpetuating illegalities and irregularities - all while exercising powers U/A 226, 32 of the Constitution of India. It observed that "the extent of damage caused to public employment due to judicial rulings is too much to be retrieved."

A few years back (2002), a former Chief Justice of Supreme Court Mr. Patnaik aired his views to a TV Channel that Chief Justice needs more powers to discipline judges. I am not able to understand. On one side Supreme Court said that no cognizance of an offence of bribery be taken without Chief Justice permission. There is also reservation to refer in-house enquiry reports (proved one) to FIR. So, these are two steps backward and clamouring for more powers with one step forward makes no sense. **Therefore, judiciary and Government need to undo the existing wrong decision/actions.**

Very often we hear from our beloved Netas that law will take its own course. Here, in respect of corruption of judiciary, law taking its course has been halted by judicial rulings.

Delays in trials, disposal of appeals, and revision in both criminal and civil matters, petitions under writ jurisdiction, pronouncement of judgments after the conclusion of hearings are all voiced and concern expressed. Was any judicial functionary, lower or higher level at any point of time in the history of our Republic held accountable for the same? Of course, there are alibis for delays, shortage of judges, funds, accommodation, etc. It is not quantity that matters but quality and will power of judicial leadership that counts. Court procedures, criminal rules of practice, disciplining defence advocates, choice of government advocates, all matter in cutting down delays etc. Unending arguments, lengthy judgments, entertaining frivolous litigation, etc., have nothing to do with more money or staff. I recall two Chief Justices in Andhra Pradesh Mr. Obul Reddy and Gopal Rao Ekbote, who were competent to discipline judges. Therefore, under the system, not even a fraction of accountability is answered. Impeachment and removal by Parliament answers 50% of accountability. **Comprehensive accountability includes removal from service followed up by criminal proceedings for acts of corruption.**

One Hafiz Saeed, leader of a Terrorist outfit in Pakistan is released by Lahore High Court on 2.6.2009. There was diplomatic uproar in India as he was suspected to be responsible for 26.11.2008 terrorist attack on Mumbai. **In many democratic countries, judiciary became a state within a state or a super state making the task of the state to fight terrorism that much more difficult.** Litigation in India is becoming big. Courts in Metros are thronged by litigants, both civil and criminal. Crime and litigation reflect poorly on the quality of civilization levels.

Unless Supreme Court accepts Accountability and Transparency in full measure by setting an example for other institutions, it will not carry credibility with public and Nation.

But the moment it accepts, it will become a National Icon and rallying point to damn the corrupt and criminalized polity. It will command the respect of intellegentsia, media, rights groups in civil society and other state institutions like Police, Bureaucracy and Army etc. While grudgingly accepting the obligation to declare the Assets, it has opted that information on the Assets of Judges is not in public domain.

Judiciary .....cont'd

The biggest casuality is Accountability and Transparency in judicial Governance. It is becoming a Herculean task even to get Judges declare their assets, forget about their punishment which will never happen in our Constitutional scheme. (For judicial non-performance, corruption and other wrong doings). **When the empowered classes such as political executive, judiciary, bureaucracy are not Accountable and transparent, democracy is defeated to its last detail.** Judiciary blocked all the doors to be Accountable and transparency. There is no **proactive** approach to identify the rotten apple though there is reactive approach to the allegation levelled against a particular Judge. Mr. D.P. Dinakaran episode reveals that point. There is no legal or Constitutional mechanism to enquire or investigate allegation against Judges. Collegium is not legal. In the case of Dinakaran, District Collector in Tamil Nadu sends report on a reference from Supreme Court on land encroachments. **These adhoc and extra legal mechanisms of enquiry like collegium will not bring any measure of uniformity in the enquiry process.**

As the book goes to print, there is this unfortunate rather sad developments in public values. On a petition filed by a concerned citizen, the High Court of Delhi rendered a judgment that the Chief Justice, Supreme Court is a "Public Authority" and that he needs to disclose details of his assets under the Right to Information Act of 2005. The Supreme Court deliberated this and choose to contest the case through its court officers before a bench of Delhi High Court, before it comes to itself for final hearing. A highest legal authority (Apex Court) indulging in litigation like an ordinary citizen and where there is no violation of rights is a strange and bizarre development. **A mere disclosure of assets will in no way according to me affect the rights of the declarant. Nor does it impinge on the autonomy of the institution of judiciary. Autonomy or independence is not absolute. Nor can it be divorced from Accountability and Transparency.** Moreover what degree of autonomy, the judiciary should have is a matter left to the public represented through Parliament. **The judiciary is therefore trying to place itself above the law of the land.** By a catena of judgments, it took away or usurped.

- The Constitutional role of Executive in the appointments to higher judiciary (Art.124 and 217). It has bent the above Constitutional provisions to enhance its position.
- Placed itself above The Prevention of Corruption Act of 1988 by pronouncing judgments that no cognizance of an offence of corruption and investigation can be done by state agencies against a member of higher judiciary without its permission.
- Is now attempting to place itself above RTI Act 2005 by refusing to make assets public.

What a contrast when we compare it with a few decades gone by. Gandhiji gave up what little tangible assets he had. He had only

- Material movable assets in the shape of a loin cloth to cover the lower part of his body, a goat, a few nuts to mulch.
- Intellectual assets as reflected in his writings.
- Mental and physical assets of indefatigable energy - action, constant action in fighting social evils in society, against unjust laws and in driving out the British rulers.

The Nehrus who were propertied class sacrificed almost all their tangible assets to the Nation.

What hardships, sacrifices did our Lordships make? Are Court hearings and delivery of judgments an arduous or risky job so as to place them in a separate category in the eye of law granting without admitting such a position?

Mr. B.N. Srikrishna famed Retd. Judge, Supreme Court in an interview to November 2009 issue of "Readers Digest" stated that 7 judges of Bombay High Court were boycotted by the Bench in 1990's as they were found to be corrupt. It is understandable, if not justified, the corruption of a one time MLA, Minister. But it is difficult to understand corruption by a Judge of High Court or Supreme Court who have fixed tenure of service and who can practice post retirement and particularly where the Constitution clothed them with power to do justice. What justice can an aggrieved citizen expect when Judges turn corrupt? Is it not the case of fence eating the crop?

Namby-Pamby political leadership of the last 20 years has acquiesced in the violation of laws and Constitutional provisions by the judiciary all in the name of judicial autonomy and independence. For there is no independence or immunity for acts of corruption and wrong doing by any Institution of State and if that were to be the case, it ceases to be a Democratic one.

Sri Dinakaran's episode spilled over into hooliganism when lawyers in Bangalore disrupted Court proceedings and rioted. (Media report dt. 10.11.2009). There were similar incidents a few months ago in Chennai High Court. The ugly face of our Democratic institutions and professional groups like lawyers is now open to International Media. The root causes need to be tackled viz., Accountability in its total form for judicial misconduct and incapacity. **Towards that end we need.**

- Comprehensive Accountability law like the Right to Information Act 2005.
- Mechanism to enforce the same by the Chief Commissioner's and Commissioner's similar to the RTI Act 2005. The Chief Commissioner may be a high judicial functionary with other Commissioners drawn from different walks of life known for integrity and impartiality.

- Weak and impractical existing mechanism of Accountability for judicial misconduct such as impeachment process needs to be activated invariably.
- Total Accountability in this case includes (a) removal of Sri Dinkaran from service (b) prosecution if he violated any law (c) the collegium of Supreme Court which selected his name should be made ineligible for the job of selecting Judges.

The crisis of Accountability in judiciary needs to be addressed urgently as the institution enjoys total Autonomy where power is likely to be abused more often.

Unless the Constitution of India makes Accountability and transparency, the corner stone of its scheme, I am afraid that it serves no useful purpose to the citizen at large. Mr. Gorbachev "Glasnost and Perestroika" brought in silent revolution in Russian Communist regime paving the way for Democracy. **In the same way Accountability and Transparency in India on the lines suggested by me if implemented will pave the way for real Democracy.**

NSG in Hyderabad

News reports in June 4th week suggest that Government of India is creating National Security Guard (NSG) hubs at various state headquarters. Are they necessary? Cannot a well trained State police force do the job? Does our economy permit the proliferation of such and similar organizations? Is it a change? I am not against these hubs coming up. But first there needs to be an answer as to why the attacks are not prevented. We first allow Mumbai (26-11-2008) Terrorist like attacks to take place and then try to find answer in NSG. What has NSG got to do with prevention and occurrence? **That is essentially a job of state police including its intelligence wings.** How many Mumbai type terrorist strikes are anticipated and what measures are evolved to make State police forces to get them or an attempt to get them prevented or occurred? Is the creation of NSG and other superstructures in the Security Establishment a propaganda piece for Governments or ill-thought out proposal? NSG is useful for hostage taking situation but not for acts of sabotage or open shoot outs in public places. These are all some of the questions that need satisfactory answer. In Andhra Pradesh there are about 3 types of Special Police forces apart from civil police. If a small percentage of the special units are trained in the job profile of NSG, that is a better option. NSG and similar units need elaborate infrastructure and there is no certainty that they will be called to duty atleast even once in an year.

We therefore need to cry halt to the triumphalism of sloth, corruption and mediocrity, inefficiency of civil police forces, its leadership in particular. In order to breath life into police functioning, merit and integrity, the quintessential human resources of merit and honesty are needed to replace numbers in police ranks, creation of special units, sloth and inefficiency. Nothing is taken seriously at any level of police functioning including the prevention and investigation of grave offences.

Merit

Merit is not a myth in administration as viewed by sceptics. In all revenue yielding departments, higher revenue collection by the head of department in a period of 3 to 5 years, should be a benchmark for efficiency and rules that promote him to next higher rank represent a change.

Faulty, non-transparent, Annual Confidential Reports, subjective assessment by departmental seniors lead to non-performance and mediocrity being crowned as king. Time bound promotions to next higher rank based on such defective ACRs, lack of Accountability for inefficiency, corruption and partiality put administration in reverse gear. Correcting this defective format of ACRs, objective assessment by a committee chaired by one outside member based on comprehensive data of performance, promotions based on such objective assessments (merit based not time bound) represent a positive change and moving into a forward gear.

Ragging

News reports suggest different and wide 'definition' of the offence. Very good! But accountability also needs to be wide/ comprehensive which includes the following:

- Immediate suspension of the offender from classes
- Domestic enquiry and follow up measures
- Criminal investigation by Police and charge sheet
- Court framing charges after hearing initial arguments for prima facie guilt. "Presumption of guilt" in place of presumption of innocence needs to be provided for so that accountability for crimes is easier in court conviction.

Once that is done, the following additional action is needed

- Notifying offender for disqualification from public employment
- Notifying private employer about the criminal past of the student
- Disqualification for issue of passport to go abroad in search of employment
- Derecognition of the educational institution for repeat of acts of ragging.

A Slew of Measures Probably will help to Control the Menace

One needs to study the pattern behind these offences, whether they have got to do with affluence and economically well to do sections of students and scholarships recipients alone or whether it covered the poor or lower middle class family students. Lax supervision in University administration is one reason. So it is not only a wider definition of the offence of ragging that is important but also wider accountability process as indicated above.

Cases of CBI/Anti-Corruption Agencies

The phrase "abuse of office" is a criminal offence under The Prevention of Corruption Act, 1988. In Government expenditure, where loss is caused malafide, the offence is registered and investigated. But these agencies, to the best of my knowledge, have not registered similar offences for causing revenue loss due to corruption. The action of a municipal official, undervaluing assessment of house tax due to corruption, squarely falls under the phrase "abuse of office". So, to improve government revenues, cases need to be filed. Government needs to plug the twin loopholes viz., wasteful public expenditure and loss of public revenues. Public exchequer will be sound. Any way, statistics can be looked into.

Sec 377 IPC 1860 – Gay Rights

In June - July 2009, Spokespersons of Congress Party kicked up the issue of Gay rights as though we do not have more serious problems on hand. **They are soft on Terrorism and corruption and want to extend their soft silken touch to gay rights.** The Delhi High Court added fuel to the fire with its direction to decriminalise the acts. The judiciary brought this under Art. 21 dealing with Fundamental Rights through that omnibus architecture of interpretative powers. The legal aspects were debated by Mr. Soli Sorabji etc., on TV channels. He says that the Court did not totally strike down Sec. 377 IPC and the same will not apply to minors subjected to sexual abuse. Apart from these legal quibblings, we need to look at it from a larger angle. It promotes permissiveness in society. We already have the heavy problem of ragging in colleges. It may spread to schools also embracing an entire lot of young students. We then have acid attacks on girls / women by jilted lovers. Third it may lead to unsuspecting children (young minds) falling prey to active gays. Jilted spouses are also in the race of violence through acid attacks. Uncommonly women also are involved in inciting attacks directly or through kith and kin. Already we have enough of TV serials which lend encouragement for permissiveness. The business interests of Cinema, TV Serials, Advertisement by business classes, political interests, interpretation by certain Judges laid seize to or conspired against the traditional Indian morality, wailed one observer. So there are a whole lot of issues involved.The judgment leads to Gay marriages. I am happy that BJP and Samajwadi Party are opposing the move set by Congress Party. The Muslims clergy in particular took a firm view against dropping Section 377 IPC. So too are Hindu and Christian religious bodies. The Media with its front page news (both print and electronic) is doing a disservice to society by glamourising it. We find Congress Party not eager to pass strong anti terror law when so many innocent citizens, security personnel lost their lives annually. Yet Congress Party has let the cat among the pigeons by taking up gay rights. **Instead of West being a model, it is better that neighbouring countries are a model on these rights.** Where are the Indian politics leading the country? This is not to say that there are no sins in society. But accepting them, legalising them is a different issue with deleterious consequences. **Any legal provision needs to reflect the will of majority.** Every thing minority has been the panache of some political parties. Minority gay gender rights fits into the grand political design of vote banks. Governments have more serious problems to face with a higher degree of responsibilities.

If individual choices have primacy over public good, abortions and other sexual offences also acquire legal character which means that State Laws need to fall in line with individual choices of minority. Anarchistic indivisualism is harmful to society. The judgement and the divided debate by Media, intelligentsia, a section of polity affects immature adults who fail to make a fine distinction between legality and morality. Understanding right and wrong, sin and virtue, sin and major sin gets confused.

Our imperfect faith, where God's existence and supremacy is not firmly rooted in hearts, except that many pray God for selfish ends and ritual centric which paved the way for 1/3 of United India becoming Islamic, our liberal Democracy based on a Constitutional document modelled on the Constitutions of western countries, liberal, very liberal interpretation of Constitutional provisions by our judicial fraternity drawing inspiration from the rulings of American Supreme Court (not from the judicial rulings of neighbouring countries that include Japan), our implicit obedience to the resolutions of United Nations in making laws affecting our culture, economy and politics have all impacted our political, economic and cultural moorings with all their attendant ill effects. Dr. Urusa Mohsin, Faculty of Law, Unity Degree College, Lucknow observes, that homosexuality is acknowledged but not approved. Only 0.3% of the population as against 99.7% are homosexuals. He referred to its disapproval by various denominations of churches in Europe and America. It also did not find acceptance according to him in Islam and in Hinduism. He refers to Buddhism which has not explicitly condemned this evil. According to me Buddha condemned sexual misconduct in no uncertain terms. Probably in those days, the issue has not got the attention it now obtains. Present day focus on rights, international and national lobbies on such rights, media ever eager to commercialise these issues, liberal interpretation of legal provisions by judiciary all contributed to make it an issue in human relations which was otherwise marginalized.

The following points need consideration by the Hon'ble Supreme Court of India before whom an appeal against the Judgment of Delhi High Court is pending.

- Whether individual choices even if they are wrong outweigh public good?
- Is law capable of preventing certain sexual "offences" where public morality can?
- Whether certain legal provisions in IPC 1860 which criminalise lewd gestures also be decriminalised in favour of individual choices?
- Cannot Sec. 377 IPC 1860 be made a non cognizable offence where permission by Judicial Magistrate is needed for taking cognizance, if it is the case of Naz Foundation that the above section paved way for police to harass gays? Three years of minimum punishment and non cognizability is an alternative to decriminalisation.
- Can individual acts which offend public morals or sensibilities be decriminalized by judiciary. Does judiciary possess such a power, not withstanding the power of judicial review? Is that power unlimited in scope?

Where are we, the Nation being led by the political and judicial leadership? Is it a minority Dictatorship where minority over powers the view of majority? Why not our controversial laws be put to referendum by suitable amendment to the Constitution?

One only hopes that the NGOs (Non Govt. Organisations) particularly the likes of NAZ foundation, the petitioner before Delhi High Court are not influenced by the International Gay rights lobby. There is poor regulation of NGOs in the country and very poor Accountability for the funds expended and activities carried out. It is unfortunate.

Higher Levels of Education and Public and Private Values

Sania Mirza, Tennis ace of India was betrothed to a local boy recently. Just before that two highly educated youth were found loitering around her house and professed infatuation for her. Is education a handicap to values? Does technology, Cinema, TV Serials, advertisements of business products, Pop music and song, Tollywood and Bollywood versions of such song and dance, internet, websites ruining values? Does ragging in colleges, suicides of students for not passing examinations, acid attacks by jilted lovers, posing semi nude for money by models, actors, gay unions, abortions, trafficking in women by Members of Parliament reflect our Educational advancement? Every where conservatives, traditionalists are on retreat before the market forces of liberalism, consumerism, culturalism, rights activism. Democratic Governments are particularly vulnerable. **Unlettered, uneducated persons of the previous generation were superior to the present generation. International rights lobbies find soft Indian state and society as a fertile soil for their cultural seeds to grow.**

Public Order, Law and Order

To the best of my knowledge, they are not well defined. They find "expression" in Chapter X of the Criminal Procedure Code 1973. The title of that chapter is "Maintenance of Public Order and Tranquility". Sec. 129 Cr.P.C. deals with dispersal of "unlawful assemblies" or an Assembly or 5 or more persons likely to cause disturbance to public peace, the nature of force to be used, the Authorities Competent to use such force. Other sections in the above titled chapter deal with (a) public nuisance (b) urgent cases of public nuisance or apprehended danger (c) disputes as to immovable property. But the above chapter has not covered **organised crime** of criminal syndicates of various colours and hues. Public order stands threatened steadily, subtly and continuously in a society by organised crime unless it is checked effectively and timely though its impact is widely dispersed and not immediately felt. Members of organised crime are not only criminal in nature but also hardened blood thirsty type. A brawl in public place, sporadic incidents of student violence etc., are not essentially **criminal in nature** so as to affect public order / peace and tranquility. So organised crime, Terrorism are potent foes of public order.

Criminalisation of Wasteful Public Spending

On 30-6-2009, TOI news reported that a public interest litigation (PIL) is pending in the Supreme Court of India. It is against spending of public money sanctioned by the Legislature of Uttar Pradesh Government to erect statues to Dalit leaders that include present Chief Minister of the State. The amount involved is Rs.1200 crores which may not be big. But the issue is the principle involved – whether public money can be spent on such and similar less prioritized or grandiose projects. Some Chief Ministers are proposing to acquire Air crafts each worth Rs. 200 crores. The list of items purchased covering public expenditure is too big to be listed. In all my writings I have raised the issue of wasteful public expenditure at the **level of administration**. They run into lakhs of crores annually – purchases made by various departments, works carried out for the beautification of offices, guesthouses, residences and in acquiring luxurious transport etc. etc. But nobody questioned this wasteful public spending by the administration in any court. There is no legal provision before which accountability of the culprits can be established for such wasteful public expenditure as long as there is no personal gain to the person who took the decision of spending. While even Rs.100 loss incurred in the purchase of an item above the market price attracts the offence of "abuse of public office" (Sec.13(1)(d) of The Prevention of Corruption Act, 1988). Similarly if one accepts Rs.100/- which is not a legal remuneration, it also becomes an offence under the above Act. But if one spends even Rs.1,00,000 crores on wasteful items, it is not an offence. So this wasteful public expenditure needs to be defined as an offence prosecutable and punishable. For large wasteful public expenditure running into hundred of crores life imprisonment provision needs to be prescribed. Wasteful use of **resources** particularly energy also needs to be taken care. Recently the Governments of Punjab and Haryana faced with energy shortage, ordered Government offices to switch off Air Conditioners. **Over staffing** of Govt. Depts., PSU also needs to be reviewed to save public exchequer. Private companies are also over staffed. The financial burden is passed on to the consumer. Wasteful water leakages in canal irrigation also need our attention. However, I am doubtful whether such a legal provision will be ever made because it hurts the interest of the political, administrative and judicial establishments who are the beneficiaries in the process. Wasteful Government expenditure, unproductive wasteful Government subsidies to various sectors, Goverment stake in non- profitable PSUs made the country a poor cousin economically instead of being a power house if not economic giant like China. Financial prudence is needed. A penny saved is penny earned. Foreign companies are shy of investment because like the Indian Business and Industrial Class, they are not familiar with the nuts and bolts of Indian Administration and polity. Local Businessmen have a network of people loaded with underhand deals to deal with Bureaucratic - political class. Union Budget presented on 06.07.2009 focussed on massive and unprecedented spending.

Headlines Today English TV Channel reported on 30.07.2009 about 15 lakh tons of imported pulses are rotting in our ports creating artificial scarcity. Corruption is also alleged in unnecessary imports.

If public funds are spent without wastage, corruption, the lot of targetted groups will improve two or even three fold. Late Sri Rajiv Gandhi is on record to state that not more than 30% of public funds allotted reach the targetted.

Writing in the Economic Times, dt. 03.05.2010, M. Bhubnarmath quoted 13 Finance Commission observations:

- 3000 crore grant to States to encourage enrolment of beneficiaries under PDS, NRGES.
- 5000 crore grant to reduce infant mortality.
- 5000 crore grant for better delivery of justice to judicial infrastructure

The Author of the article observed that public expenditure is marked by poor outcomes. According to me wasteful public spending is an insignificant issue in our country. Whereas in Western developed Democracies, the USA in particular, it is a key electoral issue.

The Luxury of Neo-rich

There is so much money with so few in India that helicopter travel for political, business or politico-businessmen or business-politicos became a fashion, indeed an addiction. In the 3rd week of September 2009, one Minister took a motorcade of 600 to Edupulapaya to pay homage to YSR. People are reminded about traffic jams that extended up to 20-30 km. There is booming business for motor and Aviation industries. Luxurious Innovas, Scorpios to our Netas, Bada babus, senior cops is the order of the day. The bug has bitten judiciary too. Not one vehicle but 2 or 3 at the disposal of each. **Car industry in India thrives on the establishment**. In 1968, when I purchased Ambassador car from Auto Fins for Rs. 18,000/- there were hardly a dozen cars in the district. When I purchased Maruti 800 in 1989 and happened to visit my native district Kadapa, it was a treat for onlookers, sleek and silent performer. There were hardly 100 to 200 cars in the entire district. After 1990's liberalization of economy, the loot of Nations' resources, exploitation of public work contracts commenced and now district Netas own a fleet of Innovas and Scorpios. The Marutis are for the use of their personal staff like PAs, drivers, gunmen, etc. This luxurious lifestyles, working styles is one of the sore points with our Maoist leadership, which they describe as the bourgeois life and working style of the establishment. True middle and lower middle classes possess cars, motorcycles, cell phones, TVs and other electronic gadgets. But many in the middle class possess them at the cost of neglect of nutritious food and comfortable living apartment. Certificates of fantastic economic growth follow from West. **The establishment's growth in terms of numbers and wealth is well assured.** I doubt the economic growth of teeming millions.

Modernisation of Police

Modernisation and professionalism do not go hand in hand. **Without commitment to duties, no amount of modernisation of police forces will help. The bulk of police functions covering preventive, detective, investigation duties including maintenance of public order duties cannot be linked to modernisation.** Of course modernisation of special police units dealing with Terrorism of various kinds is needed. But the traditional crimes that include sensational grave offences like murders, frauds, corruption cases need no great modernisation. In the past 10 to 15 years large amounts of funds were allotted in the name of modernisation. But the percentage of detection, conviction are far below the corresponding previous period. This is notwithstanding scientific aids to investigation and development of forensic sciences laboratories. **So the human element of commitment, integrity are more important than modernisation of the police force.** Take the case of prime investigation agency – the C.B.I. Can any one vouch that the sensational cases handled by them lead to greater success than the pre-modernisation period? Therefore honesty, efficiency, impartiality of not bowing to pressures from political and other quarters will improve the detection, conviction rate of crimes more importantly the grave crimes. **So modernisation did not result in much desired professionalism of police**. It also needs to be looked at from another angle. Has modernisation improved discipline? Has it brought down (a) custodial deaths, (b) unwanted use of fire arms in public order duties (c) fake encounters of outlaws and Terrorists? According to me these wrongdoings or crimes are on increase, compared to pre-modernisation period. **So the proof of pudding lies in eating.**

More Numbers and Money, More Powers under Laws

The alibis of more funds, man power more power to give better performance are common to bureaucracy and police too. There are several functions which have nothing to do with more finance, more staff. Duties such as permission for gun licence, passport screening, checking hooligans, illicit brewing, unauthorized liquor shops checking, beat service, investigation/enquiries, proper and prompt registration of crimes, right arrests, maintaining police data or records etc., do not call for any extra funds or staff. Of course, special problems like Terrorism do need funds and staff. But outside this terrorism, 60 to 70 % of police functions are either neglected or carried out in unsatisfactory way. Let us take municipal permission for building traffic checks, fixing manholes, electric bulbs, etc. need public official's service and not funds and staff. Funds are required on policy matters such as establishment of hospitals, schools etc., at the government level. At any rate, with all this pumping of funds for modernization of police forces, the rate of crime did not come down, nor detection or conviction rate improved. We have so many forensic science labs with lie detectors, dog squads, finger print experts, cameras, clues teams to detect offences. A lot of transport etc. is given. Did anyone audit and evaluate whether detection figure has improved due to all this technological or experts' services? There is a zero improvement. All of them are not substitute for the human element of dedication to duty, career long dedication. **It is not numbers which is a human resource but talent and dedication.** Existing powers under law need to be rightfully exercised and performance of an assigned job in the present station in life perfectly and honestly is justice done to the job.

In an article dt. 15.09.2009 in The Hindu, Mr. P.S. Appu, Former Central Land Reforms Commissioner and a former Chief Secretary of Bihar observed follows:

"A polity that incurs colossal wasteful expenditure on a bloated government machinery, some avoidable subsidies, the supply of free electricity to prosperous farmers, distribution of free colour television sets, the installation of statues of megalomaniac politicians and so on should not grudge a large outlay on projects targeted to benefit the weaker sections"

Parliamentary Oversight of Regulatory Bodies Sought

'They are taking big decisions involving huge amounts of public money'. Expressing anguish over the lack of parliamentary control over independent regulatory bodies constituted in the post-liberalisation era, Rajya Sabha member and deputy chairman Planning Commission of Bihar NK Singh mooted appointment of a separate parliamentary standing committee on regulatory bodies under the Ministry of Law.

Mr. N.K. Singh delivering a lecture on 'Improving Parliamentary Oversight' at Administrative Staff College India (ASCI) observed on 17.09.2009 as follows: "He felt that the independent regulatory authorities like TRAI, SEBI, Petroleum regulator authority, Director General of Hydrocarbons and others were not under the purview of the Parliament. No standing committee could review the independent regulatory bodies under the present set up of Parliament. As these regulatory bodies were taking big decisions involving huge amounts of public money, their functioning should also be reviewed by the Parliament".

For this he suggested that the auditing of these regulatory bodies should mandatorily be done by Comptroller and Auditor General (CAG). So that, the Public Accounts Committee (PAC) of the Parliament could review the functioning of regulatory bodies, Singh said. Otherwise, the Parliamentary oversight should be redefined in such a way that the a new standing committee under the Ministry of Law should be constituted to review the functioning of the regulatory bodies.

He recalled the controversy over the sale of spectrum by TRAI which involved Rs. 1,500 crore. As the TRAI was outside the purview of CAG and Parliament it could not be reviewed, he said. Parliament shutting out such issues was found only in India, he said. Singh also expressed unhappiness that there was no **'budget transparency' in the Parliament** and no amendments were made while passing the Appropriation Bill. **"The passing of Budget by Indian Parliament has fallen short of international bench mark,"** Mr. Singh said.

He pointed out that 32 per cent of the precious time of 14th Lok Sabha was wasted due to din and bustle in the House. But, the 15th Lok Sabha and Rajya Sabha had a good beginning and there were so many educated young persons who were elected MPs. However, Singh, observed that MPs hardly had an access to research on the issues being discussed in the Parliament. He also felt that the Standing Committees were hardly reviewing the burning and contemporary issues and only digging out past issues."

Contempt Law

The Supreme Court of India is a great champion of freedom of speech and expression. But the same is not true when it comes to the question of criticism of judiciary. This is so even where there is no malice in speech and expression. Contempt law is invoked and the contemner punished. The journalists of Mid-Day newspaper in Delhi were punished notwithstanding pleading truth as defence. *Second-* There is no set procedure in the trial. This is anti-law. *Third-* The court becomes an investigator, prosecutor and a judge. This is Anti-Rule of Law. Because no one or an institution can sit in judgement over its own action. **I give a more concrete instance of the difference between Law and Rule of Law.** During 1980s, two former Chief Ministers Mr. Jagannath Mishra and Smt. Nandini Satpati faced corruption charges and charge sheets were filed against them. When they were returned to power in the next round of elections, they withdrew the criminal case against themselves. True Sec.321 Cr.PC 1973 permits such withdrawal from Courts records. But such withdrawal will be in tune with Rule of Law provided that Governments led by others (not the accused Chief Ministers) permit such withdrawal. I have dealt the subject in a separate chapter in my book "Challenges of

Governance". I revert back to the question of trial and conviction for contempt law. Granting without admitting that judiciary can sit and decide on the challenges of its own action and sentence persons, I would suggest a middle path. Appeal against such convictions can be heard by a legal forum or a court of appeal constituted from out of eminent members of Rajya Sabha (Upper House of Parliament). This will be in tune with Rule of Law. Constitutional amendments are needed.

Maoist Threat – June 2009

Lalgarh in Midnapur District, West Bengal State became a battle ground between Maoists and security forces. Land mines are blasted and Guns are blazing. There is bloodshed. In the State of Orissa bordering West Bengal, the situation is no better. Several schemes, flagship schemes of Government meant for people's welfare are mired in corruption. Their full benefits have not accrued to the public. **Justice is denied.** Grievance and frustration grew giving room for Maoists to step in. Access of people to the public official is absent. There is no caring bond. It is not this lack of caring bond alone but also utter contempt of the public official to the people's problem that resulted in this discontentment in the people. This coupled with ever eager and un-ceasing monopolistic effort of the Business, Political and Administrative classes in the loot of Nation's tangible and intangible resources by blatant abuse of state power provided a fertile ground for the Maoist propaganda to thrive. The Central Government according to Media reports rushed its security forces to establish Rule of Law. **But Rule of Law is some thing higher and nobler than Law. It is essentially a Principle of Justice and fair play. All laws, decisions of the public authorities that include judicial decisions need to conform to Rule of Law. Where Rule of Law prevails, there is higher level of political civilization.** Therefore where justice and fair play in the implementation of Government's scheme is thwarted, where there is no transparency, Accountability of Administration, where people become foreigners to the public official, Rule of Law does not prevail. True, the Maoists can be beaten by the security forces and Law and Order established. But to establish Rule of Law, one need to reconnect the caring bond between the people and public official. By a robust Administrative response to the people's problems or grievances we can open up the doors to Rule of Law and many times that situation will preempt law and order situations. I have touched upon the issue of grievance redressal at some of the pages in the **preface** to my books. It is not public alone who have grievances against the administration. Even Government official, Army and Policemen have their own grievances against Government, their own superiors. We have witnessed an ugly spectacle of Army jawans, policemen killing their own officers (fragging). Grievances are there in families, private organizations etc. **It is a whole world of its own.** If poverty in India is limited to 300 million people, grievances will extend to a billion or billions. Because each individual will have several grievances. A raise in the price of vegetables, food stuff, exorbitant service charges give raise to grievances. They need to be taken care by the concerned. Every grievance cannot be rejected on the ground that it is not covered by the law. On 30.06.2009, I had a grievance against the local Maruti Motor Servicing Station for the exorbitant service charges billed. They have not exhibited rate of service charges in their premises. I telephoned the Dy. Commissioner of Police, Cyberabad. He answered the call on his cell phone. Even before ascertaining my grievance or a complaint, he said that he is in a meeting and that I can contact him afterwards. I said that he can as well call me after his meetings. That my grievance is redressed or not is a different issue but whether he attempted to know what my complaint or grievance is an issue for academic debate. So I have one more grievance on that day against the DCP. Unless one is a powerful person, a rich or even a power broker or even further a person who massages the ego of high caste All India Service officers, you are never sure that your grievance is even heard much less attended to. Therefore grievance removal though appears innocuous or responding to such grievances promotes cordial relations in families, amongst friends, colleagues, juniors, seniors in any organisational set up. It reflects on quality of Administration and democratic way of functioning. **Indeed life is a bundle of grievances.** Ignoring them leads to disputes, conflicts and violation of Laws etc. **As religious thought teaches us life is made up of little things in which kindness and meeting small obligations are what wins hearts.**

I had earlier expressed the view and I repeat that poverty is only one cause for the growth of Maoism. Failure of administration and loot of nation's resources by governing classes are the other potent causes.

So some of these root causes need to be addressed before the phalanx of Law and Guns (soft and hard power) in the armoury of Government are displayed and put to effective use.

Grievance need not necessarily be grounded in violation of a right. It can be found in a sense of wrong that visited one. Grievance in a sense of wrong (greased cartridges) led to the famous 1857 revolt of Indian Sepoy against the British Government. At the same time one need to discount imaginary or bogus grievances. Grievances are not poverty centric. They do not spare a king or emperor.

It looks to me that Imperialism, Colonialism, Capitalism largely gave birth to Democracy. Though the idea is imported from West, it struck roots in third world countries and across the globe since masses are attracted to it like a pin to a magnate. British Colonial rule dabbled in the democratic institutions in India in late 19th Century. Democracy in its turn gave birth to unbridled individual freedoms, wide spread corruption, hedonistic consumerism and cultural degradation in the form of posing for nude, semi nude photograph, cat or ramp walks, live in relationships, raggings, gay rights, gay marriages etc. Top political leaders in India are sitting on mountains of money a part of it stashed in Tax havens. Members of business class became capitalists largely due to financial bonanza to industrial class in the form of writing off Bank debts, pumping public money into unviable public sector undertakings and bailing out fraudulent transactions of private companies through public monies. Governments negligence deliberate indeed, to effect proper tax collection, soft approach to recovery of contested tax aided the Indian Business class to become capitalistic without that much needed self effort and money investment. The contribution of this capitalist class to the growth of economy, creation of permanent National assets have come to be questioned. 400 top private companies contribute less than 6% of G.D.P. As the loot or mortgage of Nation's resources by political and business class including the naked resource of Govt. land in various cities and towns is going unchecked by the public institution like police, bureaucracy and judiciary, there is no better alternative than the left parties like communists to take to agitational path some mildly violent, yet largely peaceful. This situation also explains the birth and sustenance of revolutionary movements like the Maoists in the Indian political scene. Maoist movements neither weakened nor withered away despite the great modernisation effort of police forces or the so called palliative welfare schemes.

The civil liberty groups in A.P. led by Varavara Rao etc., want **root problem** to be addressed. The root problem has different perceptions. Some say it is poverty. Other say it is land problem. Yet others talk about development (infrastructure in the form of schools, hospitals, connectivity etc.). There are no concrete suggestions on solving poverty. Is it by welfarism of the state which is available in abudance atleast in A.P. State? Does state benevolence has the effect of making people dependant thereby depriving them of developing self sustaining trades and skills or even hard effort?

As regards land ceiling, I reject it outright. Land holding came down to the minimum from more than 1 lakh acres before Independence to 10 acres of wet land and some 30 acres of dry land in the present day. Is further reduction viable for rural economy and agricultural output? Moreover, why will land owning farmers (not landlords) part with the tangible asset handed over to him from one generation to another in which blood and sweat have gone in to build the land asset. Yes, if Govt. wants to take away these meagre holding and distribute to landless, let it pay market value or let Govt. provide employment to one child for every 5 acres taken from that family. 10 acres acquisition means two children should be provided employment. **This is justice.** You cannot rob Peter to pay Paul.

Left Wing intellectuals wax eloquent on land ceiling. Why will the farmer whose property is handed over by their father, fore father part a portion of 10 acres of wet land? it is legal property and meagre holding. Let Govt. Concentrate on illegally acquired agricultural land (acquired through crime and corrupt money) which is in tens of thousands of acres in the hands of Industrialists, Media barons, political class and senior Bureaucrats in benami names. According to CBI Spokesperson Telugu TV News, dt. 24.11.2009, Ramalinga Raju of Satyam Infos has 6000 acres of land.

As regards development, of course, I do agree that development is a prerequisite to prevent alienation. Medicare, education more importantly vocational education and drinking water, electricity etc., are a must. It is taking place of course with misplaced priorities but steeped in corruption. Four lane and eight lane road infrastructure is not an immediate priority. If the Naxalites want to eliminate corruption, let them target concerned corrupt Minister and Bureaucrat. Why are they targeting all and sundry and killing at will? Therefore after

- Poverty
- Development
- Land reforms
- Exploitation of state resources by the politician and business classes.

Discrimination and indignities on dalits are championed by civil rights groups. True they should be knocked out. Laws are there. They need implementation. If implementation authorities fail, let Maoists target them first? **I find exploitation of state resources by the politician, business combine as one strong reason for resultant struggles by Maoists.** This needs to be addressed. I am with Maoists on this point.

Rights Enforcement

Basically we must view the problem of Maoism from Rights Enforcement. There are several rights arising out of various laws in favour of SC, STs etc who are attracted to Maoism. Some of them relate to land problems. The tribal lands are under occupation and cultivated by non tribals. **This needs urgent resolution**. The rights available to the STs are usurped or stolen by non tribals. This is not the same old slogan of land entitlement through land ceiling laws for none has a right for such a land belonging to others. **If you abolish right to property to eradicate poverty, it is outrageous.** Of course Govt. lands, Temple lands etc., can be allotted to landless, even where they have no right for such a land. **It is measure of economic justice.** In the same way there are thousands of cases where poor are in enjoyment of Govt. lands but due to machination of vested interests in villages and the officials who got influenced by them attempt to deprive them from the enjoyment of land. **This is a question of rights violation which accrued to him by virtue of land being in his possession and cultivation.** The administration is responsible to correct this kind of injustice and to restore rights to the eligible. **For all this Govt. is responsible. But where administration is weak and corrupt, rights get violated.** But that does not mean Govt. is a villain and its policies and programmes are bad and it should be overthrown by the barrel of the gun. The Hindu News paper reports that one B. Sammi Reddy was shot dead by Naxalites on 25.09.2009 in Karim Nagar district. The cause is that Sammi Reddy created false documents and deprived or attempted to deprive poor villagers who were cultivating Nizam's lands. For all this administration (Revenue and Police) is responsible. The villagers acquired some rights by way of cultivation and those rights are being or attempted to be snatched away. Therefore this murder by Maoists. Yes I perfectly agree that protection of rights is a powerful cause and where administration fails, Maoists have presence to champion the cause. But should not the Maoists warn the Govt. officials once or twice to correct the land records in favour of the villagers? So mindless killing of villagers need avoidance. At any rate, rights violation, whether it is poor man's or middle class or rich man's give cause for grievance, alienation in society. **It is a powerful factor**. This need protection by Govt. by punishing the Govt. official for failures. **When Naxalites handed out death sentences to Sammi Reddy, the Govt. can atleast suspend the officials concerned to send right message in the administration.** I reject once again the often repeated slogan of Varavara Rao and his friends for land reforms for there are no landlords in rural areas. Excess land may be with Business tycoon and political class in different denominations to avoid ceiling laws. I have no objection if Govt. touches their land or if Maoists occupy their lands. But they have no guts to occupy their lands for one thing, they are highly protected and have the backing of Govt. machinery or their money sometimes influences the Maoists course of action (party funds). In this archaic social conditions, why target small land holder of 8 to 10 acres of wet land and 30 acres of dry land and attempt to legally snatch away his holding? Arm chair left wing politics will not pay. Why not the civil rights groups move around districts, compile data on rights violtion such as the one in Karim Nagar district and place before Revenue Minister or Home Minister for correction before summary punishment of death sentence is carried out? Are they not part of the programme of abetment of violence of by Armed Naxalites?

Maoists/Naxalites - Intellectual Hypocrisy and Distortions

Now in addition to the several issues, we have one more politicized issue of terrorism whether it is Islamic or Maoist terrorist

- Unwillingness to pass strong anti-terrorism law by Parliament till December 2008 and lack of will power to implement the amended Unlawful Activities (Prevention) Act, 1967.
- Unwillingness to approve State anti-terrorism legislation by the President.

- Not imposing ban on certain terrorist outfits.
- Lifting such ban without considering the pros and cons and on thorough discussion and debate with Police.
- Coddling with terrorism in the proactive field operations of Police and Security agencies.
- Covert understanding of certain political parties for electoral benefits.
- Soft peddling the Maoists by calling for dialogue saying that there are good Maoists and bad ones.

What all is expected of Political leadership is nothing more than will and willingness to put down terrorism. **If that will is available, Police, security forces will complete the job to curb terrorism.**

Now, after the so-called attack on Rajdhani Express train on 26.10.2009 by Maoists, there are lot of TV chats and articles in Print Media on Maoists and the ways and means to tackle it.

True, there are certain issues which remain unsolved by the State and which gave raise to leftwing terrorism. Party and bureaucratic corruption, gross inefficiency, unresponsiveness to people's problems, highhanded acts, insensitivity of Police and administration are some of the causes. Not necessarily the land ceiling laws or the SEZs. Of course on the issue of exploitation of Nation's resources by the multi-national and national companies, a second look needs to be taken to blunt Maoist criticism and violence. Monied classes representing business and industry, political classes, administrative, police are in concert with each other in the loot of nation's resources.

Be that as it may, I have to clarify a few points. Half baked left intellectuals or their thinking coloured by their prejudice against democratic form of government, express views that the violence of Maoists is a reaction to the exploitation of Nation's resources by business and governing classes. They justify it. And Maoist violence is mindless and most brutal covering

- so-called informants
- innocent citizens

- some citizens who transgress laws
- some public properties
- property of business and industry
- public authorities such as police and political leadership.

It is understandable, if not justifiable if they target the last category. But they have no business to target the rest. So the justification of violence by Maoists by these intellectuals is meaningless. At the same time, these left intellectuals and half baked intellectuals condemn violence by State.

State Violence

True, there are some incidents where security forces and police resort to fake encounters. Only that part of it is not justifiable. Bu in all genuine "gun battles" with terrorists or Maoists, the violence and killings that follow are all admissible in law. This is so even in developed democracies or even in China. For no society or country will have laws which exclude powers to use force in the suppression of riot, disorder, terrorism, etc. So, State violence is another misnomer with which these intellectuals are confusing the public of this country of one billion population. No Nation on earth allows unlawful possession of arms, ammunition and explosives by citizens or criminals and bandits, while all Nations permit possession of arms by Police, Army, etc.

So, unless certain wrong views stand corrected and understood by a large section of society, terrorism, Maoism and the accompanying violence becomes inevitable. They can be isolated by projection of right views on the subject and it is not just media, authors, intellectuals, but people who control cinema. TV serials can help to correct this intellectual distortion.

If government passes or initiates the enactment of strong anti-terrorism law, it is attacked as draconian or legal terrorism of State, even though the Supreme Court upheld such legislation as right. There is therefore, large space in media for these left and half backed intellectuals to distort views and unless we defeat such views, the society gets misguided.

Fifty percent (50%) of Arms and ammunition with Maoist is the result of loot of them from Govt. armoury or from police stations / police parties. This happens because of slack and negligent **defensive strategy** of police and security agencies. This loot gets repeated because of lenient attitude in taking disciplinary action against the guilty (from top to bottom). In some serious cases, this negligent act needs criminalisation, so that the guilty can face the charges in a court of law. Second: The Govt. and security / police forces need to evolve **pro-active offensive** strategies to go after recovery of Arms and Ammunition. We need to disarm the enemy. **The story of Karna, Mahabharat Hero can be recollected.** Constant meticulously planned field operation need to be undertaken in pursuance of this scheme. Third: Explosive material flowing to Maoists similarly need watch and curtailment. Fourth: Money flow from

- Small businessmen
- Contracting community
- Sometime from out of Govt. funds (as in the case of North East) needs to be stopped.

The problem need to be addressed in a comprehensive way. During 1990, the ban on Maoist was lifted. They were organising political campaigns. One such was in Chabala village, Vuravakonda Taluk, Anantapur Dist., A.P. Mr. Gaddar was organising it. I was Superintendent of Police, Anantapur. No criminal action against such meetings was permissible. But I kept vigil over the activities. At a tri junction leading to the village, I kept intelligence staff to monitor the movements of vehicles and the volume of it. The party noted down vehicles and passed it on to me with the numbers etc. I got it checked up with Bangalore police. One of them was one Govind Reddy. We went to question him. This had its effect in snapping connection with regard to supply of transport to Maoists. So each detail needs to be worked out. **Low key operations** against Maoists in urban areas is another aspect. Preventing flow of money and arms to Maoists through effective laws, enforcement is another **low key operation.**

Speaking on the side lines of a seminar on preparedness to fight terrorism organised by Mumbai Police Mr. K.P.S. Gill and Ajay Sahani observed as follows - Indian Express News, dt. 24.11.2009.

Gill, who retired in 1995, said that before blaming Pakistan for rise in terror activities, India should set its own house in order. "Today, there is a political consensus on corruption rather than fighting terrorism. Our political leaders have agreed that it is all right to loot the country to any extent," Gill said. Seconding his opinion, security analyst Ajay Sahni said, "It is not just terrorists who are using hawala transactions to transfer money. It is being used by several others including corrupt officials and politicians."

Special Economic Zones (SEZ)

There are allegations that they are misused and becoming real estate proposition. The industrial classes are large beneficiaries of land allotment policy of Government. Land around cities is very costly. Instead of urban lands, Government can allot thousands of acres of arid land, poramboke etc., at cheap rate and which are available in interior rural areas with the stipulation that they develop it into agricultural and cultivable one half of which can be distributed to the landless, retaining the remaining half with the Industrialist. This will help to solve the problem of Agricultural land reforms to some extent. Government-Industrialist participation is necessary for the betterment of the lot of common man.

Land in and around big cities is an invaluable tangible state asset. Unfortunately, it is falling into the hands of

- Industrialists (SEZ)
- Cine Actors, Producers for starting Cine Studios or hubs
- Land grabbers
- Bourgeois Administrative, political class such as MLAs and creamy layers in society including the journalists for various co-op. housing societies.

- Unproductive, wasteful sports stadiums etc.
- Corporate Hospital Management

All this is nothing but capitalistic approach and orientation of Governments of the day. Governments can start public schools (high schools) and hospitals, housing colony for poor, middle class at least in the available vacant urban lands or by resuming a part of such lands allotted to the above category or grabbed by land grabbers. The Government by its policies of establishing schools, hospitals etc., can atleast protect existing vacant lands from being encroached upon by land grabbers and save valuable land.

Land Laws, Tax and Mining Laws - All benefit the establishment, the companies, multinationals at the cost of Justice to common man

Royalties from mining are meager. It effects state revenues. The implementation of mining and tax laws, even interpretation by courts caused injustice to state Exchequer. The land law legislation and its implementation benefited companies.

Delivering a lecture on "Hunger Dispossession and Quest for Justice" at the convocation of the class of 2010 of the Asian College of Journalism (ACJ) Dr. Binayak Sen, Vice President of people's union of civil liberties observes:

1. While the Directive Principles clearly mandated that all exercise of state power should be for the promotion of equity, recent trends in the use of state power clelarly violated this mandate and actually resulted in increasing inequities in the areas of livelihood, education and health.

2. "Development in tribal areas is not only about building roads or buildings but about the operationalism of equity, social justice and peoples Sovereignty. While everyone talks about peace, genuine pece cannot mean acquiescence in an exploitative and unjust social order, but rather it should be the result of a movement for equity and justice," Dr. Sen said.

3. Natural resources in the country are under threat as vast tracks of land, forest and water reserves are being handed over to Indian affiliates of International finance capital under cover of the eminent domain doctrine, or the state's pre-eminent ownership of land according to Binayak Sen. (The Hindu News, dt. 04.05.2010).

Graduated income Taxes which lighten the burden upon small incomes by its transference to the swollen revenues of the rich and famous so characteristic of our present times will help to reduce the gap in unjust tax law provisions. Wealth Tax receipts are reported to be less than the cost of collection. Only a tiny fraction of country's wealth is subjected to tax. In India only 30 million people pay Income Tax.

The natural or material resources of nation such as land, water, minerals, oil, gas etc., are a subject of worst exploitation by predatory capitalism, representing multi companies acting in concert wtih Native Business Houses. The complicity of political and administrative establishment is an open secret in such exploitation. It is a grave injustice to the common man and the community. The recent Supreme Court judgment involving a dispute between Reliance Industries Ltd., and Reliance Natural Resources Ltd., of the Ambani brothers brought out in public domain the worst features of exploitative culture. Justice Subhashan Reddy representing the minority judgement made the following obervation- The neo-liberal agenda brought vast benefits to a few, modest for some, while leaving everybody else, the majority behind. For those at the bottom of Scoial and Economic Pyramid, it appears that the Nation has forshaken those goals as unattainable at best and unworthy at worst".

Educational Institutions in Cities

They lack infrastructure of large space for games and sports. They are all crammed. Village schools have large playgrounds. Therefore there is need to allot Government land at cheap prices nearby to thé cities and towns for those who want to start schools and colleges. The beneficiaries can similarly allow concessional rates of boarding and lodging fees to the students. They will grow in the healthy environment where there is free play for physical activities in leisure time instead of getting glued to the Internet, TVs etc.

Law Makers, Enforcers, Interpreters Turning Law Breakers

Law makers and enforcers breaking law has become routine. Even Judges of High Court, Supreme Court are said to be reluctant to declare their assets and liabilities. Army personnel, police very often take law into their hands. On 06.07.2009, according to Media reports, Army personnel bashed up railway police in Hyderabad. It was so even in September 2006. It takes place in all parts of the country. Army men also beat-up civilian co-passengers travelling in train even on trivial provocations. They are becoming law unto themselves. This malady of law makers, interpreters, police, army men turning law breakers is deepening in our Democracy. It poses a threat to Democracy itself. Very often army men draw weapons from armoury in any altercation with police. This intimidates the police and public. I do not think this sort of things take place frequently even in undemocratic nations for fear of International reaction and public outrage. **Every wrong doing in our country goes by the name of Democracy.** There is very weak accountability. The concerned Chief Ministers have to treat these incidents of Army men taking up arms, beating up and injuring policemen as an issue of "public importance" and order enquiry by a Judge under the Commission of Enquiry Act 1951. Besides they must address (immediately after occurrence) the Defence Minister for prompt disciplinary action not only against lower ranks but also against the slack supervisory ranks who allowed arms to be taken out from Armoury. Only then some sense of discipline can be put into their behaviour. Discipline does not lie in their starched uniform, wearing the badges of rank, holding a baton, doing drill. **Discipline is responsible behaviour both on duty and outside duty.**

Invoking Rain God

Both in the years 2008 and 2009, there was no rainfall in the month of June. Varunayagnam by the Tirumala Tirupathi Devasthanam priests was performed at the initiative of Hon'ble Chief Minister, Andhra Pradesh. I have also observed Muslim citizens offering mass prayers invoking rain God. Similar gesture is also needed from Hindus and Christians. Particularly, the large farming community which depend on rains need to do this. It can be led by local Member of Legislature. Mass community prayers may help. At any rate, there is nothing wrong in prayers more so for a common cause. The BJP which harps on religious agenda can also organise its cadres for similar effort.

Ancient Temples, Forts – Relics of Hindu Heritage, Culture

As Sri Satya Sai Baba of Puttaparthi said, there is no need to build new temples. Existing ones can be renovated, maintained and funded where needed. There are several such magnificent ancient temples across the length and breadth of the country. Similarly, financial aid can also be given to select Mosques and Chruches, but with strict audit and accountability. After all we maintain a large network of Guest houses (Roads and Buildings Department), a retinue of watchmen, supervisors, on monthly salaries. Funds for maintenance etc. are also sanctioned annually. We also maintain our Governor's bungalows, their staff running into hundreds for each Governor on Govt. funds. There are hundreds of such wasteful expenditures. There is therefore nothing wrong in aiding financially in all deserving cases for the maintenance of places of worship. There is nothing anti secular about it.

Similarly, ancient Forts, relics of our past history also need attention by Government not in rebuilding them but atleast to see that they are protected from further decay and despoilation. I had occasion to see some forts, temples built by Kings and Emperors of yore. One such is the latest one visited by me on 5.7.2009. The ruins of the fort are in Anantagiri Villege, Karimnagar District which was built in 14th Century A.D. It is on hill top about 3 to 4 hundred feet height. From there one can view the surrounding smaller hill features. It is a 4 or 5 storied hill feature. It gives glimpse of the artificial ponds just below the main palace (small water tanks) available in those days for use by rulers because they stored rain water. Water to be brought from the plains is difficult. The ponds were well secured on all sides by heavy, chiselled stone. Only the main gate of the fort survived. Why the Fort was situated at great height and in uninhabitable position is difficult to comprehend for want of historical accounts. It can be guessed that insecurity from invaders is the reason. Muslim invaders were spreading to every part of the country. The fort also became target of robbers and dacoits who have lust for Gold. They broke parts of main entrance and also a small temple for hidden treasure. These well cut huge granite, their positioning on walls, roof, plus the architectural stone carving remind me of the tribute Professor K.M. Habibullah paid to Hindu genius in this field-particularly the Backward Classes in the Hindu Community. These Master builders and sculptors in our civilisational ethos were not remembered or their names recorded in our history texts or not even mentioned on the stone carvings they themselves made. They had to labour, give their best skill, make several sacrifices for the name, fame and pleasures of somebody - the rulers of the day. There was abundant and unparalleled talent for exquisite and intricate carvings on stone, wood, gold etc. apart from the Master Masons, builders, weavers in India which the world could envy. Kondaveedu Fort Complex near Guntur, A.P., built by Reddy rulers in the 14th century contains on the ruins of temples marvellous sculpture carved on stones.

Inflation

Third week of July 2009 witnessed scanty rainfall and prices of vegetables, essential commodities hitting skyhigh. Redgram selling Rs. 80/- per kg, vegetables very costly, water melon fruit of 1 kg Rs. 40/-. A few years ago water melon was costing Rs. 10/-. Of course there is enough money with people in business and establishment to buy any variety of fruits and at any cost. American grapes are sold at Rs. 300/- per kg and there is market. Apple is costing Rs. 25/- branded as American, Newzeland, Australian. One TV channel (Telugu) reported on 22.07.2009 that there is fake branding of apples. Ambanis, Premzi's entered retail chain of markets. There is monopoly of business. Monopolies Trade Restrictive Practices Act is forgotten by rulers. There is some action by Government to control prices of essential commodities. The Vigilance & Enforcement, the revenue authorities are conducting raids and seizing stocks. But so far there is no enforcement of Preventive Detention law against defaulting traders. **I remember that when I was Superintendent of Police in Vigilance and Civil Supplies in Visakhapatnam in 1987-1988, I have booked at least a dozen people under the P.D. Law.** Soft and kid glove approach to control inflation will not pay. Price of whisky is skyrocketing due to Government's policy of higher excise duties. in the neighbouring states beverages cost much less. The Government realizes higher revenues from excise duties only to pump them into populist schemes. You rob Peter to pay Paul. And what about quality? very poor. In olden days, a bottle of **Peterscot** brand of whisky was very cheap and had scotch flavour. Now even when you purchase **Teachers** brand of India made foreign whisky, it will not have the flavour of Peterscot. Teachers whisky is costing some Rs. 1300/- per 750 ml bottle. So much for the Mallayas and et al! in brewery industry on quality of whiskys. So much so, there is a mad rush for foreign brands of whiskys like Johny Walker, Red, Black, Green Label. And here too there is a racquet in spurious bottles. The consumer is at the mercy of manufacturers and peddlers of spurious whisky. The Indian Army, Navy, Airforce are the single biggest guzzlers of beverages. In Hyderabad there was one Rustum Fram run by Parsi Gentlemen, the community known for honesty and hardwork. I knew them since 1962 when I came to Hyderabad. It is shifted out due to its proximity to a school or place of worship. I was told, they wound up their business. Apart from Rustum Fram, you are never sure of the quality of whisky drawn from the other wine shops. Paints are of inferior quality. Lime stone powder (chunnam) is better than the present day quality of paints.

Mr. Y.S.Raja Sekhar Reddy did well in the soft function of doling out public money on populist welfare schemes, construction of chain of roads, irrigation projects. But he needed to show his capacity in handling tough functions of controlling crimes, corruption, serious ones, roll back power brokers, land grabbers in the state and contain inflation in order to make his name in history of A.P. as an able administrator. In present days 10 years mandate is a long period to make one's mark. Dr. M. Channa Reddy got disproportionate blame during his tenure as Chief Minister in 1978. When he came back in 1990 as Chief Minister for a second term, he wanted to get rid of this blame and desired to entrust excise portfolio to a trusted Minister so that party fund reaches the high command. In his 50 years of long political career as Minister at the Centre and State, as Member of Parliament he did not get any blame for corruption. It is unfortunate that he has been badly maligned in 1978. Reputation is an intangible right and asset of an individual. There are several lobbies and groups in society, Government which target the reputation of an individual. One needs to guard against these lurking conspiracies to malign a person. There always exists a school for scandal in politics or in any other organisation. For the rulers, soft functions are easy options. Take privatization or disinvestment of PSUs. It is a soft decision. But running PSU's efficiently over a period of 10 years, is a tough job. **But surely, Mr. Y.S.R. gained upper hand in handling Maoism by the end of his tenure.**

Anamoly of Statistics

The present police records on statistics of their work do not adequately reflect all work such as

- Preventive police duties carried out in a month
- Bandobust duties in a month
- Public order maintenance duties
- Duties connected with the security of state (Intelligence Wing)
- Checking of illegal fire Arms, Explosives, bad character, hooligans (non-investigative functions)
- Dispute resolution
- Traffic regulation in towns, cities, highways etc.

Unless this (the above type of work) is taken into account, it is not easy to assess true work of police official based only on detection, investigation and convictions of crimes.

Secularism

In the month of July '2009, the High Cout of A.P., on a Public Interest Litigation directed Government that allotment of funds for Christian minorities to go to Jerusalem is impermissible. I think the amount involved is a couple of crores. Petty amount. One thing I want to make clear, if all communities, Hindus included are given funds to go to Mount Kailash etc., that will not give scope for communal discrimination. The question here is discrimination. Not secularism. Secularism is getting increasingly abused by a section of Indian polity, and it is unfortunate if judiciary also falls to appreciate this. Now let me take Games and Sports. I think Government might have spent some ten thousand crores atleast for this purpose in the last 2 decades. All without making India proud in International arena. Then we have Governors and their staff. Each Governor should be having a huge staff, very big salary, maintenance bill running into hundreds of crores in a month (on all Governors). Even if we do not abolish the post of Governor, the amount spent can be cut by 50%. Like that, there will be dozens of wasteful expenses where the hierarchy easily makes money. Spending 100 crores in the year for pilgrims of all faiths to visit places of worship and further spend another Rs. 100 to 200 crores on maintenance of temples yearly is a small drop in the ocean of Government spending. It is not correct to bring in secularism here and stall such a move by Government. After all the Government needs to cater to the religious sentiment of people who want to go on pilgrimage but yet unable to make it due to lack of money. I am reminded of the leave travel concession available to mammoth Bureaucracy in India (30 million strong). Every year alteast a thousand crores will be drawn by employees and some of the claims on Travel were found fake. Some Chief Ministers are purchasing Air craft costing 100 to 200 crore for the official cum private trips. Does this spendocracy fit into our secular, politics? Secularism that occurs in the Preamble of the Constitution with no precise definition has become a play thing of our political class and judiciary has come to interpret it in different ways.

When State Governance is bad, it is religious leadership which needs to raise its voice. Similarly when religion is abused, state needs to step in to correct abuses. There is no water tight compartmentalization between State and Religion.

My views on the subject are dispersed in my writings in all the books. The views need to be codified and edited properly by those who are interested in Academic Excellence. On 03.09.2009, I saw Bollywood heavy weight Salman Khan joyously participating in the immersion festivities of Lord Ganesh. I took another hard look at the concept. We need to practice secular politics. But politics is also pursued in the wrong sense of the term that helps harvesting vote Banks that keep political parties in power. This needs correction in favour of right approach. The initiative of Salman Khan needs to be picked up by personalities in cinema, cultural, intellectual, academic, public life. Govt. or political parties need to be facilitators. In the same way Hindus representing different shades of civil society need participation and share the sentiments of minorities in the celebration of their religious festivities. This builds mutual trust and bridges the gap in the divide. The second is finding solution to Ram Mandir - Babri Masjid issue etc. Here too Govt. or political parties can act as facilitators for the initiative of civil society and religious leaders etc. We need not depend on judiciary alone for solution to the problem. The third area of dispute is annual celebration of Lord Ganesh and Dassera festivals where Hindu processions pass infront of Masjid to the accompaniment of music. There will be hardly 5 or 6 flash points one such is Bhainsa town in A.P. State. It is not difficult to arrive at right understanding and agreement which form basis for rule book for enforcement. For this too respective community, religious, members of civil / society, academia, intellectuals need involvement to iron out differences to come to mutually acceptable solutions. I have given concrete solutions elsewhere in my books. The fourth is removal of places of worship of all communities on thorough fares. Here too community involvement is needed. Govt. can even spend Rs. 1000 crores for construction of new places of worship in the place of demolished ones. There is nothing anti-secular about the move for giving funds. Govt. land can be allotted at suitable places or Govt. can acquire land in the vicinity too.

I do not want to draw water tight compartment between social justice and secularism. Now in Hindu fold, we have dalits who are discriminated in the matter of access to village temples, common wells, and also the practice of untouchability. No doubt legal provisions and police enforcement are there to prevent this discrimination It is not enough. Affirmative action by community leaders, political leaders etc., is needed to remove it and bridge the gap in divide. There is no point in washing one's hands off by mere passing laws which action is not adequate to fight this discrimination that divides Hindu society. It promotes both social justice and secularism. **Secularism according to me is tolerance not only to other religious sentiments but to their rights and views.**

Religion remains a powerful force in civil society as discovered from data collected by Prof. K.N.Panikkar (Article dated 7-9-2009 The Hindu). 90% of the respondents claimed themselves as religious or very religious. He finds that use of religion for political ends has substantially increased in the last 3 decades.

This needs the attention of genuine intellectuals (not Sarkari or pseudo intellectual, the Mafia in media) concerned citizens, groups in civil society to create awareness / spread message about the actual or true secularism or social justice. That is one way of uniting communities because once, we correct the prevalence, practice of **false views** on secularism or any other concept, we have won a major battle in the realm of ideas and that paves way for practice.

Violence, Welfarism, Developmentalism

Another issue is the might of violence and money in politics which is also called as political banditry. Violent politics like false secularism, social justice, social engineering has become a credo of our political parties which are considered the life blood of democracy. While wrong views on secularism, social justice etc., are openly advertised and practiced, violent politics is silently practiced. It is practiced at the time of electoral battle and even afterwards to retain power. Close on the heels of this issue come welfarism, developmentalism. This was more marked in A.P. under late YSR's leadership. A plethora of welfare measures for all targeted groups and at the same time developmentalism were undertaken. Mr. Chandrababu lost the race to Y.S.R. the moment he discarded welfarism. His development agenda cost his party defeat in 2004 and 2009. Though he promised unbounded welfarism in 2009 election, he did not carry credibility like Y.S.R. Now welfarism kept the marginalised sections content, while development catered to the acquisitive instincts of the politico–engineer–contractor–bureaucratic class. We now have super class contractors with companies (construction companies). The inspiration is West. Since 1990, West's influence in India's internal economic policies, external policies is pronounced. Development breeds considerable amount of corruption running into thousands of crores, a part of which goes to party High Command. **Political parties in India need additional dose of money to boost their RBC cell count where anaemia has set in due to failure of Governance though they sustained on the philosophy of welfarism, secularism, social justice and cultural Nationalism.**

The business tycoons are the kith and kin of the ruling establishment. Their interests are first looked after before welfarism of masses is commenced. They are frequent visitors to the PMO, CMO, Ministries etc. **Even union annual budgets are fashioned to their likings if not to their dictates.** The business tycoons are "time serving operators" who with Governments connivance have transferred economic assets to offshore zones and stashed away their profits, illegal commissions in foreign banks. The business tycoons are inalienable part of Western Democratic model. West has a stake both in Democracy and in business. We waive Banks bad debts, hand out bail outs through public money for the companies involved in frauds and corruption. All this is called by Russian intellectual circles as nothing but a sort of **Nationalisation of losses** in the operation of flawed or nascent Democracies. Writing off losses of PSUs also falls in the same category.

So our Democratic political parties are wedded to various political philosophies such as secularism, social justice, social engineering, cultural nationalism, welfarism, developmentalism. Old political philosophies such as Democratic Socialism, Communism, Capitalism have been eclipsed. And in this pursuit of this political philosophy, the philosophy of Governance, Good governance is irretrievably lost. One example of failure of Governance is the raise in Court litigation. The hands of Courts are full with work. Even High Courts are full with work. Enforcement of Article 226, for violation of rights of citizen is a common feature. And not more than 30% of the aggrieved avail the relief for fear of costs involved. **Failure of Governance leads to increase in Court's work.**

I give one recent instance of failure of Governance leading to Court's intervention under Art. 226. The Director of State Libraries A.P. gave advertisement in 2007 inviting Authors / Publishers to submit books for selection. I sent 6 titles, out of which 4 were selected by a Committee of Academics. After selection they were communicated to the District units for purchase after going through some formalities. The District units including Hyderabad city gave advertisement in September 2008 calling for samples of Books. Though it is duplication of work relating to selection, I sent my Books. 2 crores of rupees as admitted by Authorities were allotted for purchases. Suddenly the Authorities (the Secretary, City Library Unit and Chairman who is a political drop out in regular elections) cancelled the process of purchase. I approached the A.P. High Court u/s 226 for performance of public duty at considerable cost as a matter of principle. The matter is under hearing, I made it clear in my affidavit that I am more concerned about performance of public duty (correcting inaction) more than purchase of my books not withstanding 4 of them having been approved in 2007. **Now**

it is February 2010. The matter lies in Court. I give one more example. Warangal and Visakhapatnam districts did not make payment even after the supply of books. The delay is more than six months. I believe that Government issued an order to withhold payments. This Government order is arbitrary. In case, if there are irregularities in purchases the Library staff needs punishment and not the Authors or Publishers. I asked my Advocate to file supplemental affdavit to challenge this arbitrary order.Therefore failure of Governance leads to increase in Court work load and I remind the reader that all cannot afford court litigation. So there are millions of cases of inaction, violation of rights which Govt. fails to address. It leads to court intervention. And from a Clerk to I.A.S. officers all are united in inaction, wrong action and corruption, against which a single individual and a High Court Judge are pitted against.

It is very sad that Ministers who swear to discharge their duties fairly and effectively take no action to correct the inaction of Bureaucrats, police etc.

The issue was also brought to the notice of the Director of Public Libraries and Government by me and nothing happened even after the entire Class-IV staff of the Library Department complained to the Chief Minister of the State for action against the Director of Public Libraries. **All this is the indication of collapse of governance where massive inaction and corruption rules the roost.**

NGO

Like the development slogan, N.G.O. is another institution in our civil society which is product or child of western culture. There are around 20000 NGOs in the country for which nearly some Rs. 10000 crores of public money is doled out. Why should public money be given to them? Its role is to aid the welfarism of masses, supplementing State effort in welfarism. They network with lobbies in politics and administration and are easy breeding grounds for misappropriation of funds by persons manning them in connivance with public official. This N.G.O. has no space in West or in Arab world. **They mushroom**

here because they largely benefit the establishment and marginally benefit the targeted groups. CAG needs to be empowered to supervise NGO's.

Legislative Power of Parliament and State Laws getting approved by the President

The respective powers of Parliament and State Legislatures to pass laws is contained in **Article 246** of the Constitution.

The lists and subjects are in the **7th schedule** of the Constitution.

List I called the **Union List**

List II called the **State List**

List III called the **Concurrent List**

Entry 9 in List I relates to the power of Parliament to pass Preventive Detention Law pertaining to the "Security of India" viz., defence and foreign relations. It does not include "public order" matter. **Entry 1 in List II** relates to "public order". But Parliament can pass certain laws that probably include "public order" in "National interest" (Art. 249) and when emergency is imposed in a State. Under List III called Concurrent List, both Parliament and State Assemblies can legislate on criminal laws etc. **Anti Terrorism Law is a criminal law to meet public order situations.**

Now a legal controversy is raging between the Central Government and the Government of Gujarat. The Central Government says that the provisions of the Act need to conform to the Parliament Legislation viz., The Unlawful Activities (Prevention) Act 1967as amended in 2004. The Gujarat Government feels that the above Act of Parliament is weak in several respects. But the Central Government says that the State Legislations which are inconsistent or repugnant or in conflict with central laws will not be given assent. The centre relies on Art. 251, 254 of the Constitution.

But these words repugnancy, inconsistency, conflict are not spelt out not even in the interpretative process to the best of my knowledge or are they, as it happens the luxury of legislative expressions used mechanically by borrowing from the Western Constitutions?

The following points need discussion and analysis.

- Is a stricter law or even a weaker law of State legislature to be tested on Art. 251, 254 to determine that they are repugnant to law passed by Parliament?
- Is Art. 254 itself consistent with the totality of Constitutional scheme where "public order" is the domain of the State and powers given to State Legislature to pass laws on that subject?
- Does Central Government have independent, sufficient enforcement machinery like police under its exclusive control to enforce criminal laws under the Constitution?
- Can Central Government supplement state effort in maintenance of "public order" or substitute its role for that of State Government? Does Central Government possess Constitutional powers to substitute state's role in maintenance of "public order". If not, Art. 254, and Central Government's intervention in states in passing laws affecting "public order" becomes redundant.
- Or alternatively, the Central Government by amendment to certain Constitutional provisions can treat. Terrorism as "National Security" issue (not public order issue) and then proceed to exclusively legislate and deal with the problem of Terrorism in which case, it needs to own up responsibility to handle the problem instead of meddling in the problem as at present. Therefore bogus legal claims are made on behalf of Central Government based on Art. 254, to interfere in State legislations - all based on the literary meaning of words inconsistency, repugnancy of laws. But nobody raised the point whether such inconsistent provisions conflict with the **public interest** or promote it. And **public interest** needs to dictate the course of Constitutional and legal scheme. Public interest, let me remind the readers, is something above the interests of criminals and Terrorists.

Art. 200 and 201 are reproduced below for a clear understanding.

200. Assent to Bills– When a bill has been passed by the Legislative Assembly of a State or in the case of a State having a Legislative Council, has been passed by both Houses of the Legislature of the State, it shall be presented to the Governor and the Governor **shall declare** either that he assents to the Bill or that he withholds assent therefrom or that he reserves the Bill for the consideration of the President:

Provided that the Governor may, as soon as possible after the presentation to him of the Bill for assent, return the Bill if it is a Money Bill together with a message requesting that the House or Houses will reconsider the Bill or any specified provisions thereof and, in particular, will consider the desirability of introducing any such amendments as he may recommend in his message and, when a Bill is so returned, the House or Houses shall reconsider the Bill accordingly, and if the Bill is passed again by the House or Houses with or without amendment and presented to the Governor for assent, the Governor shall not withhold assent therefrom. :

Provided further that the Governor shall not assent to, but shall reserve for the reconsideration of the President, any Bill which in the opinion of the Governor would, if it became law, so derogate from the powers of the High Court as to endanger the position which that Court is by this Constitution designed to fill.

1. **Procedure–** Article 200 deals with the procedure to be followed when a Bill has been passed by a Legislative Assembly or Legislative Council of a State and is applicable when there is no House of Legislature.

2. **Reserving Bill for consideration–** Article 200 does not stipulate that the Governor shall give his assent and thereafter, when the Bill has become a full-fledged law, reserve it for consideration of the President. Only such Bills as are passed by the House or Houses of Legislature may be received for the consideration of the President, and not 'laws' to which the Governor,

or the President, if reserved for his consideration, has already given his assent.

Art. 201. Bills reserved for consideration– When a Bill is reserved by a Governor for the reconsideration of the President, the President shall declare either that he assents to the Bill or that he withholds assent therefrom:

Provided that, where the bill is not a Money Bill, the President may direct the Governor to return the Bill to the House, or, as the case may be, the Houses of the Legislature of the State together with such a message as is mentioned in the first proviso to Article 200 and, when a Bill is so returned, the House or Houses shall reconsider it accordingly within a period of six months from the date of receipt of such message and, if it is again passed by the House or Houses with or without amendment, it shall be presented again to the President for his consideration.

From the perusal of the said Articles it is no where clear that the Governor need to send a bill for President's assent except when the legislative measure undermines the power of High Courts. If it is any other subject, the Governor has no discretion to reserve a bill to President's assent except that he is acting as an agent of Central Government which is always the case.

There are a lot of politics in legislation which involve Constitutional Authorities such as Governors and the President of the Republic. There was a silver lining to several of these intractable legal problems when A.P.J. Abdul Kalam held the office of the President. Though he is a shining example of private and public values, he too failed to address some such problems that include not only the topic under discussion, but also the question of the President refusing to swear in a Minister who had record of crime and corruption by taking a high moral ground.

Again Supreme Court's intervention and sound judgment on the competing claims of the disputed legal issue is needed to answer the **call of justice.** The voice of genuine intellectuals, not pseudo intellectuals or sarkari intellectuals needs to be heard by the Authorities for a sound decision on the subject.

Terrorism

I have written enough on the subject. Recently anti terror legislation of Gujarat was not approved by the Central Government.

True an anti terrorism law is not a panacea to the problem of Terrorism. But

- Not passing a strong Federal Law on the subject till December 2008 and not implementing the amended Unlawful Activities (Prevention) Act, 1967 effectively.
- Not approving state anti- terror legislation.
- Not executing death sentence on Afzal Guru.
- Premature release of life convicts as it happened in the State of A.P.
- Failure or tardiness in creating State Anti terror cells and equipping them suitably has the following adverse effects.
    - Sends wrong message to the Terrorists and the Nations supporting Terrorism. They are emboldened.
    - The same message goes to the public.
    - The same message to intelligence and police agencies. Their morale will be down consequently.
    - Intelligence collection will not be of high grade.
    - Police will not be too keen to detect existing cases under investigation, effect arrests.
    - Police will not exhibit zeal and dedication in the field operations etc.

And the ill effects of all this needs to be kept in mind by the Government, well informed public as well as my kith and kin in intelligentia before debating the pros and cons of anti-Terrorism Law.

Terrorists know no religion. In Pakistan, they are targeting co-religionists

Tackling Terrorism is no ordinary responsibility. It is a colossal task for police forces and the state.

Village Courts

This agenda is pushed down the throat of the Nation by UPA Government. Mr. Moily is an enthusiastic supporter of it. It involves some thousands of crores. I am sceptical about the system being viable and practical. For certain, it serves Congress Party agenda of vote banks and also serves the burgeoning legal fraternity with employment in judiciary and self employment as a practicing lawyer.

I have given my views on court delays from practical experience and observation. I have also quoted late R.K. Jain's views on the subject. He is an Authentic Commentator on the Constitution of India and the judicial system. A few points are made or added to the existing suggestions:

- "Public officials" incharge of decision making need to do it fast, fair and transparently so that 50% of them will not reach court for adjudication. Decision making at administration level involve a joint, single or two sittings spread over one month. Joint decision means involving inter department officials related to decision making. Files cannot be tossed around. Minutes need to be typed and signed in the second sitting by all concerned.
- "Judicial officials" from Magistrate to higher ups need to perform their functions efficiently and speedily. For this, **periodic performance appraisals** need to be evolved. Such appraisals should be written by a Committee. There needs to be accountability for performance at all levels of judicial work. This will to some extent relieve the judicial official from the vicious hold the Lawyer community exercises over him. When adjournments are asked, he will tell them that he grants them at the peril of his career. This helps to cut down delay by 50%. Even a District Judge or High Court judge when sought to be elevated need to be assessed on **performance criteria**. Similarly a Chief Justice of High Court aspiring to be Supreme Court Judge.

- Incorrect decisions of Judges whether of District Judge or High Court Judge, when they are reversed by a bench of Judges or by Supreme Court need to go against such a Judge. There needs to be data compilation of such cases when one is considered to be elevated.
- When a Chief Justice of High Court is sought to be made Judge of Supreme Court, it is not his individual capacity for fast and fair disposal alone that counts but also how he motivated his junior colleagues and District Judges in justice delivery that needs to be considered.
- Short judgement, not exceeding 50 pages should be incorporated as a rule. Pedantic; extensive quoting of previous judgments are not needed.
- 3 months time limit for delivery of judgement after conclusion of hearing and one week in simple cases.

I have filed a writ petition U/A. 226 in March 2009 for issue of appropriate writ in A.P. High Court against "inaction" of Public Libraries (Hyderabad City Branch) to purchase books even after receiving Rs. 2 crores and after having given advertisement and receiving sample copy of books. My affidavit is 3 pages. Counter affidavit can be 3 or 6 pages. There is no evidence taking, cross examination, re-examination, examination-in-chief in these matters. It is not yet decided. It is the individual Judge / Judges will power, comprehension that is needed in this type of cases U/s. Art. 226 of the Constitution. Creating more number of High Court Judges is not a panacea.

Pandit Nehru emphasized the importance of efficiency, meaning **action**. According to me it is no less important than honesty. So the Govt., media, intellegentia need not wax eloquent on integrity of Judges alone but also need to focus on performance.

Development

It is the name of the game in our Democracy. The western Multinationals are also behind this. They need market for their products to sell. It suits the Indian political class to launch grandiose projects all in the name of people. But the priorities need to be set. Second, development mantra should not be for the sake of party or individual interests.. Third, corruption needs to be cut to the barest minimum in developmental works. All this is not happening. The big beneficiaries are the political class, the superclass contractors, the engineers, bureaucrats etc. There is no transparency in the tender system. Suppose if a project costs Rs 1000 crores, estimates are prepared that it costs Rs 1500 crores and that extra amount is pocketed by political class at decision taking level even before the project is grounded. Development was there even during British days. Large irrigation projects on Godavari, Krishna and Thungabhadra rivers were built. They built a large network of railways, roadways, ports etc. and they were of high quality. Kadapa-Kurnool irrigation canal that carries water of Tungabhadra river is a quality canal work that lasted for 100 years, with repairs of course here and there and the assured irrigation is for 2 or 3 lakh acres and the target is almost fulfilled. The same is the case with the irrigation projects on Godavari and Krishna rivers. The story now is different. Telugu Ganga Project was launched by late NTR some 25 to 30 years back (Krishna river water to Kurnool-Kadapa and from there to Chennai for drinking). Its assured irrigation potential was 7 lakh acres. Even after 25 years it did not irrigate one third of the above figure. The major beneficiary is the Establishment. In the same way, on the same river, there is a right branch canal in Kurnool district carrying water upto Kadapa District. It is also 20 years old. Canals were dug up even before the irrigation projects came into existence. It did not irrigate even one fifth of its targeted acreage. Canal system is of very poor quality. They are getting dilapidated. In the process the Establishment profited immensely. **Establishment is highly developed.** Local MLAs , lower functionaries entered the public contract works directly or in benami names and reaped Himalayan economic fortunes. Who has to be held accountable for this wasteful public funds in tens of thousands of crores? Right from political leaders who launched the projects and down to the lowest public officials accountability needs fixation for wasting public funds, for poor quality of works, for not meeting the targeted acreage. The works carried out on similar projects by Britishers, Nizam of Hyderabad state were 100% superior in quality than the present day works. **Roads in some areas of Hyderabad are repaired every year with the onset of monsoon.** Accountability is now demanded for the category of wrongful omissions and commissions of politcians and police. What about accountability of engineers, contractors, bureaucrats for condition of development projects. Did any one, any agency study, review the working, utility, optimum utility of these works and clamour for accountability?

Violence and Crimes

Police statistical format on crime (if it does not exist) needs to take into account the following :

- Violence abetted, sponsored by political parties,
- Organized labour
- Organized criminals
- Terrorists
- Maoists
- Urban Mafia
- Forest Mafia
- Adulteration Mafia
- Communal and caste riots
- Domestic violence
- Violence in Schools and colleges
- Election time violence
- Political factions
- Village factions
- Land Mafia
- Video piracy
- Gambling and prostitution

Business of Profit by Holders of Constitutional Posts

I have been in all these 15 to 20 years arguing against this. Now after the raids and filing of cases against Madhu Khoda, former Chief Minister Jharkhand State and the political storm created by Gali brothers in Karnataka where they own several iron ore mines and other businesses, a section of political leadership, the left in particular awoke to the new dimension of money and political power in dictating Govt. policies. Mr. Prakash Karat, General Secretary CPM (The Hindu News, dt. 17.11.2009) decried the involvement of Business in politics and politicians in Business. He lamented "Business tycoons sit in parliamentary committees that decide on policies. There are Minister in Union and State cabinets who are actual businessmen by profession". "Political business and business through politics is becoming the norms", he further observed. Mr. Karat identified only ministers. There are thousands of MPs and MLAs across the country who have business interests. **Business of profit, I have argued need prohibition by a law.** Art. 191 prohibited holding "office of profit" which is a far lesser evil by holders of Constitutional posts compared to business of profit. Now the country awoke to my call to prohibit "business of profit" by holders of Constitutional posts direct or benami. Atleast owning and running big businesses need legal prohibition. The second most important point which I mentioned in all my writings on this subject is that you cannot book these people under The Prevention of Corruption Act, 1988 for possessing assets disproportionate to the "known sources of income" (or legal sources). They will take the plea that their assets are built on the legal sources for which they are paying taxes and that the assets are not the result of illegal incomes from unknown sources but legal income from known source of business. **Senior party post holders like Presidents, Vice Presidents, General Secretaries also need to be legally disqualified to do businesses of profit.**

The issue caught public imagination in mid 1980s when late NTR as Chief Minister, A.P. was producing and acting in a film called **Viswamitra**. It was challenged by D. Satyanarayana, M.P., Congress Party by way of PIL in High

Court of A.P. for issuance of appropriate writ to unseat NTR from the post of Chief Minister as it was considered as unlawful to engage in business of profit. A division bench of the said Court threw out the challenge as there was no legal or Constitutional provision under which the relief sought for can be granted. Conventions and democratic practices obtaining in Western Democracies are of no use for the Court to give relief. Since then I have been writing on this issue and it finds expression in my books. But writings have no value to bring about desired changes to laws because of vested interest of political class as a whole. Now in November, 2009, the mighty event of wrong doing or crime of "abuse of public office" by Madhu Khoda and the political events of destabilising the elected Govt. of Mr. Yedurappa in Karnataka by Gali brothers brought the issue once again into public imagination. But I am sceptical of the success of the legal / political reform. Except the fringe political formation of left (CPI-CPM as it stands now) no political party is keen on this reform. Indeed in America, the mother of Democracies, Multinationals influence the working of Democracy. In India Multinationals, Indian Business and Industry have enormous influence on our Democratic practices and policy decisions. This situation is similar to the premise of Karl Marx that means of production and exchange of commodities determine the general social order or even political order at any given period of time where Government Institutions are impacted by Industry and Commerce and where Business and political leaders are **Comrades in Arms** in the loot of Nation's resources.

In the 3rd week of November, 2009, there were media news about Industrialists Mr. Kampani and Ambanis coming to the rescue of one Media baron in A.P. when its finances were in red by purchasing shares at very high value to the tune of Rs. 1400 crores. Kampani was co accused in the Nagarjuna group of companies fraud, now subject of criminal investigation. He jumped bail and is absconding. There were also counter allegations in Media about the purchase of share value of Rs. 10/- at Rs. 1400 (Raghuram Cements, Kadapa). It is reported that Dalmia's are involved. So there is a whole lot of mix of politics and business for mutual benefit at the cost of Nation's interest. The industrialists are not mere anchors for political party funding. They are active in pumping their surplus money into the sinking fortunes of companies owned benami by powerful politicians or by Media barons which have the support of powerful political parties or party leaders.

The Systems

The laws, the institutions created by law or the Constitution, the persons who head these institutions, the rules and regulations make up a system. Some intellectuals, editors of reputed English fortnightly like Vinod Mehta fell into the trap of blaming individuals (NDTV, dt. 13.11.2009). "The systems are as good or as bad as the persons who operate them" he lamented. I have no hesitation to reject such views for otherwise they will be in currency dominating our public life and thwarting right reforms of system. **I will give a few examples.**

- Art. 361 gives immunity to the Governor from the consequences of his actions which are often wrong in invoking Art. 356, Art. 164 (now in Andhra Pradesh by appointing Chief Minister without proof of majority in CLP). Therefore Art. 163 and 361 need right amendment to the effect that as and when a judiciary holds Governor's action wrong, he should quit office or get disqualified from public life. That will put sense in Governor's mind and prevent abuse of power.
- Prior to 2005, the country did not have Right to Information Act. With the enactment of such a law, in 2005 there is a degree of transparency in Governance. Persons manning Govt. departments have a degree of responsibility to furnish information. If it is further amended as suggested by me in my previous writings, where Accountability for failure to furnish information is severely punishable, persons heading departments will become more responsible.

- We do not have Accountability Law or an infrastructural mechanism to enforce it on the lines of RTI Act 2005. If we have such law as part of our systems, even recalcitrant person heading the organisation will be careful in respect of corruption, inefficiency and wrong doing.
- There were individual Chief Justices at the Supreme Court and High Court level who were well intentioned, honest and determined to fight corruption, wrongdoing in higher judiciary. But the Constitutional and legal guarantees in favour of judicial independence minus Accountability for corruption etc., made their task a impossible.
- I give one more example with reference to criminal justice. The primary system is law. Sub or support systems are enforcement agencies, interpretating agencies, prosecuring agencies etc. Even political executive like President, Governors, Govt. have power to prematurely release convicts that include murder case convicts. They can also delay execution of sentences as in the case of Afzal Guru indefinitely. If the law prescribes the time limit to dispose of mercy petition is one year maximum, the President, Governor are bound by it. So systems need improvement first.

The Systems Consist of Political, Judicial, Administrative etc.,

Rahul Gandhi

Mr. Rahul Gandhi was interacting with students of Loyola College, Vijayawada in the third week of November, 2009. A student questioned him about the problem of tackling corruption. His advise was to tighten the belts by students. *Prima facie,* Rahul's advice is immature. The right answer is an assurance to strengthen law and implementation. Just as pilot of a plane needs to know how the systems operate, the future prime ministerial candidates need to know (if not deep knowledge).

- Constitutional law
- Basic criminal laws etc.
- The public institutions created by laws.
- The systems and sub systems in political, judicial, administrative and police institutions in order to steer the ship of the state in the rough waters.

In addition, Prime Ministererial candidates need to study special problems like corruption, terrorism of different kind, flood and other natural calamities, law and order problem thrown up by certain agitations launched by T.R.S. etc., covering 10 districts in Andhra Pradesh. True these are the subjects to be handled by Chief Ministers of concerned States. Yet there is scope for youngsters like Rahul to make a good administrator if he keeps abreast of all such issues by case study of each problem.

Paying Homage to 26.11.2008 Mumbai Victims

People lit candle lights on 26.11.2009 on the first anniversary in memory of the victims of Mumbai carnage. MHA Government of India paraded commandos on the streets and also showcased their skills. On the other side Ashok Kamte's wife in her book "To the last bullet" bemoaned how her husband and others on the field battling the Terrorists were let down by command and control by not reinforcing, the forces and not rendering timely medical aid to the wounded. Mr. Gaffoor, Former Commissioner of Police, Mumbai is also on record to state that 4 IPS officers shirked the call of duty on 26.11.2008. Yet the Govt. is behaving that there was nothing wrong and everything is all right. **We will be paying homage not by lighting the candles or showcasing the skills of commandos, but by holding the guilty in the political, police and intelligence establishment to Accountability by drastic disciplinary action.** The first step in that direction should be a judicial enquiry to apportion guilt.

3

Police Encounters-Instant Justice or Injustice?

- Fake encounters go against the grain of justice.
- Genuine Encounters or Armed gun battles are "legal killings"
- Capital punishments awarded by Judiciary after Court trial are "judicial killings".

When we check or elimiate fake encounters, we remove a kind of injustice.

Have the Legal Provisions Precisely defined

- Police Encounters
- "Armed battles" fought in forests, hills, riverines, urban centres between security forces and the Terrorists/Maoists, where the latter are launching attacks in stealth such as blasting claymore mines(sabotage) and daring direct attacks, lead in hundreds of numbers.
- Is the "right of private defence", 150 years old legal provisions in IPC 1860 to be proved before executive magistrate or a court of law?

- Can right of private defence be weighed on golden scale of balance when confronted with mob violence of burning, looting, indiscriminate killings?
- Is the degree of accountability same for wanton police killing of students accused of ragging, acid throwing and close range "gun battles" between terrorists and police?

The various situations where police use force in line of "Authorities" before whom it is justified are discussed comprehensively.

Use of Force by Police in Discharge of Public Duty and Self Defence

Law enforcing agencies use force resulting in inujries or deaths in various situations. Law permits citizens to use force to defend themselves.

(a) Citizens acting in exercise of right of private defence

(b) Police acting in 'self defence' outside their duties. On 01-05-2009, A.P. police while visiting a temple in Dharmasthala, Karnataka opened fire in an altercation with temple authorities and public.

(c) Where police act in 'self defence' in discharge of 'defensive duties' such as protecting a post, a VIP, stationary or moving.

(d) Where police use force to defend themselves against assualt by violent mobs. (Section 100 IPC)

(e) Where police are 'mandated by Law' to disperse unlawful Assemblies(Section 129 to 131 CrPC).

(f) Where police are called upon to engage in 'gun battles' with Maoists or Terrorists.

Use of Force by Police not Connected to Public Duties

(g) Fake police encounters(no legal sanction).

(h) Death in police custody(no legal sanction).

For the acts of causing deaths at (a), (b), (g), (h), taking cognizance under Section 154 CrPC and trial in Sessions Court is relevant. Acts figuring at (c) to (f) are in 'discharge of public duties' and taking cognizance of these acts under Section 154 CrPC prior to an adverse enquiry report of Executive Magistrate or a Judge is not a correct legal position.

Use of Disproportionate Force

One Bihari youth Rahul Raj aged 25 years was shot dead by police on 27-10-2008 in Mumbai while he was trying to intimidate fellow passengers in a bus. The above youth is not

- A terrorist, Maoist, member of Mafia or a dreaded criminal.

The youth was emotionally charged up against anti-Bihari feeling in Mumbai whipped up by Raj Thackrey, a leader of a political party. There are several alternatives to shooting a person dead in such situations. They are

- He can be overpowered by police men well trained in martial arts.
- The bus can be immobolised by removing air of the tyres or bursting the tyres.
- The assailant can be overpowered by water canons.
- By throwing chilly powder in the eyes.
- By wielding a wooden lathi on his hands.
- By using gas which will send him into coma.
- By Shooting to injure and not to kill.

All these options were not even thought of not to speak about availment. Only after exhausting one or two options, the police can use fire arms. This unfortunately is not taught in the police training institutions, Academies, both at the initiation of training and in in-service courses. The District Police also need to have plans drawn to sketch to fit into each such situations as far as possible. Panicky reaction and opening fire is not a right approach. There is no denying the fact that the youth is a threat to co-passengers. But it does not justify extinguishing his life at the first provocation where neither a citizen nor policemen had injury or even a scratch on their bodies.

In all my writings through these years, I have been urging for accountability for grave wrong doings of the police such as lock up deaths and the use of fire arms in controlling **mobs or a single individual etc** as in the present case. Unless we have adequate legal safeguards, I am afraid that the police will go berserk in the control of unlawful assemblies or indivisuals in our defective legal systems. There needs to be enquiry by independent legal forum and in case, the enquiries hold the police action as justifiable, the police party and its leader indeed needs to be recognised and rewarded even by giving out of turn promotion.

Batala House Encounter : It is a Gun battle between Terrorists and Delhi Police. One M.C. Sharma was felled by the Terrorist bullet before the police party retaliated in self defence causing deaths to Terrorists.

Warangal Encounter : In the Warangal Encounter no Terrotists or Maoists were involved. But students responsible for acid attack on a girl who later succumbed to injuries were picked by police and allegedly shot dead. There were no genuine injuries to the police party. It is an extra legal death caused by police to assuage public sentiment against such acid attacks.

Various Situations of Accountability where Public Servants that include Police cause Death

- Custodial death or injury of a suspect in an offence in police custody or police station.
- Excessive use of force (disproportionate force) causing injury or death to a person or a group of unlawful persons.
- Fake encounter deaths or extra judicial deaths caused by police when the victim is in its custody.
- Genuine encounters or Armed battles between a terrorist or a group of terrorists and the police party resulting in deaths on either side.
- Death caused in arresting a murder case accused.

There are Various Reasons

- Politically inspired encounter deaths as in the case of Warangal Encounter in December 2008 in which 3 persons were allegedly shot dead by police in a fake encounter to assuage popular sentiment against acid attack on a college girl.
- Personal aggrandisement of police officers seeking popularity, promotions and gallantry awards.
- Corruption inspired fake police encounters resorted to by police officers in connivance with politico-mafia leaders, real estate mafia etc.

Right of Private Defence

In the context of a large number of encounter deaths at the hands of police, there is need to examine the legal parameters and the realities on the ground.

The legal position is laid down in IPC 1860 (Sections 96 to 106)

SECTION 96: Nothing is an 'offence' which is done in the exercise of right of private defence.

SECTION 97: Every person has a right of private defence of the body and of property subject to restrictions contained in Section 99 to defend:

First : His own body, and the body of any other person, against any offence affecting the human body;

Secondly: The property, whether movable or immovable, of himself or of any other person, against any act which is an offence falling under the definition of theft, robbery, mischief or criminal trespass, or which is an attempt to commit theft, robbery, mischief or criminal trespass.

SECTION 98: It speaks of right of private defence against the act of a person of unsound mind.

SECTION 99: It speaks about acts against which there is no right of private defence-such as against 'acts which do not reasonably cause apprehension of death or grievous injury' done by "public servant" acting in good faith.

PROVISO TO SECTION 99: Right of private defence does not extend to inflicting more harm than is necessary for the purpose of defence (use of disproportionate force as in the case of Rahul Raj who was shot dead by Mumbai police).

SECTION 100: When the right of private defence of the body extends to causing death. - The right of private defence of the body extends, under the restrictions mentioned in the last preceding section, to the voluntary causing of death or of any other harm to the assailant, if the offence which occasions the exercise of the right be of any of the descriptions hereinafter enumerated, namely-

First - Such an 'assault' as may reasonably cause the apprehension that death will otherwise be the consequence of such assault;

Secondly - Such an 'assault' as may reasonably cause the apprehension that grievous hurt will otherwise be the consequence of such assault;

Thirdly - An 'assault' with the intention of committing rape;

Fourthly - An 'assault' with the intention of gratifying unnatural lust;

Fifthly - An 'assault' with the intention of kidnapping or abducting;

Sixthly - An 'assault' with the intention of wrongfully confining a person, under circumstances which may reasonably cause him to apprehend that he will be unable to have recourse to the public authorities for his release.

SECTION 103: Deals with Right of private defence of property:

"When the right or private defence of property extends to causing death.—The right of private defence of property extends, under the restrictions mentioned in Section 99, to the voluntary causing of death or of any other harm to the wrong-doer, if the offence, the committing of which, or the attempting to commit, which occasions the exercise of the right, be an offence of any of the descriptions hereinafter enumerated, namely—

First - Robbery;

Second - House-breaking by night;

Thirdly - Mischief by fire committed on any building, tent or vessel, which building, tent or vessel is used as a human dwelling, or as a place for the custody of property.

Fourthly - Theft, mischief or house-trespass, under such circumstances as may reasonably cause apprehension that death or grievous hurt will be the consequence, if such right of private defence is not exercised".

SECTION 106 IPC: This section deals with right of private defence against deadly assault even when risk of harm is involved against innocent persons.

Rahul Raj's case (Mumbai) is one of using disproportionate force against a single person armed with a pistol who is emotionally charged up against anti-North India bias of a section of Maharashtra politicians. He is not a criminal or a terrorist. No right of private defence existed as there were not even injuries to police personnel.

In the month of February 2009, the High Court of Andhra Pradesh delivered a judgement (Full Bench) on the course of action in incidents commonly known as "police encounters." The High Court felt that in all cases of police encounters or extra judicial killings there should be issued FIR against the police or security personnel involved in the incident and investigations taken up for approval by the concerned judicial Magistrate. The High Court wanted cognizance of the offence under section 154(1) CrPC. Hitherto, the practice by the police is to issue FIR under Section 174 CrPC and conduct further investigations by itself. This judgement of Andhra Pradesh High Court placed the Government and police agencies in an embarrassing situation. After all, these agencies are called upon to act when there is serious threat to public order or to the lives of individuals.

I have already made a subtle difference between the case of Rahul Raj and that of the Warangal encounter. In the former case, there is a single person sitting in a bus with a small fire arm like pistol and threatening individuals when he was shot dead by police. **This is excessive use of force. It is not a false encounter.** The case of Warangal encounter or similar such cases fall under the category of fake encounters or extra judicial killings, wherein unarmed persons responsible for the acid attack were allegedly abducted by the police and shot dead.

Encounters have been shortcut to success. **The phrase police encounter has no legal definition.** The judgement of High Court of AP caused considerable concern, indeed consternation in police circles, particularly in the wrong quarters of police circles who are addicted to this wrong doing of fake encounters.

However, there are also adequate legal safeguards particularly in all cases of genuine police encounters with criminals or occasional offenders. Section 100 IPC listed several situations where death can be caused by a 'public servant' on "reasonable apprehension" of an assault that causes injury to his body or possible death.

Furthermore, **sec. 106 IPC 1860** goes to the extent of justifying causing death of innocent person in the cause of right of private defence if the public servant or a person is so situated that he cannot exercise such right of private defence without risking innocent lives. Therefore, there is adequate elbow room in the law itself for police and security agencies to operate against rioters, and other unlawful groups. The very sight of an armed group confronting police with deadly weapons is also a sufficient ground to give "reasonable apprehension" of death or grievous injury to the police party.

JUDGEMENT IN WRIT PETITION NO. 15419 OF 2006, 26358 OF 1999, 7906 OF 2000, 14475 OF 2002, 440 OF 2003 AND 857 OF 2008 BETWEEN THE STATE OF ANDHRA PRADESH AND THE CIVIL LIBERTIES COMMITTEE, ANDHRA PRADESH DECIDED BY HIGH COURT OF ANDHRA PRADESH ON 6TH FEBRUARY 2009

Analysis and Dissertation of the Judgement

Law has envisaged the following situations in which force can be used by the police (public servant)

Section 46 (1) of CrPC 1973 .. The Section relates to making an arrest by a Police Officer. While making the arrest the police officer shall touch or confine the body of the person to be arrested, unless there be submission to the custody by word or action. **Sub section (2)** ..speaks about all means necessary to effect arrest but does not spell out precisely what these means are. There is legal vagueness. **Sub section (3) ..**Nothing in this section gives the right to cause the death of a person who is not accused of an offence punishable with death or imprisonment for life. Which means that the police officer can also cause death in respect of an accused who is concerned in an offence punishable with death etc. if such a person refuses to submit to arrest or attempts to escape. **Section 47** CrPC empowers police officers to search a premises and to break open the same for the purpose of arrest. **Seciton 48** CrPC authorizes police to pursue an offender into any place in India.

Proportionality of Force

Section 129.. it speaks about dispersal of Unlawful Assemblies by use of "civil force". Civil force is used by Magistrate or police officers.The quantun of force is not spelt out.

Section 130, 131.. speak about dispersal of Unlawful Assemblies by Army personnel. The force employed should be minimum.

Section 132.. gives protection against frivolous prosecutions.

Section 149, 151.. speak about power to arrest to "prevent" commission of cognizable offence. **But what force to be used if the power of arrest is resisted is not spelt out in law.**

Section 152...speaks about police **interposing to prevent injury to public property** that includes a mark used for navigation. Here too there is legal vagueness as to what force or degree of force that needs to be used when such interposing by the police fails to protect public property.

Sections 154,190, 192 CrPC.. speak about power of taking cognizance by police and judicial Magistrate.

However, the above legal provisions and the provisions of 'self defence' are wilting in a situation of "Armed Battles" which have become a regular feature in handling the Maoists and the Terrorists. There is a situation of a Proxy War (Insurgency conditions) which requires proclamation of Emergency provisions of the Constitution in areas affected by it calling for more deterrent Laws to deal with this extraordinary phenomena of Proxy War or low intensity war. But Govt. is not invoking emergency provisions in part of a state for reasons best known to itself.

Accountability of Police in Investigations and in Causing Deaths/Injuries

Registration of a Complaint

I. **Section 154 (1):** The above legal provision requires that information relating to the commission of a cognizable offence shall be entered in a book in the form of an FIR. This mandatory provision of issue of FIR is usually not followed. Instead, the police practice is to cause enquiry into the complaint before issuing an FIR. This police practice circumvents law and delays or frustrates issue of FIR. The judgement of A.P High Court makes it clear that issuance of FIR is a must, a legal requirement as the word used in the above section is "shall". **Second stage:** when a Station House Officer refuses to issue FIR, the complainant can approach the Superintendent of Police under Section 154 (3) who can cause such an FIR to be issued. This legal requirement which is a check on refusal to issue FIR at police station level has been highlighted in the judgement. **Third stage:** when there is no action to issue FIR at the level of S.H.O or Superintendent of Police, the complainant can approach Judicial Magistrate under Section 190 (1) r/w. 200 CrPC requesting the court to take the cognizance of the offence and proceed to issue process for enquiry. All these safeguards have been highlighted and focussed in the judgement. All of them will answer in some measure or other **a degree of Accountability of the police in the discharge of their functions at the initial stage of regestration of a complaint.**

II. **Section 174 (1)** CrPC: This is a slightly different legal provision. This section deals with suicides, accidents, suspicious deaths or where a person is killed by another or even cases involving suicides, death of women within 7 years of marriage etc. **But the Section does not cover injuries/death caused by police in discharge of their various duties.** Therein lies the limitation of police investigations into deaths caused in dispersing unlawful Assemblies or in gun battles with Maoists etc. Even if such cases are included in Section 174 CrPC, it offends **Rule of Law** as the police become judge of its actions. At any rate the present practice of investigation by police into the cases of deaths or injuries in "gun battles" with Maoists under Section 174 CrPC rests on legal phantom.

III. **Section** 176 CrPC deals with "inquiry"by Executive magistrate into cases.

    (a) Where a person dies in police custody.

    (b) Cases of women's suicide or death within 7 years of marriage. This Section also does not cover acts of police causing injury/death while dispersing unlawful Assemblies or in fighting "gun battles" with Maoists.

There is a legal vacuum as to the authority, who has to inquire/investigate cases of injuries/deaths caused by police/security personnel in the "dispersal of unlawful Assemblies" or even in fighting "gun battles" with Maoists(all in discharge of their duties).

IV. **Therefore High Court of A.P in its judgement dt. 6-2-2009 shifted the gears from Section 174 (1) CRPC to Section 154(1) and 156 (1) CrPC where investigations into such type of deaths are supervisable by Judicial Magistrates and finally by the Sessions Court which has competence to try an offence of "culpable homicide" not amounting to murder (304 IPC). This according to me, is expected to answer a rigorous degree of Accountability of the police**

actions in encounters of Maoists. The discretion to pursue investigation or to drop investigations by the police according to judgement **is not unfettered**. Further, final report of investigation submitted by the Police under Section 156 CrPC to the Judicial Magistrate is not conclusive and that the Judicial Magistrate has to apply his mind to the police report and if need be he can take cognizance of the offence disregarding the police report. **Thus, the right of private defence claimed by the police officers is to be decided on merits finally by a judicial process involving the Judicial First Class Magistrate and the Court of Sessions competent to try the offence of culpable homicide. Further, the court quoting section 105 of Evidence Act of 1872 held that in a charge of culpable homicide not amounting to murder, the burden of proving the plea of self defence rests with the police. This in effect is a very rigorous standard of Accountability and possibly impractical in the current situation of Proxy War that is confronting the Indian Nation.**

Defining the contours of self defence, the court observed as follows:

"Non-exculpatory public policy defences include Statute of limitation (Section 468 Cr.P.C); double jeopardy (Article 20(2) of the Constitution read with Section 300 Cr.P.C.); diplomatic immunity; testimonial immunity [Article 20(3) of the Constitution]; plea bargained immunity (Chapter XXI A, Cr.P.C); Judicial, Legislative and Executive immunity (Section 77 and 78 IPC, Article 361 (2) and (3) of the Constitution); incompetence defenses (Sections 82 and 83 IPC. Defense of this class are not based on the lack of culpability of the actor. They are pure public policy arrangements. The immunity from conviction flow not on account of established non-culpability of the actor or the innocence of the defendant but on account of the countervailing public policy interests recognised, accommodated and provided by the Legislature.[Paras 85, 86].

"In justification defenses, the offence caused by the justified behaviour remains a legally recognised harm. Excusing conditions as defense constitute part of justification defenses and are available so long as the condition has been caused by a disability, transient or permanent and is present at the time of the offence. Under the special justifying circumstances however that harm is outweighed by the need to avoid a greater harm or to further a larger societal interest. Self-defense or defensive force justifications are all based on a threat in response to which the defensive force is justified. They are often distinguished by one another by the nature of the interest threatened. Statutes too often make special alterations or exceptions to the basic principles of defensive force justification depending on the interest threatened. **The general exceptions enumerated in Sections 96 to 106 in Chapter IV of the IPC fall within this category of defences".**

The High Court of A.P observed that the "State does not claim nor suggest any special or extraordinary legislative authority, for employment of lethal force against a Maoist/ extremist/naxalite and adopts the position that the deaths in the police encounters are invariably as a consequence of the exercise of the right of private defence by police officers, it is mandatory that the governance process, including the recording, investigatorial and where warranted the charge and trial processes must conform to the injunctions of Article 21".

The Court at para 8 of the judgement further observed "the Executive and Judicial Sanctions against life and liberty must be explicitly spelt out in Legislative Authority".

According to the judgment of the A.P.High court it is not only in the cases where police cause the death of a person acting or purporting to act in discharge of official duties or in self defence as the case may be which have to pass the test of the principle of " right of private defence" in a trial before a competent court of law, but also such cases falling under Section's 76 to 95 IPC 1860.(General Exceptions in Chapter IV). The court reiterated that self defence justification cannot be assumed as proved or established without a focused investigation and trial by a court.

Not withstanding the above decision, there need not be undue alarm in police circles. There may be trauma of FIR and investigation against police. Sec. 132 CrPC mitigates the trauma of trial. **Government's permission is needed for criminal prosecution.**

Keeping in view the above observations, and also from my own understanding of legal provisions and practical requirements, I am of the opinion that the Accountability process for deaths caused in "Armed Gun Battles" between the police and security forces on the one hand and the Maoist and Terrorists on the other hand needs to be more simpler than what has been presently envisaged in the judgement. **In the first place, an "Armed Battle" needs to be legally defined by placing them at a level higher to unlawful assemblies.** The mechanism of Accountability for deaths in such battles may rest with the Executive Magistracy headed by the District Magistrate and finally the Government of the day. Alternatively, judicial enquiries can be discretionarily ordered and only on its adverse findings an FIR against the police and security forces can be issued. **The Military Operations such as the one undertaken by the Indian Security Forces led by NSG in Mumbai on 26-11-2008 against Jihadi Terrorists form part of such "Armed Battles".** To issue FIR compulsorily against such security forces and conduct further investigations by police, and still further by the Judicial Magistracy have the effect of demoralising police forces and defeating the National object of fighting terrorism or low intensity wars aided and abetted by hostile nations.

The State of Andhra Pradesh made the following submissions before the High Court of Andhra Pradesh in defence of its policy of not issuing FIR against the police party which participated in encounters under Section 154 (1) CrPC. The state contended that death caused by use of force by police in the course of duty does not amount to an "offence". "**Sections 149 and 152** of the Cr.P.C obligate the police to interpose themselves between persons contemplating or actually committing offences and the rest of the society. **Sections 129 to 131** Cr.P.C authorize the use of force by police officers to disperse mobs and unlawful assemblies. Protection against prosecution is accorded under Section 132 even where the use of force in such situations results in death. **Section 151 Cr.P.C** authorizes any police officer to arrest any person, where he has knowledge that such a person has a design to commit a cognizable offence. **Section 46 Cr.P.C** authorizes use of force by the police officer in the course of effecting an arrest. Such use of force, which may result in injury to body or even a fatality, would not constitute an "offence". The provisions of Section 6 IPC read with the general exceptions contained in Sections 76 to 106, specifically Sections 76 to 79 enjoin that where injury is caused to a human body or death occurs due to such injury on account of employment of force by police officers in the course of duty, such conduct does not constitute an "offence". The contention of the State was that in view of the above legal position, the conduct of police in encounter death **does not constitute an offence.** There is considerable force in the arguments of the state.

Clubbing all police encounters involving violators of Law or criminals with that of "gun battles" with Maoists or Terrorists is to miss the wood for trees. Proceeding to issue FIR in respect of death of a Terrorist treating it as an "offence" is difficult to comprehend. All cases of injuries, deaths caused in

- Effecting arrests
- Dispersing of unlawful Assemblies
- Gun battles with Terroists/Maoists such as the parliament attack case 2002, the Mumbai attack case 2008.

Do not become offences *ipsofacto* as they are caused in discharge of public duties where injuries and casualities to the police are not uncommon..

These types of situations apart, the scale and magnitude of the oprreration, the type of weapons and ammunitions that the Terrorists are equipped with, the rapidity with which the operation is to be conducted to the satisfaction of the society, the care and caution excercised to save as many lives as possible from po;ice side need to be taken into account while judging the force employed by police. Some of the Terrorist groups are armed with military weapons such as rocket launchers.

Deaths or injuries caused by 'public servant' in effecting arrests, dispersal of unlawful assemblies or in gun battles in the course of discharging duties are "admissible form of harm" in law. Where the P.S. causes injuries in individual capacity, or individual citizens similarly causing injury/death in self defence is also a "legal harm". But there is difference in the forum where accountability is tested. While the latter needs to establish the right of pvt. defence in a court of law, the public servant needs to do it before Executive Magistrate or a judge appointed to enquire the test of self defence or proportionality of force employed. Only when the right of self defence fails or proportionality of force is excessive, the public servant needs to face an FIR U/s 154 CrPC. **Death or injuries caused by P.S. acting under the command of law do not become offences ipso facto.** There is no denying the fact of fake police encounter of Maoists, Criminals or even occassional offenders of law (illegal harm or extra legal harm resulting in deaths), even while purportedly acting in discharge of public duties. But they are not part of public duty or done at the command of law. Therefore, while attempting to correct the above forms of legal worng doing, the courts cannot embark on sweeping legal fiat that all cases of deaths at the hands of police, be sent up for trial of police officers before a Court of Sessions. A better legal option(where govt. fails to act to appoint a judge to enquire into the case of fake encounters) is for the superior judiciary to excercise its writ jurisdiction on a complaint by individuals, civil rights groups or media reports and direct the govt to order a judicial enquiry to determine truth before facing trial in a Sessions Court.

Three Categories of Acts which are not offenses *per se*

(I) Sec. 76 to 95 IPC 1860 (Chapter IV General exceptions) recognised "unintentional harm" caused by an act of a judge, a child of certain age, an act of person acting in good faith as not offences. (II) Sec. 46, 129, 130, 131 CrPC 1973 dealing with powers of arrest, dispersal of unlawul assemblies by use of force by Police, Executive Magistrate or Army recognised "legal harm", which is not an offence unless the force used is disproportionate. (III) Sec. 96 to 106 IPC dealing with right of private defense available to persons and public officials.

Gun Battles

Injuries or death in "gun battles" between police/security forces on one side and Maoists and terrorist groups on the other is another form of "legal harm", that is caused in discharge of public duties. **But it has no definite legal expression in CrPC.** They are not the same as the act of dispersal of unlawul assemblies in ordinary law and order situations. At any rate, legal harm accompanying these gun battles needs to be tested on the principle of right of private defence and proportionate use of force to find out whether an offence has been caused or not.

Police Encounters

It is a colloquial term for extra judicial deaths, where police indulge in shooting down criminals, or sometimes casual offenders of Law etc. They have no legal sanction.

These are all "legal defences" for all the above categories of deaths or injuries caused in the discharge of duties. (Except for fake Police encounters) They will not become offences ipso facto like the ordinary offences complained of for taking cognizance, investigation by police or judicial magistrate unless an independent legal forum such as executive magistrate or a judge appointed under the Commission of Enquiries Act enquires and reports that the right of private defence is exceeded or disproportionate "legal harm" is caused and such reports are referred to by government to the authorities competent to take cognizance of an offence. **It is a middle ground between the extreme degree of Accountability requiured by the High Court judgment and the feeble degree**

of Accountability demanded by police viz investigations and determining their fate by police u/s 174 CrPC whereby police become a judge of its own actions. This middle ground accords with Rule of Law. It is therefore difficult to agree with the view of AP High Court that all cases of deaths caused in gun battles be automatically taken cognizance on a complaint, investigated and put up for trial before Sessions Court for an offence of culpable homicide. **It is posible that civil right groups sympathetic to maoist abuse the "legal process" of taking cognizance of "offence".**

Solution to this intractable problem to be found in legal reforms:

- "gun battles" resulting in death/injuries need to be added as a separate legal provision in the form of Section 131A CrPC. Sec. 100 IPC 1860 providing for self defence against an assault on police by unlawful elements/Terrorists is inadequate legal provision in tackling Terrorist acts. Basically it is a defensive legal provision when police are subjected to attack. But when Terrorists, one or two in number go berserk in killing spree as it happened in Mumbai on 26-11-2008, police have to go on offensive operation of neutralising the Terrorist or shooting him dead. Police cannot wait for attack on them to retaliate in self defence. Therefore, new legal definition for the suppression of murder and mayhem unleashed by Terrorists is needed.
- U/s 176 CrPC executive magistrate has power to inquire into deaths caused in police custody and other offences. Death caused in "gun battles" need to be added to the list to remove multiple source of taking cognizance of an offence by police or judicial magistrate.
- Similarly deaths caused in the "dispersal of unlawful assemblies" also need to form part of Magisterial enquiry u/s 176 CrPC as they are not enumerated therein.

- Amendment to Sec154 (1), 190, 192 CrPC excluding the power of taking cognizance of deaths caused in "gun battles" by police or judicial magistrates treating them as offences even prio to an adverse Executive Magisterial report or a report of judge appointed under the Commission of Enquiry Act and where such a report is referred to the authorities by the government. This suggestion is in stark contrast with existing judicial rulings that no cognizance of an act of corruption by a judge is taken though the act of corruption is not in the discharge of public duty or a part of such duty.

Neither Sec. 129 to 131 CrPC which speak about use of minimum force against unlawful assemblies or Sec. 100, 103 IPC 1860 dealing with right of self defence are relevant in controlling violent mobs or in the Gun battles with Maoists / terrotists. Minimum force will not work with violent mobs armed with deadly weapons or incendiary material. Right of private defence is relevant when police come under attack. Police need to suppress voilence, stop death and destruction of citizens and their properties before they themselves come under attack and react with fire power. This third party viz citizens and their properity need protection. All police duties are not reactive duties. Here there is proactive element in duties. So Sec. 100, 103 IPC are not applicable to proactive duties. The same logic holds good about Gun battles where police need to be proactive and not reactive. In the 26-11-2008 Mumbai carnage, terrorists were killing citizens indiscriminately. In such situations, police need to stop further loss of life by proactive operation using force.

The AP Suppression of Disturbances Act, 1948: To some extent the State of Andhra Pradesh had a law namely, **The A.P. Suppression of Disturbances Act, 1948** (Act No. III of 1948). **Sec. 5** of the above Act is reproduced. 'Power to fire upon persons contravening certain orders in disturbed areas: Any Magistrate, and any Police Officer not below the rank of sub-Inspector may if in his opinion it is necessary to do so for restoring or maintaining public order, after giving such warning, if any, as he may consider necessary, fire upon, order fire to be opened or otherwise use force, even to the causing of death, against any person who in a disturbed area is acting in contravention of any law or order for the time being in force in such area, prohibiting the assembly of five or more persons or the carrying of weapons or of things capable of being used as weapon'. **This Law is an improvement over Section 100 of IPC, 1860. or the provisions of Sec. 129 to CrPC 1973.**

The century old Cr.P.C. amended in 1973 has recognised "unlawful Assemblies" in Sec. 129, 130, 131 and used the words "minimum force" to disperse such Assemblies. The code has not spelt out.

- "Armed riotous mobs" with deliberate purpose of unleashing violence.
- "Armed Gun battles" between police /security forces and outlaws that include Terrorists.
- "Subversive Gatherings" or groups of Armed people who blaze their guns and blast landmines and procure and prepare guns and landmines.
- "Mass upraisings" against atrocity perpetrated by person or a group in society or even committed by police and security agencies.
- Situations: Where intelligence inputs suggest that Terrorists are planning to strike targets. Are we to wait for them to strike or preempt such a strike timely and decisively?

In September 2009, there was a media report about the judicial enquiry report of Mr. S.P. Tamang, Judicial Magistrate of Ahmedabad into the cause of death of **Ishrat Jehan** in exchange of fire with the police. The report went against police. Meanwhile the High Court of Gujarat stayed the said report as it was made public without its permission. The said High Court appointed a **three member committee** of chosen police officers to investigate and report on Ishrat Jehan's death. Then there are Gujarat C.I.D. police investigation reports which determined the death as genuine encounter. Then again the Supreme Court has appointed one **Geetha Johri**, a senior Police officer of the Gujarat cadre to investigate and report on Sohrabuddin's death at the hands of police (investigation monitored by Supreme Court). **Thus we have multiple agencies of enquiry and investigation.**

1. Investigation conducted by State C.I.D. branch.
2. Investigation conducted by individual police officers or a committee of such officers and monitored by Supreme Court or High Court as the case may be.
3. Enquiry conducted by Judicial Magistrate.
4. There is demand by other aggrieved persons in Gujarat for CBI investigation through Supreme Court order.
5. Another agency called SIT (Special Investigation Team) headed by R.K. Raghavan was appointed by Supreme Court.
6. Commission of Enquiry headed by a Judge of High Court serving or retired (not come into existence).

It is true that High Courts, Supreme Court have power under their writ jurisdiction to pass such order or give directions to protect rights of citizen. It is perfectly legal. I learn through the TV debates in which legal luminaries participated that there is a recent amendment carried out by Central Government to Sec. 176(1) Cr. P.C. which authorizes a **Judicial Magistrate** to conduct enquiry and report. Prior to this Executive Magistrate possessed such a power. This is a better method of accountability process instead of an Executive Magistrate who is subordinate of State. As regards Court monitored investigation by another set of police officers of the state, it is not a healthy precedent as these police officers are hopelessly divided against themselves and have their own grievances against Government of the day. **Statutorily, CBI has no jurisdiction to investigate into cases reported in state without state Government's permission and overriding or encroaching the state function by Supreme Court or High Court is not a healthy Democratic practice in the scheme of separation of powers.**

It is learnt that C.I.D. branch of Gujarat police requested for Magisterial enquiry. This is not the normal procedure. The Government has to address the judiciary. So there is a free for all in ordering enquiries and it is not conducive to get at truth. **There is a saying that too many cooks spoil the broth.**

Therefore there needs to be single source of enquiry and Judicial Magistrate's enquiry fits into the scheme as he is not a subordinate of Government. But first of all Secs. 174, 176 Cr. PC 1973 need to cover as I said in my detailed writings on the subject not only

- suspicious deaths
- unnatural deaths
- custodial deaths

but also deaths caused in "exchange of fire" between police and out laws. It should be spelt out clearly. **They should not be lumped in the category of suspicious and unnatural death.** Therefore Court's intervention in police investigations etc., is an attempt to treat symptoms of disease of individual cases brought before it and not have the effect of treating the disease itself. **For this reason, well thought out amendment to laws as suggested by me are needed.**

In an article published in THE HINDU, dt. 12.09.2009, Mr. N. Rama Krishna, Advocate, Supreme Court while discussing the subject with reference to the legal developments in Gujarat pertaining to **Ishrat Jehan's** death mentioned about amendment in 2006 to Sec. 176(1) Cr. P.C. 1973 which substituted Executive Magistrate with the Judicial Magistrate. **This is a salutory legal provision in the direction of protection of Human Rights.** But it does no good if such an important amendment is not placed in public domain through media.

The bone of contention is the legal point as to whether the 2006 amendment to Sec. 176(1) Cr. P.C. has retrospective effect to cover 2002 Gujarat riots. And it is pending with Gujarat High Court.

While discussing the meaning of "custodial death" a phrase occurring in the same section; the author of the article is of the opinion that all Police Encounters are "custodial deaths" since the victims according to him however were in police custody before being shot down in stage managed encounters. The phrase "custodial death" figured the old Cr. P.C. and retained in 1973, when Terrorism was unknown or minimal and sporadic. After Terrorism has become a menace to the country, there were no subsequent amendments to Sec. 176 (1) Cr. P.C. 1973

A custodial death is relatable to a) death in police custody, in particular in police stations, where the suspects are brought for the purpose of interrogation and where torture is used some times to extract a confession or to obtain clue to the offences committed. b) Suicides do takes place in police lock ups. c) It happens that police shoot the suspect terrorist dead after they are apprehended and while in their custody. This (c) takes place at secluded places away from police station premises.

But there are cases or certain acts associated with discharge of **preventive / proactive field operations of police** which are outside the description of the "custodial deaths". **Preventive police duties are like preventive medicines. They are**

- "Acts of exchange of fire" between police and outlaws in a forest, secluded places.
- In urban hideouts.
- While the suspects are on the move in a train or car etc.
- Hostage rescue from a particular setting and neutralising the fire power of the Terrorist.

The above acts of "exchange of fire" or more succinctly called as "Armed gun battles" by me are preventive in nature and not necessarily part of investigative duties. Therefore the phrase "custodial death" is too narrow a phrase to include "Armed gun battles" or acts of "exchange of fire" which are the part and parcel of police field duties. Such field duties are common across the world. **For this reason, I have argued that Sec. 176 (1) need further amendment to include "Armed battles" in addition to "custodial death" in Sec. 176(1) Cr. P.C. For otherwise, the Executive action, judicial decisions will rest on sandy legal foundations.**

The phrase "Police Encounter" does not figure in any provisions of criminal law. It is a legal fiction. The proper description is "armed gun battle" or acts of "exchange of fire" between police and outlaws or even between outlaws and Forest Guards, Coast Guard and customs officials etc

"Armed gun battles" need legal anchor by further amendment to Sec. 176(1) Cr. P.C.

A word or two about unnatural deaths, suspicious deaths or accidents, occurring in Sec. 174 Cr. P.C. where police enquiries, Magisterial enquiry are caused. Deaths in Armed gun battles or acts of Exchange of fire between outlaws and public official are sometimes registered under the above sections of law. This is wrong because they do not fall even literally in the description of acts of "exchange of fire". **So enquires, investigations now carried out U/s. 174, 176 (1) Cr. P.C. 1973 in respect of "Armed battles" rest on sandy foundation. This is where the Supreme Court needs to zero in on and catch the law makers by the scruff of their neck.**

In the same way, the legal provision of "right of private defence" **where police stand on the same footing as a citizen** also need re-look. In the year 2007, in the aftermath of Bomb blasts in Mecca Masjid in Hyderabad, the faithful who were aggrieved against police inaction, took out a procession and when they came across a **petrol pump**, it was alleged by police, that the processionists were set to attack the petrol pump and to protect the collateral damage police opened fire killing half a dozen people. Now is the act of opening of fire and deaths caused thereon are in "self defence of police personnel" or in the defence of petrol pump and collateral damage in the vicinity? And more important question is who has to exercise the right of private defence? Is it the owners of petrol pump or the police? If the act of firing is in defence of police personnel, resulting in injuries, deaths or even apprehension of safety to their lives, it can be still justified. **These legal ambiguities need a fresh look and reforms effected.**

It is necessary to correct faulty, inadequate legal provisions, incorrect views on such provisions and incorrect

judicial decisions that follow from the above. Incorrect views, legal provisions, judicial decisions are at the heart of injustice.

It is equally a wrong view to say that only judicial deaths (hangings of murder case convicts) are permissible and that there are no other forms of death which admit of justice. But I say that law recognized various situations (a) dispersal of unlawful assemblies, rioters where force is allowed to be used causing injury or even death (b) use of force that causes death in effecting arrest of murder convict trying to escape from custody (c) right of private defense where citizen and "public official" can cause deaths (d) armed "gun battles" where deaths are caused in "Genuine" Encounters. In all these cases there is no injustice in causing injury or even death. **They are not judicial killings. But they are legal killings.** Our intellectuals, my kith & kin in the profession need to spread this message. Mere understanding of the message is not enough. **It needs to be spread to wider sections of society. That is a big service in the cause of justice - understanding right view points and spreading them.**

Fake encounters are extra legal killing. Extra legal killings are "offences" prosecutable and punished.

So there are three types of killings (1) Judicial killings (2) Legal killings (3) Extra legal killings alone are offences.

Moreover, we have to look at the causes that resulted in the disease of fake encounters and that cause needs to be addressed before treating the symptoms. **They are**

- Lack of strong anti-terrorism law to meet the problem of terrorism and other violent outlaws till about December, 2008.
- Lack of equally sound interpretation by judiciary of anti terrorist legal provisions that hands out deterrent jail sentences to the accused.
- Lack of right incentives to honest investigation, prosecution for conviction obtained to terrorists.

- Lack of Central government cooperation to clear state anti-terror legislations.

The view point of Police and Army is that failure in respect of the above by political class and judiciary have cast them in a situation as the present. Of course there are unscrupulous police officers who resort to fake encounters to advance their professional interests or to have tough image. **For this, accountability of those indulging in fake encounters is the first step to put brakes on such encounters.** It is true that fake encounters far out weigh genuine. **To club both in the same category and wield the same stick is not a right approach.**

I am sorry to say that both political and judicial leadership is not able to zero in on **the bull's eye on the target by proper** amendment to laws. That leaves us to live in the paradise or hell of Court litigation in which there is no solution to this important public issue.

Genuine Police Encounters-Are they Offences?

(Article sent to English dailies for publication)

The High Court of Andhra Pradesh delivered judgment on 06.02.2009 treating all cases of deaths or injuries in police encounters as "offences" to be taken cognizance U/s 154 Cr P.C. 1973, investigated and put up for trial before a Competent Court of Law. On appeal, the Supreme Court of India stayed the above judgment.

For an appreciation of the subject, it is necessary to know what an "offence" means

Category I – Acts of Police, Executive Magistrate, Army Officer in dispersal of "unlawful assemblies". (Sec. 129 to 131 Cr. P.C. 1973). Under the Proviso to Sub. Sec 2 (a) of Sec. 132 Cr. P.C. the acts mentioned in Sec. 129 to 131 Cr. P.C. are not deemed as offences.

The above legal provisions mandate permissible limit of "legal harm". This legal harm is not a "certain" offence.

Category II – Secs. 75 to 95 IPC 1860 – General Exceptions (acts of persons, Judge, Court official). Section 6 IPC 1860 explicitly states that every definition of an "offence" shall be understood subject to exceptions contained in Chapter-IV titled as "General Exceptions".

Category III – "Right of private defence" (acts of persons and public officials). Section 96 IPC 1860 states that nothing is an "offence" which is done in the exercise of the act of right of private defence. Sec 98 IPC 1860 explicitly states that an act which would be otherwise be a "certain" offence is not that offence by reason of youth, want of maturity of understanding, unsoundness of mind, intoxication etc.

So acts in Category **I, II, III** though causing injury or death are not "offences" unless proven otherwise in police investigations in respect of persons concerned and in an "inquiry" by an independent legal forum in respect of public officials that include Police / Army.

The **first schedule to IPC 1860** under the sub classification of "offences" commences with Sec. 109 dealing with abetment to an offence which are all "certain offences".

Taking Cognizance and Investigation / Inquiry into acts resulting in Legal Harm

An inquiry by an independent agency such as an Executive / District Magistrate, a Judge appointed under the Commission of Enquiry Act 1951 needs to precede before cognizance of "offence" resulting from the use of force is taken by the police U/s 154 or by the Judicial First Class Magistrate U/s. 190 Cr. P.C. 1973. When the acts of public servants that include police resulting in use of force causing injury or death fail the test of proportionality of force or genuineness of Police Encounter/Gun battle, such acts become offences and not before.

Inadequacy in Law as Regards "Inquiry Authority"

One has to take into account the gaps in law for the Agency or Agencies authorised to cause inquiry and report into the deaths caused in Gun battles. Sec. 176 Cr. P.C. 1973 no doubt mentioned about an "inquiry" by Executive Magistrate into cases of deaths caused in police custody and other forms of deaths and suicides relating to married women. Custodial deaths are different from deaths in Gun battles. Sec. 176 Cr.P.C. therefore needs amendment to include deaths caused in actual "Gun battles" between police and the terrorists or other outlaws.

Therefore, the judgment of A.P. High Court that Police Personnel involved in "Gun battle", need to be straight away proceeded with by registering an FIR, investigated and prosecuted before a Sessions Court competent to try an offence of culpable homicide, where police need to prove their innocence regarding the genuineness of Gun battle or the proportionality of force used does not accord well with the totality of legal scheme that covered the definition of an "offence" both in the Indian Penal Code and Code of criminal procedure. If criminal cases are straight away filed without reference to the report of an independent, intermediary agency like an Executive Magistrate etc., there will be trauma of investigation, arrest of the police personnel concerned for discharging duties mandated by Law.

This irony of incompatibility of duties mandated by Law with rigorous accountability as required by the A.P. High Court Judgment needs reconciliation by Law makers.

Gun Battles with Terrorists etc. & Dispersal of Unlawful Assemblies

Gun battles do not have **legal anchor.** They are different from dispersal of "unlawful assemblies" described in Sec. 129 to 131 Cr. P.C. Force allowed in Sec. 129 to 131 Cr.P.C. is "as little force" and "as little injury" to person and property which will not work in Gun battles as the terrorists are equipped with military type weapons like rocket launchers etc. Gun battles therefore need to be separately and explicitly spelt out in law broadly indicating the nature of force to be employed.

Relevance of the Right of Private Defence in "Gun battles"

There is yet another angle in regard to "gun battles". Sec. 96 to 106 IPC 1860 are not appropriate legal provisions (legal defences). Many of these gun battles involve a third party. In the Parliament attack case, New Delhi in the year 2002, the third party is political leadership of the country. In Mumbai attack case on 26.11.2008, it is the citizens and their properties. This third party needs protection by way of proactive military or police field operations. The right of self defence provisions in Secs. 96 to 106 IPC 1860 of reacting with force after the police party comes under assault are misplaced. Police cannot wait for an attack to take place on them before they use force against the rampaging Terrorists or Maoists. Proactive policing initiatives are different from reactive one. However the right of self defence provisions are relevant when police are guarding a place, VIPs, VVIPs (defensive or reactive operations) where the police have to retaliate when they or the VIP comes under attack.

Therefore well thought out, precise and definitive legal provisions need to replace the ambiguous and the outmoded. They will help the Courts to come to right conclusions in the interpretative process.

Supreme Court's intervention and sound decision is needed to **answer justice** to the competing claims of State represented by its police and security forces on one side and civil rights groups and perpetrators of violence on the otherside.

There is an urgent need to resolve the legal contradiction that is the outcome of inadequate law and faulty interpretation by Courts.

Responsibility of Other Agencies - Hindsight/What Went Wrong

In the scheme of the Code of Criminal Procedure, 1973, it is not the sole prerogative of police for taking cognizance of an offence and further to investigate such an offence. There is a parallel power of taking cognizance of an offence by the Judicial Magistrate and give directions to register and investigate a case by the police (Section 191 CrPC). Sub Section (2) of the same section authorises the Chief Judicial Magistrate to empower any second class Magistrate to take cognizance of the offence, inquire and try the same.

Under Section 192, the Chief Judicial Magistrate may after taking cognizance of offence, make over the case for enquiry and trial to any competent Magistrate subordinate to him. So the power of taking cognizance of offence, investigation is not an exclusive power given to police. Similarly, under section 157 (1) CrPC, the S.H.O has to send report of investigation to a Judicial Magistrate. Further, under Section 159 such a Magistrate upon receipt of the report of investigation by police, may direct further investigation or if he thinks fit at once proceed or depute any Magistrate subordinate to him to proceed, to hold preliminary enquiry into or otherwise dispose of the case in the manner provided in the Code of Criminal Procedure. The point focussed by me is that the lower judiciary has parallel power of taking cognizance of an offence, enquiry etc., in addition to possessing the power of supervision of police investigations.

In the above scenario, the moot point that was missing in our intellectual, classes, legal fraternity, police circles is that with all these powers of taking cognizance of offence, investigations by police, Magistracy, Judicial Magistracy etc. the Criminal Justice System is in a pathetic state. The Intelligentia has to analyse as to whether the above functions of Police, Magistracy and Judicial fraternity led to service to the common man or disservice to him and whether the actions of the above establishment incharge of Criminal Justice System fortified the right to life and liberty of the common man or fortified the rights and liberties of vested interests in society, the criminal enterprise, the Terrorists and Mafia and finally the political class which is nexus with the criminal and corrupt. There needs to be a public debate on this issue in the main stream print media and prime time TV channels involving the genuine intellectuals in society.

Judicial and Political Decisions-Impact on Criminal Justice

The judiciary evolved several jurisprudential principles touching procedural law, law of evidence, substantive law. In respect of bail which falls under procedural law, the judiciary has been very liberal to the accused. It evolved the dictum or jurisprudential principle that bail is a rule and not jail. This ran riot in the decisions rendered by the lower courts in day to day bail matters which will be in thousands. This encouraged the criminals to continue their criminal activity without fear of law. The judiciary evolved, the concept of interim bail which is not traceable to any legal provision in the criminal procedure code. It has been very liberal to grant anticipatory bail. On the side of the law of evidence, the judiciary evolved criminal jurisprudential principles of "proof beyond all doubt", "benefit of doubt", "natural justice" etc. All these weakened the case of prosecution and helped the criminal or the terrorists. They made proof in a court of law almost impossible. On the side of substantive law, the judiciary evolved rarest of the rare cases principle which also caused damage to the criminal justice system. With regard to sentencing policy, the courts never gave full term of imprisonment prescribed by law even though the convictions are given after a case is proved beyond all reasonable doubt. For example if the legal provision provided 7 years imprisonment, courts give 2 or 3 years. All these weakened the criminal justice system. The criminals and outlaws were emboldened. Resultantly, some of the fake encounters have become common particularly, in Metropolitan Cities where police are called upon to control big criminal mafia. **On the political angle.** The politician has always been soft to the offender and criminal for various reasons. There is interference in criminal investigations and prosecutions. In fact, prosecuting agencies is the pocket borough of the politician. The political executive have the power to commute prison sentences awarded by the courts. Life convicts are coming out of jail in less than 14 years because of the existence of sec. 432 to 434 CrPC and liberal exercise of executive power to commute prison sentences under the above section. So all these make up a sum total of the weak links in the system of criminal justice which are giving scope for the so-called fake encounters. The moment we remove all these weak links in the chain of command in judiciary, political executive, police agencies, it is possible to drastically cut down the rate of fake police encounters.

OFFENCE, TAKING COGNIZANCE, INQUIRY

S. No.	Sec. of Law	Description of Offence	Legal Status	Authority to take Cognizance	Remarks
1	2	3	4	5	6
1.	Sec. 76 to 95 Sec. 96 to 104 IPC 1860 Chap IV General Exceptions in IPC 1860	Official acts of a Judge, acts done in good faith, accident is doing lawful act, acts of person bound by law to do it, acts of child of certain age, acts in self defence of person or public servant	These acts of "unintentiona harm" or "legal harm" or even "harm caused in self defense" are not offences perse until they are proven otherwise.	Police can take cognizance except where public servant viz., police is acting in self defense	Sec. 6 IPC 1860 states acts become offences subject to general exceptions in Chapter IV.
2.	Art. 361 of the Constitution of India	Actions of the President of the Republic, Governors of States in exercise of power while in office	Absolute legal immunity	No cognizance can be taken by any authority	
3.	Sec. 46, 129, 130, 131 Cr. P.C.1973	Acts of police in effecting arrests, Acts of police, Army, Executive Magistrate in ordering use of force to disperse unlawful Assemblies	Permissible "legal harm" in discharge of duty. Not offences until proven that force used is unwarranted or dispropor-tionate.	Cognizance of the Act can commence by way of "inquiry" by independent legal forum.	It is a postulate of Rule of Law that one is not Judge of one's own action. In case of Police or Army acts of employing force, Executive Magistrate can inquire while in case of Executive Magistrate is involved, a judge appointed under the Commission of Enquiry Act, 1951 can enquire and report on points at Column 4.
4.	All other offences under Criminal Laws	Difficult to enumerate here. They will be in thousands	Offences	Police Judicial Magistrate etc., can take cognizance	

S. No.	Sec. of Law	Description of Offence	Legal Status	Authority to take Cognizance	Remarks
1	2	3	4	5	6
5.	Response of Law Enforcement Authorities is faint or there is misapplication of existing legal provisions such as Sec. 100, 103, IPC 1860 which empower causing death	Large scale violence of unlawful mobs resulting in loss of life and properties.	"Legal harm" in discharge of public duties	Independent legal forum such as Executive Magistrate	In large scale violence of the type in column 3 there are three parties (1) unlawful mobs (2) citizen and properties of public and private (3) Police. Right of private defense in Sec. 100 extends to cause death to ecsape from an assault likely to cause (a) death (b) grievous hurt (c) attempt at rape (d) attempt at unnatural lust (e) kidnap (f) wrongful confinement. Sec. 103 IPC mention about self defense extending to cause death to escape or protection from robbery, house breaking, mischief, theft, tresspass. These two sections are inadequate to meet large scale violence resulting in death to third party viz., public and property and not merely against the offences stated therein.
6.	Legal response on the nature and extent of force to be employed is not specified. Force described in Sub(2) of 130 Cr.P.C. inadequate. Force to the extent of causing death in Sec. 100 IPC misplaced.	Gun battles between Terrorists, Maoists Vs the Police, Security Forces	Legal harm not offence perse	Independent legal forum in the form of "inquiry"	Sub Section (2) of Sec. 130 Cr. P.C. mandates as "little force as possible" and do as "little harm against person and property" This does not work in gun battles. Sec. 100 IPC 1860 is misplaced because police cannot wait till they come under deadly assault. Police need proactive operation to neutralise or kill Terrorists before they kill more. Sec. 100 or 103 IPC 1860 are not appropriate provision in proactive operation against Terrorists or Maoists. The spirit of Sec.100, 103 IPC is reactive.

4

Accountability of State and Criminals

Accountability and Transparency determine the quality of governance. The concept is tricky and complex. Some say that Accountability is for Law. Others say it is for the public as the sovereignty in a democracy rests with public. Yet some others say it is for the Government or employer. In respect of public representative like M.P. M.L.A etc., the public is supreme in the Accountability process. They are accountable in periodic five year term of elections for performance. But if it is for corruption and crime, they are also accountable to the law of the land. But both need not go hand in hand. It happens as in the case of some politicians, even if they face criminal charges, they are returned elected to the Assembly in the periodic elections. After the issue of non-performance, crime and corruption the issue of wrong doing also figures. **Public wrong doing involves nepotism, casteism, favouritism, wrongful commissions and omissions in exercise of public power. Only the public can judge on this wrong doing and law cannot sit in judgement over this for the reason that this type of wrong doings do not fall under the definition of "criminal misconduct" attracting the provisions of the Anti Corruption Law.**

The subject of Accountability has been written about by me in my books atleast for the last one decade. Basically there are three components deciding Accountability.

- Accountability for traditional crimes committed by offenders which are in millions in a year.
- Accountability for acts of corruption of Governing classes called the "establishment" which are also in tens of millions annually.
- Accountability for "wrong doings" of the establishment in particular.

There is no ambiguity in understanding crimes and corruption. But clarification is needed for "wrong doings" Wrong doings can be enumerated as below:

(a) Delays, inaction, serious inaction in public order duties which disturb social harmony in a community.

(b) Arbitrary action.

(c) Highhanded acts of police.

(d) Ill considered and ill thought out actions.

(e) Non-participatory and undemocratic decision of single authority.

(f) Negligent act

(g) Non-transparent act

(h) Acts of claiming false credit

(i) Usurping powers and functions that belong to others

(j) Sensationalisation and scandalisation of news.

(k) Spreading false views knowingly and unknowingly.

(l) Misuse of Government facilities like housing, transport and personnel.

(m) Lack of puctuality and accessibility

(n) Motivated action like foisting of false cases and white-washing genuine cases (Ex. St.Kits against V.P. Singh's family in 1990s by CBI is a glaring example of implicating the innocent).

(o) Unauthorised phone tapping

(p) Favouritism based on caste, community, friends, party affiliation.

(q) Nepotism

(r) Constitutional authorities **doing "business of profit"** and also heading sports bodies like BCCI which generate profits.

(s) Discriminatory action based on gender, caste etc.

(t) Squandering of public money on wasteful items of purchase and development.

(u) Exploitation of nations resources (natural and human resources) by companies and multi-nationals in connivance with the Government of the day.

(v) Rewarding and promoting the wrong doer (Ex. Several Intelligence Chiefs who undertook the job of telephone tapping that include the phones of former Prime Minister Sri Chandra Sekhar were rewarded).

(w) Silence of the society for the above wrong doings.

(x) Misuse of high cost resources such as helicopter by the establishment.

It is difficult to enforce Accountability in respect of wrong doings in the Indian context because they are not criminalised.

Crimes

There is some measure of accountability for the crimes committed by the offenders. But it is not *foolproof* at the stage of enquiry and during the course of formal investigation as several offenders are not brought on record by registration of the First Information Report (FIR). This is due to the factors like corruption of the Investigating Agencies and political influence. Such unregistered crime should be in millions annually. The offenders escape Accountability for their crimes. Enquiries are closed. Investigations are also closed as mistake of law, mistake of fact or for want of sufficient evidence. The next stage is the trial in a Court of Law where charge sheets have been filed by the Investigating agencies after obtaining satisfactory evidence. In this category, only a fraction of Accountability is answered where not more than 40 to 50% of the offenders are convicted and sentenced to jail. The rest of them are acquitted by Courts due to archaic rules of evidence and procedure as well as the principles of criminal jurisprudence evolved by judiciary. In grave offences like murder that involves the high and mighty, the conviction rate is less than 30%. That makes the Accountability process a laughing stock.

Corruption

Corruption is all pervading. But Accountability is negligeible. The reason is that not more than 10% of corrupt acts are detected, registered and prosecuted. And out of this 10%, 50% only get convicted and answer the Accountability process. In respect of the high and mighty in politics, bureaucracy and judiciary not even 2% of the cases are detected and registered. This is because the Investigating Agencies like CBI etc. are under the control of the political executive. A few cases which were registered and investigated are due to·the initiative of public spirited persons who approach the High Court and the Supreme Court to order investigations. In respect of the senior bureaucrats Accountability for corruption is equally negligible. Hardly 5% of the senior officials are booked for corruption related offences. The reason is executive instructions issued which require prior permission of the Prime Minister or the Chief Minister before an enquiry is commenced against senior bureaucrats. This is called the "Single Directive System". Though it is outlawed by the Supeme Court, it is not implemented by the Executive. Even to book cases in the middle and lower rungs of bureaucracy, there is difficulty due to shortage of staff in the Anti Corruption Agencies and also due to corruption in lower ranks of Anti Corruption Agencies. In the same way an enquiry against Judges needs the permission of Chief Justices concerned. This is due the judicial instructions or decisions given by the Courts. So much so not even 2% of the Judges are facing criminal investigations for corruption though there are reports that 50% of the judiciary is corrupt. There are ironclad guarantees that protect judiciary from Accountability. Yet again Article 226 of the Constiution, Secs. 488 Cr. P.C. and 389 Cr.P.C. of 1973 have defeated

Accountability process instead of enhancing the same. Art. 226 and Sec. 488 Cr. P.C. deal with quashing of criminal investigations or enquiries while Sec. 389 deals with withdrawal of criminal prosecution. The high and mighty in Government availed the above legal provisions liberally.

Wrong Doing

I have listed several wrong doings in the foregoing pages. The wrong doing of "favouritism" needs to be elucidated as it is a potent cause for injustice in Government and Society.

Art. 75 (4) refers to administering oath of Office to Union Minister according to the forms set out for the purpose in the Third Schedule. Art.99 refers to such oath to members of parliament Art.124 (6) refers to such oath by Supreme Court Judges. Art.148(2) refers to such oath by CAG. Art.164(3) refers to such oath by Minister in a state. Art.188 refers to such oath by members of Legislative Assemblies. Art.219 refers to such oath by Judges of High Court. The form of such oath is as follows:

Form of Oath of Office for a Minister for the Union

"I, A. B., do swear in the name of God and solemnly affirm that I will bear true faith and allegiance to the Constitution of India as by law established, [that I will uphold the sovereignty and integrity of India], that I will faithfully and conscientiously discharge my duties as a Minister for the Union and that I will do right to all manner of people in accordance with the Constitution and the law, without fear or favour, affection or ill will".

The words discharge my duties without fear or favour, affection or illwill do not admit, favoritism, nepotism or malafide decision in discharge of public duty. Therefore concerned citizens, in the absence of Independent credible mechanism of accountability for Ministers for "public wrong doing" (short of crime and corruption) can move the judiciary to make a Minister quit public office if a charge of wrong doing is held proved. **This issue is raised by me for the first time in the history of the Republic and it needs to be debated and**

acted by media, intellectuals and concerned citizens. This is an indirect and round about way to accoutability and is not a substitute to Independent Accountability mechanism. Even though there is breach of Constitutional provision regarding the oath of office referred to, it is not prosecutable with prison sentence. The only way for Accountability is to sack the concerned from the positions they are holding.

Phone Tapping

This wrong doing also needs interpretation. There needs to be good reason to violate the right of privacy - personal freedom enjoined in the Constitution. State surveillance has to be carried out according to the procedures in order to be justified and where procedures are not adhered to, such an act should be made accountable. The real issue is not about the principle of phone tapping but the motives behind it. Such tappings can be justified in the cause of internal and external security and in the interest of security of Nation's leadership. It can also be justified in the security of Nation's financial institutions. Criminals and Terrorists and those public figures or officials who are in league with them can also come under the purview of phone tapping. But phone tapping of political opponents violates the principle.

In April 2010, there was a political storm where UPA Government was accused of tapping the telephones of political opponents by the Intelligence Bureau. In Great Britain Intelligence agencies are regulated by Law and their actions are subject to scrutiny by Parliament. In India they are not regulated by the law. So too is the C.B.I. This leads to higher levels of misuse without Accountability. The Central Government has power U/A 246 (empty 8 of List-I) to legislate on Central Bureau of Intelligence and investigation. Yet such a legislation is absent and they are regulated by Executive order of Government with occasional guidelines by Supreme Court. All this is nothing but shadow boxing with legal provision which I adverted to in the preface of the Book. **Rule without law is undemocratic.** I have raised the issue in my earlier writings.

Parliamentary House Panels

Parliamentary House Panels (Committees) are expected to oversee the working of the executive and enforce Transparency and Accountability. Media reports in September 2009 suggest that three MPs from Andhra Pradesh who own Construction companies are members of these House Panels and that they made claims to the tune of some 10 thousand crores on the National Highway Authority of India (NHAI) and that such a claim is a subject of arbitration between the NHAI and the companies owned by them or their family members.This is an instance of accused sitting in judgment of their own wrong doings. **All this defeats accountability to the bone-marrow.**

Working of the Principle of Accountability

The existing legal criteria in respect of crime or corruption of political class is **conviction** by court of law for disqualification from public life or from holding a public office. The law on the subject is the Representation of Peoples Act 1951. For certain offences the conviction is for 2 years, for others it is 6 months, and in yet another set of cases there is no particular period of prison term. Minimum conviction is the criteria. This is in respect of Section 123 of R.P. Act, 1951 in which the High Court can hold a person guilty for corrupt electoral practices. I have dealt with this subject in a separate chapter "Criminalisation of politics" in the book "Threats to the Indian Republic". There I have suggested a uniform pattern of the offences that disqualifies a person from public life. I also suggested a uniform pattern of trial. Let me elaborate on the principle of conviction by a court of law. Accountability in the sense of quitting public office by a Minister etc., is not answered soon after conviction. Such an accountability has to wait until the appeal of the convict is disposed off by the Appellate Courts. This normally takes 10 years resulting in **dilution** of the concept of accountability. For this situation the judiciary is partly responsible. While interpreting the jurisprudential principle of "presumption of innocence" till convicted, the judiciary has overstretched it by holding that the person so convicted will be presumed innocent till the challenge is finally disposed off by the Appellate Courts. Therefore, both legal provisions and judicial pronouncements on the subject need re-appraisal if accountability principle is to have any impact on public imagination in our democracy.

Indictment by Legal Authorities

Secondly, conviction by courts apart, there are other areas where "political class" stand indicted for corruption and wrong doing. Wrong doings include nepotism, favouritism, casteism, communalism and also interference in administration to protect the guilty etc:

- Indictment by commission of enquiry appointed under the R.P. Act, 1951. Justice Sri Krishna Commission which went into Mumbai riots etc. in 1990s indicted politicians, police officers for crimes, connivance and slackness in the discharge of duty.
- LokAyukta findings on corruption charges against politicians.
- Similar findings by various High Courts under Article 226 of the Constitution of India.

A High Court is a Constitutional body while LokAyukta and Commission of Enquiry are legal authorities. **Their findings need to be respected in democratic governance.** For example in 1990 a CM in Andhra Pradesh was indicted for "abuse of office" by full bench of A.P. High Court. He refused to quit the office and appealed to Supreme Court. The matter is pending in the Supreme Court to the best of my knowledge. **Therefore, in such and similar cases accountability loses its value.**

There is thus a **legal chaos** in respect of Accountability of those who are facing criminal investigations and who have been convicted for crimes or corruption and this gets further murky in view of the fact that the investigating agencies are under the control of political masters.

As the establishment got more venal, corrupt, as private enterprise and public office got mixed up, as the operations of multi national and national companies spread far and wide in business areas and as the loot of Nation's rich resources continued unabated after the opening up of the economy 20 years ago, as the execution of the ever increasing public projects are handed over to the community of contractors and construction companies, and as the unholy nexus between these business classes and political class got further cemented, the principle of Accountability gets dimmer and dimmer.

In the formative years of republic, the accountability principle was not much in focus partly because the standards in public life and administration including judiciary were considerably good. There were no suggestions like the creation of **Lokpal** Institutions etc. Now the situation has changed.

Mechanism to Enforce Accountability of Governing Class

As I try to grapple with or crack the concept of Accountability, a broader picture emerges from such a thought. A wholesome mechanism of Accountability rules out departmental or domestic enquiries in Administration or "in house Enquiry mechanism" as it exists in judiciary. There is always, however noble the motives are, an element of subjectivity or departmental loyalty in assessing the wrong doings or corruption charges of subordinates and colleagues. This is inevitable. To rule out such a subjectivity, it is useful to have an independent mechanism of Accountability. The composition of the agency or the council for such a scheme should not be departmental centric or judiciary centric. There should be a reasonable representation to eminent men from outside the judicial fraternity. In the same way, in all criminal investigations that involve the political class, it is unsafe to leave such investigations incharge of Police, CID, CBI since all these agencies are controlled by political executive. In 2006-07 some of our public representatives (MPs, MLAs) have figured in such crimes as trafficking in women abroad on forged passports (identity fraud). There are also a number of traditional crimes in which they are facing criminal investigations. In all such cases, it is imperitive that investigation by police is supervised by the Sessions Court or the High Court inorder to carry credibility to the investigations and lend support to the principle of Accountability. Similarly, where investigating agencies such as Police, CID, CBI or other agencies under the Union Finance Ministry face investigations of wrong doing or corruption, it is fair that a judicial enquiry is conducted or that the Human Rights Commission can also undertake such job. In Rizwanur Rahman's death case, in Kolkata in September 2007, a CID enquiry was ordered for the involvement of Kolkata Police. This is not proper as CID is also manned by IPS fraternity. Investigations by CID will not carry credibility while an enquiry by judicial authority will carry credibility and answer the principle of Accountability. The Indian Express editorially commented on 15.10.2007 "that the involvement of police in private matter like marriage of two adults cannot be condoned and the inevitable inference is that police is acting on behalf of powerful interests opposed to the marriage". A further allegation against Kolkata Police is that it is involved in the alleged murder of Rizwanur Rahman or the cover up of the offence of murder. The dimensions of the wrong doing by Police is multifold. Even if murder charge is not proved, the involvement of the police in marriage affair which is not an **offence** is proved on the available evidence. The Chief Minister of West Bengal is said to be close to Commissioner of Police, Kolkata and that the former has supported the latter in the contest to the post of Presidentship of the Cricket Association of Bengal. I only hope that in an attempt to cover up the wrong doing of Police, the Chief Minister, West Bengal may not burn his fingers further. I believe that he is holding the portfolio of Home under which the Police Department works. **The CM is an honest person. But honesty and taking right and timely decision are two different issues.** A conspiracy of silence or inaction to punish the guilty police officers will bring down the image of the holders of public power and possibly the image of the party to which the C.M belongs.

Accountability is **the oxygen** f Democracy but it did not find expression in the Constitution or laws of the land. There is no **Accountability Bureau** as it exists in our neighboring Pakistan. How effective is that Bureau in Pakistan is a different issue. Accountability exists for crimes in a limited sense. But conviction must follow. All crimes do not end in convictions. Standard of evidence required by Courts, rules of procedure to be satisfied result in acquittals. No one is above Law whether he is a Minister, MP, MLA. But the operation of law, is a different matter. Now we move to another aspect. Can a convicted politician hold public office? Here the accountability concept hits road block. Can he contest the next election? Will he be effectively disqualified for the rest of his life. These are all the larger questions of accountability. After crime, conviction and holding of public office, contesting election, comes the aspect of performance more precisely non performance. **Generally accountability is equated with ministerial responsibility where a Minister resigns from office owning up responsibility for failure.** This is not mandatory. It is left to individual choice or to the whim and fancy of Party High Command. Thus the accountability for **non performance** of a Minister gets diluted. And failure means what? When serious allegations surface and are held proved by a Commission of Enquiry, or ay other judicial authority, resignations occasionally follow. **But there are tens of thousands of cases of non performance / inaction and malafide actions which are the subject matter of writ jurisdiction of Supreme Court and High Courts. When the Courts pass adverse verdict, it is the Minister, who needs to be held accountable.** Once a Minister is asked to resign, he will be alert and will make Bureaucracy under him work and work efficiently. But if he escapes accountability for this, he will continue to be slack and so will be the staff under him. But unfortunately, neither non-performance (in action) nor wrong actions described above are "offences" for demanding Minister's resignation. Here, the accountability concept gets compromised. Therefore for millions of inactions, wrong actions (wrongful commissions and omissions) accountability of Ministers is lacking. Even though inaction and wrong action are not "offences", a law can come into existence that adverse court verdicts on such inaction etc., meets with resignation of a Minister. That will put sense in the mind of a Minister to perform. A minister is a lynchpin in administration. He cannot make bureaucrats scapegoats. If he wants let him punish bureaucrats too. But the first principle is ministerial accountability (not for mere rail and road accidents caused by his staff) but for tens of thousands of inactions and wrong actions. Of course, only 10% of them are taken to Court and when adverse judgments are delivered in this 10%, it should form a ground for Minister's accountability. **This is democratic principle.** At present Minister becomes a white elephant in Democracy, where he misuses the bureaucracy for his nefarious ends. Therefore, a law should come up on the lines suggested by me to make accountability of the Minister real (not a vague and shadowy) for non performance and malafide performance.

The criteria of any "institutional mechanism for accountability is the credibility it carries in the public domain. It is not only failure of individuals but institutional failures are surfacing. During the emergency imposed by Smt. Indira Gandhi, all the State Institutions failed to check the authoritarian rule. It was resisted by powerful public movement led by Late Sri Jaya Prakash Narayan, the media, sections of civil society, lawyers included. Their struggles and sacrifices helped to roll back emergency and restore normal governance. The principle of Accountability is enforced by the civil society and public at large when powerful constitutional authorities like Prime Minister and Chief Ministers abuse their authority. In the contemporary political situation in Pakistan where Military dominates democracy, the principle of Accountability for the several authoritarian decisions taken by Gen. Pervaz Musharraf, then President of Pakistan could not be answered even by the Apex Court of that country. Several, public movements led by lawyers in particular are taking place in Pakistan to call authoritarian decisions of the President in uniform to Accountability.

Our Constitution, whose articles run to nearly 400 in number is silent on Accountability principle and practices. The custodians of the Constitution carried out several amendments. But, at no point of time in the history of our Republic was there an attempt to correct this omission. Nor, is there a current thinking to set right this omission.

Accountability for Gross Failure/Inaction and Underperformance in Natural Calamities

I have referred to the above subtext in my other books. Now let me discus it with reference to the unprecedented flood (not known since 100 years) that struck A.P. on 01.10.2009. Three districts were affected (1) Kurnool (2) Mahaboobnagar (3) Krishna district in that order. The worst in Kurnool. Half of Kurnool town was under 15 to 20 feet water. Alampur, a temple town with 20 thousand population in Mahaboobngar District was another. Kurnool is to the right of river Tunga Bhadra and Alampur is to its left. Mantralaya another temple town on the banks of the same river upstream is another that got affected. About 100 human lives were lost and death of innumerable cattle followed. Loss of crop and damage and destruction to movable and immovable properties was reported. The loss was estimated in the three districts at Rs. 12,000 crores. While Mantralaya in Kurnool and Alampur in Mahaboobnagar were affected due to flood water of Tunga Bhadra river which merges in Krishna river some 20 miles down stream. Kurnool was affected by Tunga Bhadra and Handri rivers which flow inside the town and due to the back water of Srisailam Hydel Project (Electricity cum Irrigation Project) on Krishna river. Srisailam is a famous South Indian pilgrim town of Lord Mallikarjuna nestling in hill ranges of eastern ghats.

There was no proper comprehension of the problem either by political leadership or at the administrative level in its totality and how to go about it to its last detail. The media reported the devastation caused by flood and reflected people's view about inadequacy of Government effort to tackle the flood. It had no concrete suggestion to make. The civil liberty groups, human rights groups, women rights groups, women empowerment groups whom we see frequently with their sound bites on TV channels were no where in proffering advice not to speak of plunging into relief operations.

Honesty is a good policy. **But imaginative planning, efficient action to its last detail and service delivery is best.** Mr. Rosaiah lacked experience in handling the unprecended havoc caused by floods. The Bureaucracy let him down. The advisors to Govt. were not trained to think out policies in meeting such a situation. The Central Congress leadership, its defence forces, paid lip service.

Smt. Sonia Gandhi made a flying visit. She had no time to halt even for a night. Had she stayed for a couple of days and gave push to the effort of the State Government with Central teams on hand it could have done a whole lot of good to her image which was low after the Constitutional coup d' etat executed by Congress High Command in installing Sri Rosaiah as Chief Minister, Andhra Pradesh. Congress leaders of the stature of Sonia Gandhi, Rahul Gandhi were keen to be the party mascots in winning elections rather than being one such with missionary zeal in tackling natural calamities. The Hon'ble Prime Minister Sri Man Mohan Singh came on 10.11.2009 stayed, slept and left the next day after a brief aerial survey. **Mr. Rosaiah was left to fend for himself.** When he visited the flood affected area on 10.10.2009, he had to face hostile crowds and his convoy was reportedly pelted with stones in Kurnool district. This is Mr. Rosaiah first brush with masses and angry crowds while his predecessor lived and liked to live with masses.

Thus there was failure

- In not regulating inflows and out flows at Sri Sailam dam down stream soon after the CWC gave warning about heavy inflows in to Krishna river (20 lakhs cusecs of water unknown in the last 100 years) - resulting in its back water entering Kurnool town and also causing breaches to Pothireddipadu Head regulator canal systems etc. **It is the failure of Project Engineers and the concerned Minister.** However Accountability needs to follow on the findings of judicial enquiry.
- The Chief Minister ought to have rushed Chief Secretary and sufficient number of experienced (not seniors in IAS cadre) officers to Kurnool to coordinate

the work of various agencies in rescue, relief operations.

- Failure in not pooling sufficient number of helicopters for rescue, relief by renting private helicopters.
- Failure in not drawing police recruits from various police colleges (instead of the over worked Kurnool civil and Armed police) for rescue and relief.
- in not promptly utilising the services of the NCC for relief operations.
- in not using the services of prisoners. Remissions or commutation of prison sentences can be linked to public service in such and similar calamities. Such public policy will be rational. While releasing them on commutation etc., on the eve of Indepdence day is a mockery of criminal justice system.
- in not pooling the medical and nursing staff from all over the district including private practitioners, if necessary by payment for their services.
- in not employing on payment people who burn or remove Caracasses, in not utilising wood in forest depot at Atmakur, Nandyal, Giddalur for burning caracasses, in not announcing one month extra salary to Municipal staff who do the sanitation work.
- in not clearing the 25 feet height mud in Kurnool town by entrusting it to the private contractors whatever be the cost.
- **in failing to engage local fishermen at the first instance whatever the costs involved in rescuing the trapped families.**
- There was chaos on the distribution of relief material, food, cloth and water donated by Philanthropists, Voluntary Service Organisation, Reliance Industries etc., all because Senior Officers of Joint Collector level were no where employed for each affected areas like Manatrayala, Alampur etc. **There was a flood of assistance in the form of food, clothes, cattle feed**

etc., by the above Non-Govt. agencies. But it did not reach the targeted timely.

Failure in not requesting army and halicopter service to be on stand by on 30/09/2009.

There was not imely Action on all the Above Issues

On 12.10.2009, I cross checked on my views with one retired police officer in Kurnool and Ex-legislator of Kurnool Mr. Gaffar. Mr. Gaffar agreed on all the points raised by me. He said that there are around 5000 fisherman families. But he was not sure as to how many boats they own. At any rate even if 5000 fishermen families have 50 boats they could have evacuated people trapped in water.

The response from Defence Establishment, National disaster management agency to send boats to rescue the marooned in Kurnool town and villages, was a bit late and the help was handicapped on account of road breaches from the side of Hyderabad and there was no imaginative coordination to rush them from Bangalore or Chennai. Coordination is a function by itself. Though boats were sent from Chennai from National Disaster Management agency, they were held up at Nandyal on 5th & 6th due to the loss of road connectivity, on account of swollen waters of Kundu river. The district administration could not coordinate well to bring the material of National Disaster Management Agency via Gooty, where one can circumvent Kundu river. Therefore the best option available for district administration was the local fishermen community and their boats

Fake Police Encounter - A Grave Illegality

Chapter 3 discussed in detail the law and practice on "Gun battles" or commonly called police encouters. Fake police encounters are outright grave crimes. But in the name of putting sense into the minds of outlaws, terrorists and Maoists, and to maintain a semblance of public order, they are prevalent in criminal justice system. This also has some support from society and large section of polity and therefore, the guilty police officers are rarely called to account for the crimes. These fake encounters according to police officials are due to failure of criminal justice, where weak enforcement and interpretation lead to a situation where criminals and Terrorists become a menace to society.

Political Parties

Accountability of political parties is a zero sum game. Political parties collect huge funds both through cheque and cash to run the party machinery and to contest elections periodically from Parliament to Panchayat. There is no proper auditing of the collection and expending of the funds by a statutory body. Accountability is defeated. At best party functionaries who misuse the funds are removed from their posts. There is no legal Accountability for prosecution and punishment in the Courts. There are other maladies such as selling of party tickets from Parliament to Panchayat to the aspiring candidates where money is made by the party functionaries. Industrialists purchase their way through money into Rajya Sabha and in States Second House of Legislatures. For all these Accountability is lacking.

Summary

For whom?

- In case of crimes or corruption, accountability is for law.
- In case of inactions, it is not for specific legal provision since inaction has not been illegalized. But rules can be enforced to punish. Punishment ranges depending on the gravity of inaction.
- In respect of wrongful action also accountability is not for law as they are not illegalized.
- For non-performance, inaccessibility of an MLA, MP, accountability is not for law but he will be accountable to the people of the constituency in periodic elections.
- Where abortions are not criminalized, accountability is not for law but for the life of still born child and to society or family.

Complexity of the Problem

- Under the Representation of People's Act, 1951, a person who is convicted and sentenced to two years is disqualified from public life. Such conviction however has to be upheld by the Apex Court. The time taken is nearly ten years. Accountability gets complex. It applies to all other crimes due to the rules of criminal jurisprudence evolved by judiciary that a person is presumed innocent not only till he is convicted but also till such conviction is upheld by Apex Court. The simple process is to disqualify a person against whom court framed charges in a serious case or set of cases or upon conviction by a Trial Court.
- A Judge of a High Court or Supreme Court is removed from his post for corruption through impeachment process by Parliament. This is a very complex process and in India it did not succeed. 2/3rd majority (not simple majority) is needed for this purpose.

Comprehensiveness of the Problem

- A Judge of a High Court even if he is removed through impeachment process for corruption, there is no comprehensive accountability. For comprehensiveness, the Judge needs to be prosecuted in a court of law.
- When an MP or an MLA is found prima facie guilty of corruption in Trust votes or for putting questions in Parliament and is suspended for the rest of the life of Parliament by the Speaker, it is partial accountability. When such an MP is "disqualified from public life" for the rest of life of the individual MP and further prosecuted criminally, comprehensive accountability is met.
- LIC of India (Institutional Investor) invested Rs.1000 crores in Satyam Infos. There is a big scam involving 7000 crores in Satyam Infos in 2008. The loss to the individual investor needs to be made up not only by punishing the officials of LIC and Satyam Infos through criminal prosecutions but also through payment of compensation for the loss of his money by attachment of the properties of the Stayam Infos

and Life Insurance Corporation of India. Only then it becomes comprehensive accountability.

- When a minister who indulged in corruption gets away with resignation, or when a judge H.C. or S.C. gets away with resignation it is symbolic accountability and not real. When they are removed from service and further prosecuted, real accountability and complete justice is answered.

The principle of Accountability in the Indian context is over simplified such as a resignation tendered by a Minister for a rail accident caused by the railway official. It goes in the name of Ministerial responsibility and it ends at that. Ordering an enquiry into corruption charges and allowing them to languish on the files of Investigating Agencies is a symbolic act to blunt criticism.

In all, lack of Accountability of State or even offenders of law in society is detrimental to the principle of justice. Accountability is no longer an intellectual concern but a practical necessity for the welfare of Nation and common man. We need a separate law on Accountability on the pattern of RTI Act, 2005.

Sl. No.	Nature of Offence or Wrong Doing	Punishments	Remarks
01.	a. Sec. 302 IPC, 1860 Ordinary Murder b.Terrorist Murder count of double or multiple figures c. Abortions, female foeticide	Death or Life Imprisonment - do -	Lacks proportionality of Accountability for crime. (PNDT) Act 1994 Practically Mother's accountability lacking
02.	a. Sec. 379 IPC 1860 theft of 6 crores of property, Alukas Jewellery shop in 2006 at Panjagutta, Hyderabad. b. Keeping rare bird (Peacock) against the provisions of Wild Life Act. c. Theft of a loaf of bread	Maximum 3 years imprisonment Minimum 3 years imprison- ment 3 years	No proportion-ality
03.	a. Govt. Land Grabbing (A.P. Prohibition of Land Grabbing Act) b.CPM, CPI land struggle to evict land grabbers 2007 in A.P. (Cr. Trespass)	6 months 3 years (Criminal trespass)	Accountability is in Topsy turvy
04.	a. Bank bad debt running into crores or 100s of crores by the elite in politics and business.	The offence is not criminalized no prison terms. Our laws not even disqualify them from public life and to hold constitutional posts.	Poor accountability

	b. Poor man	It is recovered to the last pie. Indian Express Reported On 24.06.07 that One Yadaiah died in the custody of Elite Financial Services, a firm having tie up with ICICI Bank, Hyderabad for failure to repay Rs.15,000 loan.	Disproportion-ate penalty of accountability.
05.	Political Elite facing criminal trials in heinous offences	Punishable with imprisonment. Criminal jurisprudential "principle of presumption of innocence till convicted" bails them out from disqualification from public life and to hold constitutional posts.	Accoutability defeated
06.	Purchase of Govt. Land from poor assignees prohibited under the A.P. (Prevention of Land Assignment Act, 1977)	Payment of value of land or regularization.	No punish-ment of imprisonment or disqualifica-tion from public life even if proved. Accountability defeated by the absence of strong law.

07.	a. Sec. 8 (3) R.P. Act. 1951 b. Sec. 8 (4) R.P. Act, 1951	Sitting MLA when convicted for two years ineligible to contest elections Such disability not applicable	Accountability fractured
08.	Voluntary disclosure of income under IT Act 1961.	Can get away without criminal prosecutions	Nil accountability
09.	Corruption in Parliamentary business.	No legal liability	Article 105(2) gives exemption from prosecu-tion for corruption. Nil Accountability
10.	Politicians indicted by High Court, Commission of Enquiry, Lok Ayakut for corruption	No legal provision to dis-qualify them from public life. Discretion to quit public life left to the individual indicted.	No accountability
11.	a. Holding Office of Profit by constitutional and legal authorities. b. Doing business of profit by them	Prohibited by Constitution (Article 191) Not prohibited by Constitution	Quasi criminal accountability of disqualifica-tion as M.P. No liability whatsoever
12.	a. Defection of a Member of Parliament to another Party b. Group defection	Disqualification from Parliament No disqualification	Discriminatory law and accountability

13.	a. Enquiries against Govt. servant, middle and lower level b. Sr. Officers	Allowed under the Anti Corruption Law Govt.permission is necessary	Discrimination in Govt. Action defeats Accountability in respect of senior officers
14.	Party Funds received other wise than through cheques	Not criminalized	No accountability
15.	Judicial misconduct (High Court and Supreme Court)	Art. 124, 217 envisage impeachment	No criminal liability. fractured accountability or removal through impeachment
16.	Governors and President abusing public office	Constitutional provisions give exemption from legal liability (Art. 361)	No accountability

5

Advancing Justice by Correcting Wrong Views on Values

***Truth* and *Justice* is a magnificent moral concept.** Both the words though not identical flow into each other. They are the obverse and reverse of the same coin. In common parlance truth means not uttering lies. That is somewhat a conventional or narrow interpretation. Truth in effect is *practicing* what you think and speak as rightful conduct. It is diametrically opposed to falsehood and hypocricy. **Mahatma Gandhi** laid great stress on truthfulness. At the height of freedom movement, he gave notice of intended action like Fasting, Satyagraha, Hartal etc., to the British Govt. That is straight forwardness even while dealing with an enemy. **Truth was believed to be the supreme good by Gandhiji**. Self condemnation and admitting mistakes was explicit in Gandhiji's autobiography. **Secondly**, we should not claim the credit of others as our own. That is falsehood personified. **Thirdly**, we should also not claim ideas of others as our own. That is opposed to truth. Gandhiji when questioned about his views and ideas, though some of them were unconventional, replied that his ideas are as old as the hills, thereby disclaiming any right to social discovery. **Unconventional ideas are considered as the parent of social discovery**. **Sage Socrates**

upheld truth even at the cost of his life. Courage of conviction is another component of truth. What you feel as correct, you should state and stick to it and not disown or furnish pretext when greeted with trouble. Gandhiji never shied away from punishment by the Courts of the British Indian Government. **He voluntarily submitted to the imprisonments by the Courts for his action which in law was a crime but is a duty as a citizen.** He never defended himself against the charges. He did not offer extenuating circumstances to the charges levelled. He accepted punishment of imprisonment in the British Indian jails without demur. In fact, he sought from the Court authorities, the stringent possible punishment. That is truth, self denial, a kind of self abnegation of the highest order. Truth also involves suppression of falsehood and upholding justice. If you justify the action of the corrupt and inefficient, you are suppressing truth and elevating falsehood. Lastly if you do not have correct book keeping for the monetary transactions, you will be sidetracking truth. Gandhiji said without properly kept accounts, it is impossible to maintain truth in its pristine purity.

Democratization of Decision Making and Time Limit

Time is the essence of Life as well as Governance. For this, time limit for decision making is important. It should start at a higher level of political, judicial, administrative leadership.

- There is no time limit under Article 72, 161 of the Constitution for the President and Governor to exercise clemency powers. Statutory time limit of **six months** should be set. Files should not be tossed between the Ministry and the President's Office. All concerned officials can meet the President's Secretariat officials and in one or two sittings, deliberate the issues and a note put up to the President for a decision.
- For according sanction by **competent authority** to prosecute a person on corruption charges under the Prevention of Corruption Act, 1988, there is no time limit. Six Month's time limit should be adequate

- For defence purchases, there is no time limit. Maximum of 12 months should be fixed
- The same logic applies to various administrative decisions. Time limit of 3 months should be maximum. **Participatory decision making is the spirit of democracy.**
- Statutory time limit should be fixed for court trials. Similarly, time limit for delivery of judgment should be fixed. After the conclusion of the hearing, judgment should be delivered in 60 days. In Dr. Jayalalitha's Case in 2004, one Supreme Court Judge took 14 months to deliver judgment (as reported in the media). Judicial delays go against the grain of Justice

Tentative Efficiency

I have given my views on efficiency - what it means in some of the pages of my books. The views are diffused or scattered across all the books. Efficiency needs to be built brick by brick. It is not a bolt from the blue. In the police organisation, it has to start from basic police functions such as Prevention of Crime by effective surveillance over criminals, by effective organisation of police beat service in nights, effective supervision of them, by periodic inspections, visits to police stations to supervise proper registration of all crimes, proper investigation of registered crimes, and prosecution with effective court conviction of criminals. Generally 2 to 3 thousand crimes are registered in a district in Andhra Pradesh State. How these cases are handled by subordinates at various stages of enquiry, investigation and disposal by courts is a matter of importance. Then effective bandobust to VVIP, VIP movements, to religious festivals, in controlling urban mafia, rural factions, in tackling terrorist offences are all relevant to assess efficiency. Then again checking excess use of force in law and order situations, insubordination or indiscipline in rank and file, corruption and pure criminality of the constabulary and other higher ranks matters most. Then again overseeing **political, communal neutrality** of the force under the charge of district Superintendent of Police is equally important. Conduct of periodic elections with fairness counts a lot. These are all the bench marks to arrive at efficiency of District Police Chief or even of a higher level police official. But today all the above is forgotten. **Adhoc efficiency or tentative efficiency has taken centre stage.** Opening fire in troubled law and order situations, communal riots, even where such fire is unwarranted or resorting to fake encounters once or twice in career are the benchmarks to judge efficiency. One gets the badge of efficiency and can shine with that image for the rest of the career even without doing any outstanding work in any field. **So several times, on the wrong doing of fake encounters, excessive use of force etc., the image of a tough police officer is built not only in the department but unfortunately in public.** A couple of Superintendents of Police in Kurnool, Ananthapur districts encountered "hired assassins" of a particular political group. There were allegations that money given by the opposite political rival groups influenced the actions of the police officers. These politician-cum mafia leaders are happy to part with their ill-gotten crores of money to police officials because their names will not be figuring even in FIR. So much so, even when the opposite political party comes to power in the next round of elections, and wants to pursue clues, it is not possible to proceed against politician cum mafia leaders because their names did not figure in FIR. Therefore, intelligentsia need to understand the nitty-gritty of police functions and make a truthful evaluation of their work. **Assessment needs to be based on steady and comprehensive efficiency, for fairness and objectivity in a multifaceted role of preventive, detective, investigative jobs etc.** Wrong or faulty assessment of a public official is the bane of good governance. The work done in specialized agencies like CBI, CID, Intelligence is **silent efficiency** if objective and indepth analysis of each case is undertaken and right recommendations made.

Parameters of Efficiency

- Resisting political pressure in its various manifestations.
- Cutting down corruption at all levels, in all ranks.

- Cutting down overall inefficiency, improving operational preparedness and efficiency against the terrorists.
- Cutting down inaction and delay.
- Cutting down inaccessibility.
- Lend transparency in the police, intelligence functions.
- Reducing manpower wastage at all levels in all police organizations.
- Reducing mismanagement of funds.
- Accountability, prompt and sure for all the above lapses.

When we observe the above scrupulously, efficiency is born and will blossom gradually. Efficiency is not a bolt from blue. It has to be built brick by brick. **Justice is reflected in efficient action.**

Compassion – Issues of Great Consequence

On 20-12-2003, the author watched D.D. TV Channel. His holiness **Dalailama** was interviewed by a prominent T.V Journalist Mr. Rajiv Mehrotra. Sri Dalailama was speaking about genuine **compassion** as different from personal one. If a person is nice to you, you show compassion towards him wher he is in distress. But genuine compassion for all human beings transcends this type of narrow compassion. Drawing inspiration from his observations, the Author followed up his reasoning to logical end which is as follows:

Motivation

Sincere motivation is different from insincere or dishonest motivation. We talk (in administrative culture), of motivation as the loadstar in the discharge of duties. Such sincere motivation / honest motivation is limited to 10% of the governing classes. In the 90%, there is dishonest motivation to exploit the **office one holds** to enrich oneself, friends, relations, cronies and psychofants. Several police officials sit in their offices or police stations over time so that all cases are within their knowledge so that they can get their cut in the corruption in each and every case. Entrepreneurs and businessmen are also motivated by **profits** whether they are ethical or unethical. Indeed where the criminal, delinquent, wrong doing tendencies prevail in human beings, there is this **malignant motivation** in such wrong doings. Criminals, Terrorists also have motivation in their dirty, risky jobs. How can a **suicide bomber** without motivation in his mission undertake the job?

Discipline

His holiness Kanchi Paramacharya mentioned about all round indiscipline as one of the wrong doings affecting our society and government. The Author mentioned about discipline in a limited way (pertaining to police organization) in a pamphlet published in 1988 (incorporated at P.53 in the book ***"Discovery of Human Values"* title changed to "Thoughts and reflections on Law and Government".)** My view of discipline in police organization is sincere discharge of duty more than smart dress and salutation. **Enforcing law and regulations, lawful orders of superiors is the core of discipline.** A junior police official may salute a senior dozen times a day, wait on him for hours, may be unwilling to take seat even when offered and prefer to remain in standing posture and that too in attention. All this may be to cover up one's own inadequacies in discharge of duties or to placate the ego of the senior. **In India, nobody is above praise and gratification of false sense of pride even though he is honest in the technical sense.** Everybody wants to be praised not criticized. **If there is no one to praise a person, self-exultation is generously indulged in.**

All round indiscipline which Paramacharya of Kanchi mentioned may include indiscipline in family, schools, colleges, work places and so on. Parental authority even when it is right is declining. Scant respect for the teacher, ragging and other forms of misdemeanour in colleges have taken the center stage.

French Philospher **Romain Rolland** observed that "Discipline is duty. Unfortunately those who are entrused with enforcing it may be narrow minded. **They may mistake discipline chosen to attain the ideal for the ideal itself.**

Discipline fascinates them by its rigidity for they are a kind who feel at ease only on the narrow path." The above view was held by me since the begining of my writings.

Work ethic in Govt. organisations is on decline. Punctuality in office attendance, public transport is poor. Methodical work and levels of efficacy have fallen. Whilingaway time in offices, chit chat, character assassination of seniors and colleagues, viewing TV in work places by senior officers, fiddling with computers, lap tops and cell phones are all bureaucratic delinquencies.

Men in professions, medium and small business entrepreneurs, self employed in shops and establishments, some private company employees are better in discipline and in their work ethic. **Those who live on inherited wealth, government employees who draw fixed salary from treasury have not matched the above classes in possessing that sense of discipline.** Agriculturists and that its labour are also better disciplined than factory workers where militant trade unionism has entered. I do not decry all factory workers. I do not want to generalize the issue.

Every person seems to respect **authority** more than **principle** even though such authority emanating from the head of government department or other organization is always not exercised for honest ends. **Discipline means, you have a right to point out, criticize and resist such dishonest authority.** Implicit obedience to such authority is no discipline even if it emnates from the head of a family.

Team Spirit

The Author remembers, (going back to his writings a few years ago) reconstructing similar idea on the subject of **Team spirit**. Team spirit should be focused on the service of common man or national objectives. The present culture in the governing classes is to be united for personnel enrichment and of, friends and relations. So team spirit is limited to narrow ends. Team spirit which is a noble principle is sometimes subverted to benefit superiors in an organization / hierarchy or political masters in order to promote one's own career interests. The author has written about this a few years back in an article in the Book **Discovery of Human Values.** (Title subsequently changed). What our seniors, colleagues, subordinates (majority) think about team spirit is about this negative team spirit, just as His Holiness **Dalailama** spoke about negative compassion. **Training** is essentially training of the mind to sensitize public official or police official towards his duties, responsibilities, involvement in Job, total dedication and to distance from corruption and other wrong doings in the discharge of duties.

Police Training

Of all the government departments, police maintain a large number of training Academies, Colleges, Schools. It entails considerable expenditure. There are different courses such as basic training lasting for six months to one year followed by refresher courses througout the year. **The indoor training classes have not contributed for learning the right or for unlearning the wrong. The outdoor training classes in the form of physical drill for constabulary has not improved their physical fitness.** Comparatively an average citizen and other Governmental employee might be more healthier than a constable. **This needs to be studied and examined by the police leadership.** Police are taught age old lathi drill, arms drill which are somewhat outdated. They are also taught methods of investigation and law in the indoor classes. The **police institutions have no modules or schedules which focus on courtesy, response to grievance, robust response to duty, avoidance of excesses in the discharge of duty.** Then again, how to respond to each field situations in the maintenance of law and order drawing from the experience of a series of failures and successes is the need of the hour. The training institutions also need to have full documentation of the above field situation at least for the last one decade. **It is true that police investigate crimes, but who will investigate the excesses and lapses of the police? Karate** is a form of martial art. Its focused teaching to the Police men, Home guards is essential to handle ordinary agitations, protests, processions etc. So also **Chiruta Katte** (a form of martial art where a long stick is held in hands and the stick is swung fast). It is a barrier against stone pelting at the police. 10 policemen well-versed in this art can control mobs pelting stones. This is a defensive technique and not an offensive one where police wield lathi causing violence to the public. Police training institutions need to replace lathi drill and similar archaic training forms with the above suggestions to control mobs which are not armed with deadly weapons. The **mindset** of colonial, bourgeois bureaucrat and police leadership need to change if they have to accept the above suggestions.

There is a tendency in the police department to over-react to a provocation. If a group of agitated persons obstruct or catch hold of the collar of a police person, their ego shoots up beyond proportion and they will not hesitate to pull the trigger. This tendency needs to be curbed by appropriate lessons etc, in the training institutions.

To the best of my knowledge, police firings and deaths in Independent India in situations like communal riots, political agitations, agitations launched due to regionalism, linguism, caste based reservations, workers and students struggles etc. (excluding death of terrorists in police actions) may exceed the deaths in police firing during the freedom struggle under British Rule (barring Jalianwallah Bagh massacre). Our rulers need to do a bit of soul searching.

In a recent interview to a TV channel Mr. K.P.S Gill prided himself not on his tenure as DGP of Punjab where he was instrumental in putting down Terrorism in 1980s but on his performacne as Superintendent of Police in Assam where according to him there were no police firings or custodial deaths in the district in which he worked. Mr. Sankar Sen, former DGP, National Human Rights Commission writing in the Times of India dt. 30-8-2007 says that 70% of the complaints received by the Commission are against the police for violation of Human Rights. Similarly, he has reported that State Human Rights Commissions are also flooded with complaints against police. This is a sad reflection on police in our democracy.

Loyalty

Loyalty is as old as Creation. There is always an element of duality in creation. Light and darkness, ignorance and knowledge, good and evil etc. Loyalty falls in that category. Loyalty to values and loyalty to individuals. The great men of merit and virtue in the Epic Mahabharata like Bhishmacharya, Dronacharya, Krupacharya, Karna etc., were content to be loyal to individual - prince Duryodhana. So there is nothing uncommon if ordinary people do not stick to the virtue of loyalty to values. Of course all advice and working need to be in the direction of loyalty to values. **Blind loyalty to individual without discrimination amounts to loyalty to the wrong doings, crimes, injustices of that individual.** That defeats justice.

Misleading / Misguidance

It leads to misunderstanding in families, Society and Govt. Misunderstanding is subtle, yet a potent evil. **It is not rightly understood even by my kith and kin in the intellectual circles.** On 17.08.2009 Mr. Chidambaram, Union Home Minister said that Terrorism and insurgency are the main threats to Nation. During 2005-2006, Mr. Manmohan Singh, Prime Minister said the same. I condemned this in the Book "Threats to Indian Republic" first published in 2006. **The main threats to the nation are Corruption, Wrong doing and gross inefficiency of the political, judicial, administrative establishment.** Once we arrest these, Terrorism etc., will come down or gets knocked out. Zero tolerance often expressed by Hon'ble Prime Minister can be achieved only when there is zero tolerance of crimes, corruption and incompetence of the political and other establishments. **Our Netas are misleading the Nation which means deceiving the society to think otherwise. It is very sad. It is unjust.**

During 1979-81, the Author was Additional Superintendent of Police, Tirupati, a world famous pilgrim town (abode of Lord Venkateswara). There was some trouble in Tirumala for widening the four Mada streets since it was opposed by vested interests in the town. As is the practice with me, I was there in no time. An armed police party was assembled. Some miscreants were arrested and when they still did not disperse, I asked police party to load the rifles. Considering my image for handling public order situations, the mob melted away. I thanked God because bloodshed in temple premises is not desirable. But I believe (as told by one Rama Krishan Rao (Retd.) RTO and a tennis player) that Mr. P.V.R.K. Prasad, I.A.S., then E.O., T.T.D. claimed in a magazine called "Suprabhatam" that I was pulled up by him for not acting strong on the miscreants. **I had a hearty laugh at it.** He was not even present at the spot. So every one lays claim to credit for handling a situation and mislead the readers and claim credit and honour. I give one more example. For the last 9 to 10 months, prior to this write up Terriorists' acts of violence have come down. The UPA Government is claiming credit. It is not correct. Terrorism in Indian main land came down due to Terrorist groups of Pakistan getting pitted against their own Government under pressure from USA and West. They have little time to regroup and operate in Indian mainland and Pakistan ISI's full support is also not forthcoming because of international pressure. The reader can have any number of such instances. Misguidance leads to ruination of careers. **We need to raise the levels of awareness of this to mitigate its ill effects**.

The following intangible assets are vulnerable for usurpation / stealing

- Credit and fame
- Ideas
- Powers
- Pubic employment
- Video piracy etc

Credit, ideas, power that belong to an individual or institution will fall prey to the schemes and machinations of others while for ideas and video piracy there is a legal prohibition. For the remaining, there is no such prohibition. Even public employment is vulnerable to stealing. There are cases where persons who do not belong to Scheduled Tribes produce certificates of ST status and gain entry into public employment in the reserved category. This when proved comes under the criminal offence of cheating.

It is not a question of stealing tangible assets like gold, cash etc but stealing intangible assets like credit or fame or even power which legitimately belongs to another. The former is an "offence". The later is not. I give one instance with regard to power. In an NDTV interview in Sept 2009, Mr. Anil Dawan, Supreme Court Advocate said that Supreme Court stole the power of appointment of Judges by an interpretative process which does not wholly and rightly belongs to it. According to the Constitutional scheme political Executive possessed a dominant say in such appointments. **I think intellectual property rights legislation illegalized stealing of ideas. But stealing of power, credit etc., is not yet legally prohibited.**

Help

There is no adequate understanding of this principle and people are deluded and comforted in ignorance. From my experience and a smattering of knowledge, there are three types of persons (1) Those who neither help nor damage (2) those who help whole heartedly on a large scale or those who render fistful help grudgingly (3) Those who help and also damage the image. The third are harmful type. **Secondly** what you consider as help or obligation may in fact be your duty. In 1990, Mr. J.C. Diwakar Reddy, a Minister at that time brought to my notice that one Sub Inspector in Peddavaduguru Police Station used to come to Police Station drunk in day time. I got it enquired and after confirmation transferred him out. Here I was performing a duty. There is no help or obligation to Mr. Reddy. **Thirdly** help may also turn out to be correcting a mistake. Suppose a Superintendent of Police who is doing good work is transferred out of a district due to political compulsion and if he is given a next best posting later, there is not much of help rendered. You are correcting your previous mistake of not resisting political pressure. **Fourthly** several politicians dig borewells in private capacity and also supply roti and dal for Rs. 1/- out of **selfish generosity** with an eye on Vote Banks. Here the help has strings attached. **It has yet another angle.** I helped one political family of Kurnool district whose faction activity extended to Anantapur district. They said they are related to my in-laws. **This is not help as I later understood on sober analysis.** It amounts to aiding their illegal action or criminal action. I also helped some 70 to 80 persons to get into public employment as constables, RTC drivers, conductors, two S.Is, and as amins in Courts etc., in my career of 32 years and felt proud of my generosity as there are no strings attached. **But one police officer Krishna Raju, Additional C.P., Hyderabad remarked that by doing so, I deprived the more meritorious of a place in public employment. I see some meaning in what he said.** But I do not regret because all those who got the help are poor and also deserving in all respects. May be in 10% of cases relations and friends derived some benefits. **So gratitude follows help.** But such help that goes to a family such as the one referred to above, no gratitude needs to be expected or demanded.

Many political heavyweights are known to dispense favours and are called helpful. State favours are doled out to the undeserving, be it a friend, relation or party person. **It is a wrong doing and not a help.** They also sit on mountains of black money and disburse a part of it to the people who seek it. Selfish generosities indeed fall short of the definition of word 'help'. I think genuine help that comes out of one's heart with no strings attached (such as the expectation of better future birth or a hope of success in the next elections) is more blessed. **Those who help from out of their legal incomes and for rightful causes are more blessed.**

Service

Whether the help referred to resulted in public service or whether you are acting in the best of public interest is a mother of all questions. Suppose you extend material or moral support as an individual it is a different issue. **One need to record one's public services on a weekly basis.** Satisfying the demands of political establishment is not public service, but service to the establishment. Common man or community is not served. **There is disservice largely.** If there is no political interference, we serve ourselves by personal corruption. This is self service. **Due to lack of efficiency or due to apathy / unconcern disservice to common man in political, judiciary, Administrative decisions is a marked feature and this disservice,** I am sure, will be debited (not credited) to the record of your bad karma which one carries into his / her next birth. So many false views that reign in society/ Government etc., need correction. **Once you correct false view from the minds of at least 50% of the populace a major battle is won on behalf of good in society.** Securing good is a victory to justice. Unless we correct and accordingly report on false views or incorrect ideas, they continue to dominate public and private lives. The message conveyed to society is wrong. We are decieving the society to think wrong. **Conveying a right message is service and justice while conveying a wrong message is disservice.**

Selflessness

More than a century ago, Karl Marx said that the world is divided between the haves and have nots. In the last 100 years the gulf between the two is bridged or the lot of have-nots improved. But the gulf between **selfish and unselfish, the worker and idler class** has not been bridged even by a fraction. You hardly find 10% selfless in society and in Government. **It is said that selflessness is a noble trait.**

Effort

Mother Theresa said "It is not how many good things you have done but how much love and right effort you have put in what you have done or attempted that counts". Ministers and public officials need to strive in that direction. **Efforts to promote one's image, party's image, efforts directed towards corruption and crimes are not right effort.**

Hatred, Prejudice, Enemity

In Telugu language and tradition or in any religious tradition, there is what is called (Nishkarana vairam - unnecessary rivalry) or prejudice for no valid reason. Misguidance, hearsay, inflammed ego etc. lead to develop such prejudice.

Misguidance

Misguidance by projecting incorrect views as correct or expressing knowingly incorrect views as correct by authors, writers, Media is a bigger offence than a murder case or cases because it involves a whole society and affects it. It distorts the concept of justice.

Pseudo Reform Distorts Justice

I have written on political reforms in my books (1) Threats to Indian Republic (2) Plain Speaking. It is not necessary to repeat here. I have also written on police reforms. But the subject on police reforms is incomplete. There are also economic, educational, administrative and jail reforms. A right reform covering the above subjects will carry **justice** forward.

I would confine myself to police reforms. In the year 2006, the Supreme Court of India laid down a charter of police reforms. It evoked praise as well as criticism. The following are the reforms suggested.

The Supreme Court of India issued directions in the third week Sept.2006 for the establishment of

- State security commissions to insulate police from political influence.
- Police establishment board consisting of department officials to decide postings and promotions of dy. S.P's and below.
- National security commission to prepare panel of officers to be chosen to head central police organizations.
- Police complaints Authority at State and district level headed by Retd. Judges.
- Investigations to be separated from law and order.
- Tenure postings for two years.

The first salvo against the above set of proposals was fired by Mr. K.P.S Gill (Article in the Indian Express dt 25-09-2006). His observations are

(a) The judgement reads like a proposal for re-employment of superannuated judges, bureaucrats and political hangers on.

(b) The touchstone for defining utility of proposed police reforms should be whether any such reform improves the experience of a citizen when he enters the police station. There is not one recommendation in the judgement that meets this criterion.

(c) The crisis of police is short staffed, ill-equipped, ill-trained police force.

Author's View

Reform according to me should be comprehensive and quality reform and such reform has got to be periodically tested every 5 year period in the service of public good. However the move of Supreme Court is a first step in the right direction.

Over the years there have been quite a good number of reforms such as

- Increase in the posts of senior officers in Police Services (top heavy).
- Time bound promotions and not merit based (a retrograde measure)
- Introduction of self-assessment report and categorization of official as "outstanding" in the Annual Confidential reports.
- Increase in the age of superannuation to 60 years.

All the above reforms have not contributed a wee bit in improving the levels of integrity and performance of the senior police official in particular, All India Services in general. Time bound promotions and categorization of officials as "outstanding" have destroyed whatever levels of competency and integrity that was available before their introduction. The corrupt and inefficient stole the "outstanding reports" from their seniors leaving the honest in the lurch. There is no rider in the age of superannuation at 60 years unlike in judiciary where a District Judge's performance will be assessed by the

High Court at 58th year before he is allowed the extra 2 years of service.

Annual Confidential Reports

The core reform of perfecting the "Annual assessment report" of police official is left untouched. It is a breeding ground of all the maladies afflicting police. The performance assessment of I.P.S officers should be by a Committee preferably headed by a serving Chief Justice or a senior most judge with Chief Secretary and Home secretary as members. The head of the police department would be member secretary of the Committee. Unless performance appraisal report is placed on rails, the dishonest and mediocre will continue to thrive in administration and halt merit based promotions which is at the heart of good governance. Assessment by a committee lends transparency, objectivity and credibility to the assessment. A reading of the book "Betrayal of Defence Forces" by Admiral Vishnu Bhagwat discloses that even in the Defence forces there is lack of objectivity in Annual Confidential Reports.

In a conference of Chief Ministers in 1997 on the subject, no decision could be taken to weed out All India Service officers in view of the fact that ACRs, year after year were certified as good or outstanding by the superiors. This is because of bureaucratic brotherhood in corruption and wrong doing. Media reports dt. 16.10.2009 suggest that Mr. K.M. Chandrasekhar, Union Cabinet Secretary is keen to effect change in performance appraisal reports. But he needs the guidance of experts who can draft perfect Appraisal Reports. Judging merit without reforming ACR format is like treating symptom and not the disease. Faulty Assessment Reports, promoted injustice in administration.

Investigation Function

As regards directives of the Supreme Court on separation of investigation from Law and order, I suggest a rider. Lakhs of cases are registered in a State and many of them are less important. Therefore only grave offences should be handed over to this investigation agency supervised by Director of prosecutions who is accountable to the Government or the High Court of the State. This should be applicable only to urban police stations and police Commissionerates and the CID wing.

- Reform is not merely at top level. It is applicable equally to middle and lower level and organisational structure and the multifaceted police functions.

It is about

- giving specific duties of enquiry to a literate constable which is now centralised at SHO level. Any complaint received and which does not disclose prima facie a cognizable offence, enquiry can be done by a P.C. and his report placed on record.
- In certain cases registered (which are less important) the Head Constable can investigate cases, file charge sheets and be accountable for the enquiry or investigation.

Duplication of Effort Avoidable

All cases of grave nature are routinely registered by SHO and investigation done by C.I. and D.S.P. We need to make C.I. as registering and investigating officer in certain grave cases. In specially grave case of murder, the DSP needs to register and investigate and be accountable for failure in not detecting or leading to its acquittal.

The Role of Addl. Superintendent of Police

Should he be a rubber stamp of S.P. or should be given independent charge of certain subjects with power to supervise these subjects and also write C.Rs of subordinates? According to me he needs to be incharge of all non-grave offences, their reportance, investigation and prosecution. While grave crimes, collection of intelligence, maintenance of law and order and overall discipline of police is left to the Superintendent of Police.

The Superintendent of Police

He needs to have atleast 6 years divisional experience and a couple of years as Addl. S.P. Training if necessary can be cut to 1 year. After 8 years he should be given charge of district. This is another reform. There are several posts of Addl. S.P. which are continued for well over 3 years. All of them need to be encadered so that I.P.S. recruits can be posted as Addl. S.P. Now, the moment they complete 4 or 5 years tenure of service, they are eligible for "cadre posts" as per rules. At present only a limited number of Addl. S.P. posts are cadre posts and the rest are non-cadre posts so much so direct recruit straight away get into SP's post. When all posts of Addl. S.P. are encadred, they can be posted as Addl.S.P. and work in that post for 2 or 3 years to get the feel of various aspects of administration.

Ex-cadre posts need to be abolished. Senior cadre posts need to be rationalised.

Promotions

- Promotions need to be merit based. For this ACR format needs change and assessed by a Committee headed by High Court Judge which also include a public spirited person to make ACR objective. The present system of ACR is subjective, written by a superior without any reference to work done, integrity shown.
- The percentage of promotion of state police officials into I.P.S. need to be raised to 50% from the present 33%. A Sub-Inspector recruit given his good record should get into IPS atleast after 30 years of service. **Good career prospects of lower level functionaries is an incentive for better police services.**

Smaller Police Districts

Police Districts need to be more in Andhra Pradesh. There can be atleast 35 police districts. That makes it easy for crime and administrative control.

Posts of A.S.I. in Each Station Need Creation

Armed police unit in urban police stations should be stationed (1 platoon round the clock). This will be under SHO's control. It means decentralisation of power of deployment of Armed units.

Traffic duties: Women constables, Home guards can be used to the extent of 50%. Home guards are used now for meaningless or supportive duties with no clear cut job profile.

Is there a need for CCS? Atleast restructuring of it is needed.

Restructuring District Special Branch is needed. It functions in the S.P.'s residential bungalow or office premises. It needs decentralisation with each Divisional Head Quarter having intelligence unit headed by Inspector rank official with Accountability for non-performance.

Intelligence Collection at Station Level in Metropolitan Cities

First, all the families in Police Station limits in urban areas need enumeration even if it takes one year for that purpose. Census office is also a reference point. You get to know who is who. Each house or business establishment, a call centre, an internet etc etc. will be on police records. The data needs to be updated from time to time.

Other Reforms

- Inquest reports
- DNA finger printing
- Chemical analysis of viscera
- Autopsy on dead body

Need to be Fully Transparent to Advance Criminal Justice

A few more reforms are proposed by Government.

- Registration of FIR on telephone call
- Videographing of statements recorded by Police U/s 161 Cr.P.C. 1973

Any basic reform (not the superstructure of reforms suggested by Supreme Court) will be incomplete without a reference to the **outstanding work on the subject** done by the Cyberabad Commissionerate lead by M. Mahender Reddy, now Chief of Intelligence in Andhra Pradesh. He got prepared a few booklets with a team of dedicated subordinates police officials and some professionals. They form the bedrock of various types of basic reform or change at police station level. They can be with certain modification adopted at all the higher levels of police such a S.P., D.I.G., I.G.P., D.G.P. rank officials.

The short question one needs to ask oneself is how effectively police duties are discharged in the process of reform. It is necessary to quote some of the reforms indicated in these booklets.

The booklets divided police services into several categories which when carried out will advance justice at micro level.

- Crime prevention
- Crime detection
- Crime investigation
- Effective enforcement of laws particularly special and local laws
- Court and prosecution services that include effective execution of court process such as BWS and NBWS.
- Public order services

The basic theme is

- Responsive and people friendly organisation.
- Culture of continuous improvement in service delivery.
- Community participation and greater co-ordination with public and involvement

A few objectives set before police are

- Quick response to complaints
- Integrity and transparency
- Decision without fear or favour
- Learning and willingness to change
- Responsiveness to well founded public criticism
- Treating citizen with respect
- Creativity and innovation in function

These are the basic or gross root level requirement of change or reform needed in police organisation for improving criminal justice.

Reorienting Service Delivery Process

Crisis Management

- Emergency Response
- Situational Handling
- Networking

Public Interface

- Clear and Realistic Information
- Community Partnership
- Conflict Resolution
- Petition Enquiries
- Performance Feedback
- Needs of socially challenged groups

Traffic Management

- Modeling and Integrated Planning
- Traffic Education-Engineering-Enforcement
- Stakeholders education and partnership
- Technology Adoption
- Effective Synergies

Victim Interface

- Timely and empathic response
- Respecting privacy
- Complaint redressal
- Victim support
- Progress intimation

Witness Interface

- Truthful examination
- Respecting privacy
- Witness support

Crime Handling

- Investigation
- Technology applications
- Interface with allied criminal justice agencies
- Case Disposal

Institutional Interface

- Networking
- Interface with
- Policy makers
- Media
- Pressure groups
- Government agencies
- NGOs

Constabulary as a frontline service agency (80%)
Inter human resource development

- Job rotation
- Welfare
- Socialisation
- Rewards, benefits
- Administration
- Family / children care

Enforcement of special and local laws such as Hyderabad City Police Act, Town Nuisance Act, Gambling Act, Excise Act etc., goes a long way in controlling crimes. When we control small crimes we will be able to prevent big crimes (Broken Window Theory). Traffic enforcement effectively will prevent road accidents and deaths to a large extent. Enforcement of Prevention Detention law will have the same effect of prevention of crime. At present not even 20% enforcement of the above laws is taking place due to inadequate understanding and lack of imagination and drive from the police leadership.

If enforced this itself represents a change or reform in the work ethic of police organisation.

The booklets got prepared by Sri Reddy identified basic police services and supportive services and also change in police approach, practices and procedures in their function.

Conclusion

Documentation of various police services on monthly basis will help in better assessment of police work.

Reform aimed at

- Organisational restructuring
- Creating small police districts
- Functional division of work
- Functional Autonomy
- Accountability for non performance
- Accountability for corruption
- Better career prospects for state police services etc.

Will have desired effect on better police services and consequently on criminal justice system.

Justice Delivery is not Exclusive Domain of Judiciary

A victim of injustice does not necessarily mean a victim of crime or accident. It includes within its broad fold the following:

- Victims due to inaction, wrong action of administration, judiciary and actions of political class.
- Similarly failures (preventive action) by police in preventing riots etc., leaves behind thousands of victims of injustice. Those victims due to failure of inaction become victims of crime later.
- Failure by administration to anticipate and take timely action in respect of natural calamities like flood, fire, etc., rendering several thousands as victims of injustice.
- Similar inaction or Corruption in rendering relief measures in natural calamities, leaves behind thousands of victims of injustice.

- Criminals acts of adulteration of medicines, foods, oils, leaves behind thousands of victims of injustice.
- Negligent criminal acts such as Bhopal Gas tragedy, 1980 killed three thousand people and rendered many injured and houseless.

So these millions of injustices to victims in day to day life form part of the subject of victimology and it in not only a component of criminal justice but an essential part of larger concept of social justice. There needs to be awareness and understanding of this sub text of social justice to make it a policy issue before safe guards are made through legal Enactment.

All these type of injustices can be prevented by honest action and supervision.

Our democratic politics needs to be nurtured on the plant of patriotism and national interest. If the country is to become strong in the 21st Century – Strong not in the sense of the growth in the number of billionaires and welfare of governing classes, but where political economic and social justice of all the segments of society is taken care.

Balata House Encounter, New Delhi 2008

In the third edition of my book "Challenges of Governance" (Nov. 2008) at P.XIX, while discussing the above case, I observed as follows "I am however sure that it is a genuine encounter". **My intuition came true**. At that time spokespersons of Samajwadi Party, Congress Party expressed doubts about the genuineness of encounter. Even after one of the accused Terrorist Sahzad Alam confessed to the crime of shooting down Inspector Sharma of Delhi Police, Mr. Digvijaya Singh, Congress Party General Secretary expressed doubts about the encounter. (Times of India News, dt. 06.02.2010). This is an attempt to politicise Terrorism. There is more than one dimension to it. It hurts the morale of police. Second it spreads wrong message / views in society which has to effect of subverting Truth and reality. It is a National disservice and serious wrong doing. All wrong doings pose direct threat to justice. Let us take one more instance of Padma National

Awards 2010 going to Terrorist and crime tainted. Justice is denied to the most deserving.

Two examples of wrong ideas evolved in Govt. policies subverting justice can be cited. One is Reservation in Govt. employment based on castes and communities which subverts justice to sections of society who are excluded. A uniform policy of poverty based (economic criteria) will not deprive the socially and educational backward classes of the existing opportunities. At the same time it extends similar opportunities to the poor among socially forward castes. The second is Human Rights ideas which are crime and Terrorist centric and which cause violence and injustice to victims as well as to peaceful society. Human Rights that focus on healthcare, mal nutrition, education, employment and other entitlements will advance the cause of justice to all sections of society.

False Views or Incorrect Views

False or incorrect views covering private and public life are more damaging than false evidence because they affect the society. In the Indian Penal Code, 1860, there is Chapter XI where giving false evidence in crimes or failing to give information of an offence are made crimes. Incorrect views also do not help good Governance. Adverting to Maoist attack in Silda, West Bengal where 24 police men were killed and to a similar attack in a village in Bihar where 12 people were killed, The Hindu English daily in its editorial, dt. 19.02.2000 lamented poor training to police men. The editorial wanted increase in police numbers. I could not agree with the above views. They do not help shape right public policy. The police men have police colleges and Academies where good training is imparted. What is required is mental toughness, motivation and higher levels of commitment to duties. Training is essentially training of the mind more than physical drill, law classes and target practices. The police is not participating in International Shooting Competition, to get at bull's eye. Alertness in duty, learning tactics to face sudden Maoist attacks, adapting to the developing situation and standing up to the task is the need of the hour. Increasing Police numbers is not an answer. It leads to misuse or over use by way of over protection given to political class that include even a lower level party functionary. On 20.02.2010 to handle 2000 students, 20,000 police men were deployed in Hyderabad City. Rational, effective utilization is the need of the hour. Intellectual climate in the country is not helping to shape right policies.

False views or incorrect views are not only in currency and ascendancy but also gaining acceptance. The meaning of discipline is distorted. There is no "Right Understanding". Right Understanding is one of the noble eight fold paths of Buddhism and wrong understanding leads society astray. Discipline in governance is observed more in breach of law and rules than in upholding them. A slavish mentality is equated to discipline by bourgeois and elite governing classes. Erosion of work ethic, corrosive amorality, flagging sense of national purpose are no longer symptoms of indiscipline. In running a political party, dictatorship of party leadership is accepted as discipline - whether it is in choosing a Chief Minister of a State of dropping one from ministerial posts or party posts. Mr. Y.S. Jagan's case is one example. Dropping Mr. Natwar Singh from Ministry to another. One W.R. Varada Rajan, CPM Leader, Tamilnadu Unit reportedly committed suicide for the harsh treatment, the CPM Central leadership handed out to him. Right activists of Criminals, Terrorists and Maoists have gained acceptance. Religious or moral activists are condemned as fundamentalists and branded as moral police. Maoist prisoners are described by Mr. Varavara Rao as political prisoners though it is not a recognized political party. Legitimate use of force by police is confused as illegitimate. False theological belief of suicide bombers striking innocent and reaching heaven have claimed thousands of human lives. We brand Pakistan as Mastermind behind terrorists strikes but we fail to sever the local hand which carries out such attacks on the orders of the master mind. Figures of economic growth rate given by Ministers do no tally with ground realities. Symbolism gained significant success over substance where the President of India paid homage by visiting the Coffins of slain Indians in Kabul Terror strikes on

27-02-2010. The substance lies in attacking Terrorism root and branch. Punishment of the delinquent and law breaker for violation Motor Vehicle Act or rules is replaced by moralizing "Training sessions" to the State Road Transport Corporation drivers in Andhra Pradesh. (The Hindu News dated 28-02-2010 on a spate of road accidents). Carelessness, an attribute of indiscipline by drivers and aviation pilots cost atleast a lakh of lives of passengers annually. Even as the indiscipline of pilots is treated with kidgloves by the Authorities, the later need to share the blame for loss of lives.

6

YSR Phenomenon and Post YSR Era in the State of A.P.

The YSR Phenomenon

The tragic death of Dr. Y.S. Rajasekhar Reddy, Chief Minister Andhra Pradesh in an air accident on 02.09.2009 **generated a wave** of sympathy and grief across the state with a spate of suicides. Some 600 suicides were reported in Media. Critics tried to belittle it by saying that it is a trumped-up campaign of youth congress activists which Mr. Jagan Mohan Reddy his son helped to create. However statistics are gathered by the Authorities through some agencies to know the actual number.

The Times of India in its Editorial dated 8-9-09 made the following observation. "YSR like most successful rulers, had built a system of patronage. His supporters and loyalists were beneficiaries of the patronage. They fear that a change in leadership could mean a disruption in the system. For many people, YSR represented the benevolent ruler who tweaked the system for their benefit. He alone could continue to provide the goodies, they believe. The flaws in governance help the culture of sycophancy to thrive. Politics of patronage breeds sycophancy. **Public utilities and welfare schemes are identified as contributions of the person in office and not as**

the outcome of modern government. The state publicity machinery also helps to reinforce the impression. If public institutions become autonomous and deliver the goods independent of the people in power, patronage politics will peter out. That calls for a more democratic public culture."

I want to be fair in my assessment about him, though I was not in his good books. I did not seek any favour or recognition from him after he became the CM of Andhra Pradesh in 2004. But I know him. I met him in 1984-85 in his brother-in-law late Kumar Koti Reddy's house where the latter hosted a dinner. There was another person, an Ex-public Prosecutor of A.P. High Court who was well known for integrity. Mr. Kumar requested a small favour on behalf of Mr. Kamaluddin, Ex-M.P. which I obliged. On the way back he dropped me in his vehicle at my in-laws place.

When I was Superintendent of Police of Anantapur and DIG of Police of Anantapur range, he was a dissident congressman. There was a faction in a village called Parnapally. One faction was supported by Y. Raja Reddy, F/o Y.S. Rajasekhar Reddy. On a particular day in 1990 followers of Raja Reddy came to Parnapally which is about 25 kms from Pulivendula Town. They blasted houses with explosives though a Police picket was stationed there. In these blasts, houses collapsed and injuries were caused to people. Ten cows also died. **I placed the police party under suspension for failing to prevent this crime.** Later, during the course of investigations YSR telephoned me to resolve the faction feud by involving Late Justice Challa Kondaiah and also to release the police party from suspension. I did not oblige or release the police party from suspension.

There was another occasion when as S.P. of the same District in 1990 I had to send a police party to search the house of a Member of Legislative Assembly, Anantapur Constituency as some of the accused in crimes were reportedly taking shelter in his house. The said MLA was a strong follower of YSR.

On another occasion in 1992-93 there was trouble in Tadipatri town between J.C. Diwakar Reddy faction and Mr.YSR's followers. MLAs of Anantapur and Uravakonda

Constituencies started a dharna in Tadipatri exerting pressure to arrest Mr. J.C. Prabhakar Reddy who reportedly rebuked local DSP Naganna now SP, Srikakulam District. I as D.I.G. sent Additional S.P Subbanna (in the absence of S.P) to take a complaint, from Naganna to set law in motion. But as the DSP was unwilling to give complaint there was stalemate in legal process and the pressure was built up by YSR group to get Prabakar Reddy arrested. There was threat to public peace in Tadipatri town when 3 or 4 more MLAs from adjoining Kadapa district along with scores of followers were reaching Tadipatri Town to give support to the Anantapur District MLAs. I went to Tadipatri to take charge of the situation. I stopped his followers at Penna river bank and did not allow them in.

May be on some other occasion during the same period YSR telephoned me for some favours. I do not exactly remember what the work was, but my well-wisher one Sivashankaracharya a native of Kalyandurg affirms that I obliged him on his request.

On 02-08-09 I met him in his camp office to extend invitation to my son's wedding. In the same room Mr. Balakondaiah, IPS (Retd) was also there. He was S.P. Kadapa district long time back. After sometime YSR came and accosted Mr. Balakondiah warmly "How are you sir". Later when he took a turn towards my seat he accosted me "Bagunnara" (How are you). I gave him the wedding card and exited from the premises. Though he did not attend the marriage or send a letter of Greetings to the couple, I have no grievance.

His Plus Points in Politics

- He was in the vanguard of struggles during the long reign of TDP rule or misrule as he perceived it to be.
- He breathed life to Congress party in A.P., brought it to power for 10 years (2004-2014) pitted as it is against a well oiled, rich TDP and other combination of parties like TRS etc.
- He ensured the formation of UPA government led by Congress at the centre, the fruits of which are enjoyed by central Congress party leadership.

- He launched welfare measures and developmental projects on an unprecedented scale despite fund crunch. His economic advisor tells in a T.V chat(Mr. Somayajulu) that YSR first dared to launch a project and gave thought for fund realization next.
- He had contacts with Congress workers, local leaders at grass root level. No other, not even NTR possessed that mass contact in the post Independent India in A.P. That enthused the party cadres.
- He had credibility to implement the public promises made.
- He had imagination and vision well beyond 2020.
- He brought back religious minorities into Congress fold.
- He built rapport with some sections of media persons, cinema czars (Tollywood).
- He launched pucca housing schemes built with steel and concrete. This is largely my idea which was written in my book "Reform Forward" published in 2003, which Mr. Jannat Hussain his Principal Secretary had access to. Mr. Jannat Hussain was Joint Collector Visakhapatnam District when I was S.P. CBI in 1980s.
- He sold urban lands to realize money for his projects. (This idea of selling urban lands finds expression in my letter, dt. 22.10.2005 addressed to Sonia Gandhi and incorporated in my book "Threats to the Indian Republic".
- He gave more than Rs. 1000 Crores of economic support to OBCs according to the OBC leader Mr. Krishnaiah (TV Interview dated 09.09.2009). This according to him far exceeded their expectations.
- He gave Rs. 500 Crores of economic support to EBC students, which was admitted to be a very generous grant in that direction.
- YSR beat a formidable political combination called 'Mahakutami' led by Mr. Chandra Babu Naidu. His political acumen and strategy did not fail him in 2009 elections.

- In the modern day Machiavellian politics in A.P., Y.S.R. was more than a match to his political opponents.

His Minus Points

- Crimes, Corruption grew both in public life and administration.
- Honest and straight forward senior Bureaucrats were sidelined.
- Built prejudice into principle against powerless where the causes or provocation for prejudices were unfounded. **It is understandable if prejudice is developed towards dishonest, inefficient and partial officials or persons.** People talk much, even media talks about his likes and dislikes. But correcting wrong views or likes or dislikes will help to create right intellectual atmosphere.
- Nursed dynastic ambition and promoted nepotism. favourtism.
- A class of power brokers thrived.

Though he has high credibility with A.P. masses in general and Congress party workers in particular, he lost that silken touch of credibility with the Party High Command. The High Command was not pleased with his act of filling up the Cabinet in 2009 with his chosen men who have large business interests and who got their illegal holdings legalized by Government.

YSR was at once an advocate of capitalism and development on the one hand and welfarism and secularism on the other. He was a 100% politician who practiced dextrously the politics of secularism, welfarism and capitalism.

He had a penchant for over ruling right recommendations. Times of India, dt. 11.09.2009 reported that the performance of Capt. Bhatia who died along with him in the air crash was below par professionality. He was recommended for repatriation to the IAF. But YSR over ruled this suggestion and gave him extension. By this decision he signed his own death warrant. Such an ill thought out decision contributed to his death.

He believed in the principle loyalty to the individuals more than the loyalty to values. Loyalty to the individuals is a tribal trait. Individual loyalty is good but loyalty to values is best.

He tried to please every section of society, employees, the All India Services officers and he was humble or cultivated humility to sir even some All India Service officers. This humility, of course, was a good trait.

In assessing the work of a person who held public office one needs to take into account a) whether he used public office for peoples benefit b)whether he used it to benefit self, relations, partymen, colleagues in the cabinet, MLAs & M.Ps etc., whether he used it for both. YSR used it for both ends. He is a beneficiary of the system.

The surveys undertaken after his death indicate that YSR and his son have 80% approval rating in the public. This is unprecedented in the history of Andhra Pradesh. **He carved out a niche in the political history of A.P. as people's man.** In the hey days of Indira Gandhi, late P. Bayyapu Reddy, M.P., Hindupur advised his followers not to insist on his electioneering but to carry the photo of Indira Gandhi and relay her speeches. In the same way, YSR's photographs, his speeches and programs may ensure congress victory in 2014. **But the Government needs to avoid attrocities and corruption, scandals etc.**

During his time, he was a hero, the rest of cabinet members zeros. The Home Minister Sabita Indra Reddy was reduced to a figure head. He appointed Mr. K.V.P. Ramachandra Rao as Chairperson of **State Security Commission** which provoked one Harish Rao, TRS leader to comment that YSR wields the lathi while Sabita Indra Reddy wears a hat. There is now freedom of action. Ministers are on the move after initial inertia due to the grief they experienced at the death of YSR. Sabita Indra Reddy is on the move every day. We see some action or the other. Whether she keeps up the tempo and delivers goods (police services) or not is to be watched.

By a dextrous admixture of the politics of welfarism, secularism (quotas to religious minorities), developmentalism that immediately catered to the needs of the business classes, by politely greeting senior MLAs, bureaucrats as "Sir", by tickling the egos of the political and social elite in accosting them as "Prince" (a reference to M.Sashidhar Reddy) "Raja" (a reference to Kishnam Raju, Tollywood actor and ex-Minister in Union Cabinet), "Hero" (a reference to Sri Hari, a Tollywood actor) by his endearing words in electioneering while addressing masses, so often relayed by Sakshi TV, such as "Namaste Papa", "Namaste Babu", "Namaste Akkayya", "Namaste Chellemma" (Papa is young girl, babu, a young boy, akka is elder sister, chellemma is younger sister), YSR etched his image in the hearts and minds of major sections of society. He had also soft corner for that monolith of Bureaucracy and even according to M. Rosaiah, he treated bureaucracy as part of his family. This enormous goodwill from several sources is a huge **electoral asset** to the political fortunes of his son Mr. Jagan and also the Congress Party. In the public perception YSR immortalized his name as a "Karana Purusha" - a person born with a mission in life. **Y.S. Raja Sekhar Reddy was everything for everybody. Persons who dole out Govt. goodies are being worshiped, their statues erected. We forgot to worship work.** The large majority worship money, fame, power.

True, much of public goodwill and sympathy wave that is now sweeping in favour of YSR cannot be explained with any degree of reasoning. When VP Singh opened the Pandora box of Mandal Commission, there were hundreds of suicides against the policy of VP Singh. But when YSR provided quotas to religious minorities like Muslims and Christians, there were not even sustained peaceful agitations. On the other hand, there were some 3 to 4 hundred suicides or deaths due to shock after hearing the news of the tragic demise of YSR. It is equally true that YSR used to take some ill-thought out decisions and invite the wrath of Media, political opposition, etc. One senior IAS Officer, who was Principal Secretary to some Chief Ministers, used to joke that "you people of Kadapa and Kurnool will take rash decisions and later regret. Instead, why not you think twice before a decision is taken." I told him that you better be his advisor to bring balance in decision taking by these factious or hot headed people of Rayalaseema districts.

I do not however, subscribe to the popular perception and which is often repeated by YSR himself that he is a person who does not go back on his word and will not turn back the heel ("Maata Thappadu, Madama Thippadu" in Telugu language). True, he kept his word on public promises. Privately he kept his word largely to his political followers, officials who helped him when he was out of power and gave them positions in party, various corporations etc. etc. He rehabilitated a number of retired officials and posted them to a number of posts. In the process, the honest, impartial and the efficient got raw deal in the "spoils system" of Public Employment which I have discussed in some of the pages in this Book. He also kept up his word to commute prison setences to murder case convicts, some of whom were his poltical followers. For me this does not make any sense of keeping one's words. **This public perception needs correction that keeping up one's word has a limited reach and meaning.**

Post YSR Scenario

A Constitutional Coup d' Etat has been executed in A.P. (in the aftermath of the demise of YSR) by the party High Command taking advantage of that archaic Constitutional Provision of Art. 164 through the institution of Governor.

Article 163, 164 of the Constitution

The chinks in the armour of the Article 164 were exposed in the first week of September 2009 when the Governor of the State of A.P. swore in Mr. K. Rosaiah (a Senior Congress man and a veteran of Parliamentary debating skills) as Chief Minister of A.P. This act of the Governor was said to be inspired by the designs of Congress High Command. On the other side is Mr. Y.S. Jagan Mohan Reddy, M.P. and son of Late Y.S.R. He was waiting in the wings to take over the mantle of his father. He enjoyed (largely due to sympathy factor towards his father) massive public support, almost unprecedented. Some 152 legislaters out of 157 reportedly supported his candidature and the Council of Ministers too surprisingly passed unofficial resolution supporting Mr.

Jagan's candidature. True, the Council of Ministers as well as a large number of MLAs were hand picked loyalists of late Y.S.R. That is a different matter. Whether Mr. Jagan is suitable to the job is yet another issue. **Prima facie there is nothing to suggest that he is unsuitable for he is not convicted for any offence or held guilty of corruption charges.** Yet in the presence of all these, he was sidelined and Mr. K. Rosaiah was appointed as Chief Minister and a Council of Ministers was hastily and collectively sworn in by the Governor.

It is relevant to quote Art. 163, 164 of the Constitution to judge whether they are Democratic or Transparent.

Article 163. Council of Ministers to Aid and Advise Governor

1. There shall be a Council of Ministers with the Chief Minister at the head to aid and advise the Governor in the exercise of his functions, except in so far as he is by or under this Constitution required to exercise his functions **or any of them in his discretion?**
2. If any question arises whether any matter is or is not a matter as respects which the Governor is by or under this Constitution required to act in his discretion, the decision of the Governor in his discretion shall be final, and the validity of anything done by the Governor shall not be **called in question** on the ground that he ought or ought not to have acted in his discretion.
3. The question whether any, and if so what, advice was tendered by Ministers to the Governor shall not be inquired into by any Court.

Article 164. Other provisions as to Ministers.-

1. The Chief Minister shall be "appointed" by the Governor and other Ministers shall be "appointed" by the Governor on the advice of the Chief Minister, and the Ministers shall hold office during the **pleasure** of the Governor?
2. The Council of Ministers shall be collectively responsible to the Legislative Assembly of the State.

3. Before a Minister enters upon his office, the Governor shall administer to him the oaths of office and of secrecy according to the forms set out for the purpose in the third Schedule.
4. A Minister who, for any period of six consecutive months is not a member of the Legislature of the State shall at the expiration of that period cease to be a Minister.

As the wording suggests, the Chief Minister will be "appointed" by the Governor and the Ministers will be "appointed" on the "advice" of the Chief Minister which means that Governor can appoint even a passerby on the road as the Chief Minister of a state. Legal eagles do not air their views to reform laws and Art. 164. But they want Status-Quo so that they live in a world of **professional paradise.** What is the criteria for appointment of a Chief Minister by the Governor is not spelt out. **A modicum of such criteria can be traced to the word "advice" with regard to appointment of Ministers. A few words or another sentence in the Article that the Chief Minister will be appointed by Governor "who has been elected leader of majority in the Party or combination of parties in the Legislature" could have sufficed to make it Democratic and Transparent.** In the absence of such phraseology we revert back to sound Parliamentary practices as they exist in Britain of electing a leader who commands majority in Parliament / Assembly and then communicating it to the Governor. True, such Parliamentary practices sustain when public value system is strong. That is not the case in India or in the other third world countries. So much so, Governor's personal choice, party High Command's choice, Central Govt.'s choice prevails over sound Democratic principles and practices.

True the Architects of the Constitution were guided while framing the articles of our Constitution on the phraseology of the Western world Constitutions. More over the public values of 1950s of Gandhian era were infinitely superior to the present. **They did not anticipate the present state of polluted politics.** Art. 164 is a loose legal canon, in which a Governor can appoint a Chief Minister who is not a member of the House and who is not a leader commanding majority in Assembly.

Pending Public Interest Litigation

In the absence a proviso to Art. 164 that the Assembly be convened within a time frame of one month to elect a leader commanding majority, it may be difficult to obtain clear cut verdict from Courts. The alternate course open to Mr. Jagan was to collect the flock of his supporters (MLAs) and present the list to the Governor or parade such a gathering of MLAs before the Governor. These are **political actions** outside the Assembly. However the proper forum before whom such an action plan is to be carried out is not the party High Command but the Governor. Whether Mr. Jagan can defy the party and take to such a course of action incurring the wrath of the party High Command in which absolute loyalty of his followers is not assured are all the issues involved in this Constitutional imbroglio.

The essential of Democracy are

- Elections
- Multi Party System
- Majorities in Parliament / Assembly.

The majority in Andhra Pradesh Assembly is ignored in preference to wishes of party High Command. Therefore, Art. 164 needs amendment on the lines suggested by me to prevent further abuse of party power or Governor's power in the appointment of Chief Minister. It is not this Articles alone, but many such as Art. 16 (dealing with reservation in public employment, Art. 356 (dismissal of State Govt.) etc. that are grossly abused by the Governments or party for the sake of power. **And this misuse of Constitutional provisions undermines the principles of justice.**

Who is the authority to convene the CLP to elect the leader? Is it

- Governor
- Speaker
- Party High Command

And in what time frame such an arrangement falls into place is not finding expression in Art. 164. That leaves the issue to be arbitrated by judiciary. And a conflicting body of judicial decisions makes litigation a **profesional paradise** for Senior Advocates of Supreme Court.

In this Constitutional imbroglio in A.P. in September 2009, the National English Media (The Times of India, The Hindu, The Indian Express) did not support the democratic principle and practice of electing a leader who commands majority in the Assembly to be appointed as Chief Minister by the Governor. It pontificated on the experience, the debating skills of K. Rosaiah who was appointed as Chief Minister of A.P. by the Governor. All this is done by Media which is touted as the 4th pillar of Democracy. **Concern for truth and justice alone can make Media a 4th pillar.** Splashing news on world events, crimes and wrong doing, political commentaries, salacious gossip, criticism etc., will not make Indian Media the 4th pillar.

It is not just the Corporate Media that sidetracked the larger issues involved in the appointment of the Chief Minister, Andhra Pradesh, but also the intellectuals, academia, retired justices of High Court or Supreme Court, members of the Bar associations who kept silent.

Opposition political parties (the watch dogs of Democracy) are playing the same tune and want to profit and fish in troubled waters. The aged congress veterans also fell in line of Congress High Command.

But to me K. Rosaiah the incumbent Chief Minister looked more fair in his approach to power. He was never power hungry. The post of Chief Minister was thrust on him and he is discharging his duties and responsibilities without

abdicating them. He is according to me a sane voice in present day politics in the country, and I hope to see him continue the same.

Mr. Rosaiah had a long political innings of 60 years and as Minister for some 20 years. But his administrative capacities as Chief Minister and ability to manage politics need to be tested.

He has stentorian voice. He is good speaker if not a rabble rouser and an orator. In Assembly debates, he can meet irresponsible or even vicious criticism of opposition parties. If **dynamism and dare devilry the forte of late YSR in launching a plethora of welfare measures, a clean public image is the asset of Sri Rosaiah.** He commands respect by the sheer force of his public image from any responsible opposition party / parties. The only thing is that he needs to continue existing welfare schemes, cut corruption in their execution which YSR admittedly failed, keep power brokers at bay, control political corruption and in administration and above all take care to see that no atrocities are committed against SC, STs. He needs to curb crime wave and violence in order to succeed in 2014 election if he continues as Chief Minister up to that date. On 22/9 or 23/9 in an interview to Sakshi TV Channel, Rosaiah praised YSR and admitted the limitation of his capacity to discharge the duties associated with CM's Office, keeping in view his age factor. **It shows his humility which needs emulation.**

Mr. Rosaiah lacks charisma and histrionics so necessary for hocus-pocus (deceiving the public in a Democracy). He is serious, stern and stoic and incapable of a smile much less a hearty laugh. He appears to me like a Head Master going about his job in a business like fashion.

Media reports, dt. 23.09.2009 suggest that the High Court, A.P. entertained a Public Interest Ligitation to correct injustice in the appointment of Chief Minister by the Governor. From one stage of litigation, we may move to another viz., the Supreme Court. Litigation has become a big industry in India. **We go through a hell of Court litigation only to discover or**

get disappointed over the paradise of justice. Legal fraternity, the creamy layers of it is thriving. On the eve of retirment as Supreme Court Judge Sri B.N. Agarwal, reputed to be a person of high degree of honesty said that Senior Supreme Court Lawyers earn Rs. 25 to 30 lakhs per day (Media reports, dt. 10.10.2009). A great disparity in income compared Rs. 100/- per day earned by common man.

Court litigation is not an answer for precise legislative and constitutional provisions.

Accountability of the Governor for misuse of Art. 164 is a first condition to ensure justice. The immunity for the actions of Governor now allowed under Art. 361 of the Constitution needs to be removed. Only then there will be a check on the misuse of the Article.

A rigged opinion in the Congres Legislature Party by arm twisting Y. S. Jagan or luring him into alternative political position will make entire process of electing a leader of majority party undemocratic.

True, two representatives of Congress Party, Mr. Pranab Mukherjee, Mr. Veerappa Moily attended C.L.P. meeting on 27.11.2009 and later left for Delhi to "nominate" the CLP leader after obtaining the consent of Congress President Smt. Sonia Gandhi. This procedure conflicts with Art. 164 where only Governor of a State has power to "appoint" a Chief Minister. In the second place, there is absence of signed support of MLAs in favour of Mr. Rosaiah in the CLP meeting. This makes the process of electing a leader of C.L.P. non-transparent, arbitrary and authoritarian. So both the language of Art. 164 as well as the current practice of appointing Chief Minister of a State made democracy a mockery. Only a vote taken in the House by the Speaker by raising of hands or secret ballot, then counted and communicated through proper channel to the Governor makes the process Democratic. Art. 164 lent itself to gross abuse by the Party High Command and the Governor.

Media report (New Indian Express), dt. 02.12.2009 suggests that the High Court of Andhra Pradesh has closed the pending case in the aftermath of CLP meeting and party President nominating Mr. Rosaiah. The great Constitutional and jurisprudential principles involved are not adjudicated. **The battle for political justice in favour of Y.S. Jagan is lost.**

Is Telangana Area in Andhra Pradesh Denied Justice?

Timely intervention in perceived and real injustices and correction of them will avert

- Revolutionary movements
- Separatist tendencies
- Demand for separate statehood

Telangana state was merged with Andhra in 1956 and the state came to be known as Andhra Pradesh. Kurnool was the capital of Andhra area before 1956. After merger, Hyderabad became the capital of the unified state.

There was Gentlemen's Agreement in 1956 between the leaders of Andhra state and Telangana so as to avoid misgiving of neglect and discrimination against Telangana.

The following points arising out of the unification of Telangana and Andhra were discussed and the conclusions arrived at are as follows:

1. The expenditure of the Central and General Administration of the State should be borne proportionately by the two regions and the balance of income from Telangana should be reserved for expenditure on the development of Telangana area. This arrangement will be reviewed after five years and can be continued for another five years if the Telangana members of the Assembly so desire.
2. Prohibition in Telangana should be implemented in the manner decided upon by the Assembly members of Telangana.
3. The existing educational facilities in Telangana should be secured to the students of Telangana and further improved. Admission to the colleges, including technical institutions in the Telangana area, should be restricted to the students of Telangana, or the latter should have admission to the extent of one-third of the total admission in the entire State, whichever course is advantageous to Telangana students.

4. Retrenchment of services should be proportionate from both regions if it becomes inevitable due to integration.
5. Future recruitment to services will be on the basis of population from both regions.
6. The position of Urdu in the administrative and judicial structure existing at present in the Telangana area may continue for five years, when the position may be reviewed by the Regional Council. So far as recruitment to services is concerned, knowledge of Telugu should not be insisted upon at the time of recruitment, but they should be required to pass a prescribed Telugu test in two years' time after appointment.
7. Some kind of domicile rules e.g., Residence for 12 years, should be provided in order to secure the prescribed proportion to recruitment of services of Telangana area.
8. Sales of agricultural lands in Telangana area to be controlled by the Regional Council.
9. A Regional Council will be established for the Telangana area with a view to secure its all-round development in accordance with its needs and requirements.
10. The Regional Council will consist of 20 members as follows.

    9 members of the Assembly representing each district of Telangana to be elected by the Assembly members of the Telangana districts separately.

    6 members of the Assembly or the Parliament elected by the Telangana representatives in the Assembly.

    5 members from outside the Assembly to be elected by the Telangana members of the Assembly. All ministers from Telangana region will be members. The Chief Minister or Deputy Chief Minister, whoever is from Telangana will be the Chairman of the Council. Other Cabinet Ministers may also be invited.

11. (a) The Regional Council will be a **statutory body** empowered to deal with and decide about matters mentioned above and those relating to planning and development, irrigation and other projects, industrial development within the general plan and recruitment to services in so far as they relate to Telangana area. If there is difference of opinion between the views of the Regional Council and the Government of the State, a reference may be made to the Government of India for final decision.

    (b) Unless revised by agreement earlier, this arrangement will be reviewed at the end of **ten years**.

12. The Cabinet will consist of members in proportion of 60:40 per cent, for Andhra and Telangana respectively. Out of 40 per cent Telangana Ministers, one will be a Muslim from Telangana.

13. If the Chief Minister is from Andhra, the Deputy Chief Minister will be from Telangana and vice versa. Two out of the following portfolios will be assigned to Ministers from Telangana.

    (a) Home (b) Finance (c) Revenue (d) Planning and Development (e) Commerce and Industry.

14. The H.P.C.C. President desires that the P.C.C. should be separate for Telangana up to the end of 1962. A.P.C.C. President has no objection.

All those above points were agreed upon in a meeting held on February 20, 1956. We have today further discussed about the following points, on which agreement could not be arrived at:

(1) The name of the New State– the Telangana representatives wanted that the name of Andhra Telangana (as proposed in the draft bill) be retained, while the Andhra representatives wanted that Andhra Pradesh, as amended by the Joint Selection Committee be retained.

(2) Regarding the High Court, the Telangana representatives wanted that there should be a bench at Guntur,

with the principal seat at Hyderabad, while the Andhra representatives desired that there should be no bench at Guntur and the entire High Court be located only at Hyderabad.

Again on 21.07.1973 there was a six point formula

1. Accelerated development of the backward areas of the State and planned development of the State capital with specific resources earmarked for these purposes and appropriate association of Representatives of such Backward areas in the Legislature along with other experts in the formulation and monitoring of development schemes for such areas should form the essential part of the development strategy of the State. Constitution at the State level of a **Planning Board** as well as Sub-Committees for different backward areas should be the appropriate instrument for achieving this objective.
2. Institution of uniform arrangements throughout the State enabling adequate preference being given to local candidates in the matter of admission to educational institutions and establishment of a new Central University at Hyderabad to augment the existing educational facilities, should be the basis of the educational policy of the State.
3. Subject to the requirements of the State as a whole, local candidates should be given preference to specified extent in the matter of direct recruitment to (i) non-gazetted posts (other than in the Secretariat, Offices of Heads of Department, other State Level offices and institutions and the Hyderabad City Police) (ii) Corresponding posts under the local bodies and (iii) the posts of Tahsildar, Junior Engineers and Civil Assistant Surgeons. In order to improve their promotion prospects, service cadres should be organised to the extent possible on appropriate local basis up to specified gazetted level, first or second, as may be administratively convenient.

4. A high power administrative tribunal should be constituted to deal with the grievances of services regarding appointments, seniority, promotion and other allied matters. The decisions of the Tribunal should ordinarily be binding on the State Government. The constitution of such a tribunal would justify limits on recourse to judiciary in such matters.
5. **In order that implementation of measures based on the above principles does not give rise to litigation and consequent uncertainty, the Constitution should be suitably amended to the extent necessary, conferring on the President enabling powers on this behalf.**
6. The above approach would render the continuance of Mulki Rules and Regional Committee unnecessary.

In pursuance of the above six point formula, Art. 371 D was inserted in the Constitution. The said article is worth quoting.

(1) The President may by order made with respect to the State of Andhra Pradesh provide, having regard to the requirements of the State as a whole, for equitable opportunities and facilities for the people belonging to different parts of the State, in the matter of public employment and in the matter of education, and different provisions may be made for various parts of the State.

(2) An order made under clause (1), may, in particular, -

(a) require the State Government to organize any class or classes of posts in a civil service of, or any class or classes of civil posts under, the State into different local cadres for different parts of the State and allot in accordance with such principles and procedure as may be specified in the order the persons holding such posts to the local cadres so organised;

(b) specify any part or parts of the State which shall be regarded as the local area, -

- for direct recruitment to posts in any local cadre (whether organised in pursuance of an order under this Article or constituted otherwise) under the State Government;
- for direct recruitment to posts in any cadre under any local authority within the State; and
- for the purposes of admission to any University within the State or to any other educational institution which is subject to the control of the State Government;

(c) specify the extent to which, the manner in which and the conditions subject to which, preference or reservation shall be given or made, -

- in the matter of direct recruitment to posts in any such cadre referred to in sub-clause (b) as may be specified in this behalf in the order,
- in the matter of admission to any such University or other educational institution referred to in sub-clause (b) as may be specified in this behalf in the order,

to or in favour of candidates who have resided or studied for any period specified in the order in the local area in respect of such cadre, University or other educational institution, as the case may be.

(3) The President may, by order, provide for the constitution of an Administrative Tribunal for the State of Andhra Pradesh to exercise such jurisdiction, powers and authority [including any jurisdiction, power and authority which immediately before the commencement of the Constitution (Thirty-second Amendment) Act, 1973, was exercisable by any court (other than the Supreme Court) or by any tribunal or other authority] as may be specified in the order with respect to the following matters, namely, -

(a) appointment, allotment or promotion to such class or classes of posts in any civil service of the State, or to such class or classes of civil posts under the State, or to such class or classes of posts under the control of any local authority within the State, as may be specified in the order;

(b) seniority of persons appointed, allotted or promoted to such class or classes of posts in any civil service of the State, or to such class or classes of civil posts under the State, or to such class or classes of posts under the control of any local authority within the State, as may be specified in the order;

(c) such other conditions of service of persons appointed, allotted or promoted to such class or classes of posts in any civil service of the State or to such class or classes of civil posts under the State or to such class or classes of posts under the control of any local authority within the State, as may be specified in the order;

(4) An order made under clause (3) may, -

(a) authorise the Administrative Tribunal to receive representations for the redress of grievances relating to any matter within its jurisdiction as the President may specify in the order and to make such orders thereon as the Administrative Tribunal deems fit;

(b) contain such provisions with respect to the powers and authorities and procedure of the Administrative Tribunal (including provisions with respect to the powers of the Administrative Tribunal to punish for contempt of itself) as the President may deem necessary;

(c) provide for the transfer to the Administrative Tribunal of such classes of proceedings, being proceedings relating to matters within its jurisdiction and pending before any court (other than the Supreme Court) or tribunal or other authority immediately before the commencement of such order, as may be specified in the order;

(d) contain such supplemental, incidental and consequential provisions (including provisions as to fees and as to limitation, evidence or for the application of any law for the time being in force subject to any exceptions or modifications) as the President may deem necessary.

(5) The order of the Administrative Tribunal finally disposing of any case shall become effective upon its confirmation by the State Government or on the expiry of three months from the date on which the order is made, whichever is earlier:

Provided that the State Government may, by special order made in writing and for reasons to be specified therein, modify or annul any order of the Administrative Tribunal before it becomes effective and in such a case, the order of the Administrative Tribunal shall have effect only in such modified form or be of no effect, as the case may be.

(6) Every special order made by the State Government under the proviso to clause (5) shall be laid, as soon as may be after it is made, before both Houses of the State Legislature.

(7) The High Court for the State shall not have any powers of superintendence over the Administrative Tribunal and no court (other than the Supreme Court) or Tribunal shall exercise any jurisdiction, power or authority in respect of any matter subject to the jurisdiction, power or authority of, or in relation to the Administrative Tribunal.

(8) If the President is satisfied that the continued existence of the Administrative Tribunal is not necessary, the President may by order abolish the Administrative Tribunal and make such provisions in such order as he may deem fit for the transfer and disposal of cases pending before the Tribunal immediately before such abolition.

(9) Notwithstanding any judgment, decree or order of any court, tribunal or other authority, -

(a) no appointment, posting, promotion or transfer of any person, -

- made before the 1st day of November, 1956, to any post under the Government of, or any local authority within, the State of Hyderabad as it existed before that date; or
- made before the commencement of the Constitution (Thirty-second Amendment) Act, 1973, to any post under the Government of, or any local or other authority within, the State of Andhra Pradesh, and

(b) no action taken or thing done by or before any person referred to in sub-clause (a),

shall be deemed to be illegal or void or ever to have become illegal or void merely on the ground that the appointment, posting, promotion or transfer of such person was not made in accordance with any law, then in force, providing for any requirement as to residence within the State of Hyderabad or, as the case may be, within any part of the State of Andhra Pradesh, in respect of such appointment, posting, promotion or transfer.

(10) The provisions of this Article and of any order made by the President thereunder shall have effect notwithstanding anything in any other provision of this Constitution or in any other law for the time being in force.

Notwithstanding the agreements and Constitutional and legal guarantees, Telangana area witnessed several movements for separate statehood some of them violent indeed. During 1968 to 72 Telangana movement for separate statehood was launched by Dr. M. Chenna Reddy. Nearly 300 people mostly students died in suppression of the movement by government through police. I was D.S.P. Bellampalli Sub-division of Adilabad district and Nizamabad sub-division of Nizamabad district during that period. All this separate statehood movements were inspired by perceived neglect and injustices to Telangana area. Some of the alleged irritants and discriminatory policies are

- Govt. of Andhra Pradesh while giving high priority for irrigation spent around 12000 crores between 1956 and 2002 which constitutes 25% of the total plan outlay from the II plan to IX plan. Of this expenditure 90% was allocated to major and medium irrigation while minor irrigation received 10%. Though net irrigation area under major and medium irrigation rose from 28 lakhs hectares to 55 lakh hectares between 1955-56 and 2001-2002, meagre allocation of funds for minor irrigation such as for tanks etc., on which Telangana area depends resulted in impoverishment of the area in agricultural production.
- Benefits of major irrigation (canal system) went to Coastal Andhra area copiously – the 4 districts of East Godavari, West Godavari, Guntur and Krishna. Nearly 60% of the net area irrigated under canals is located in these 4 districts and the balance of 40% is shared by the rest of 17 districts. The area irrigated under canal system in 9 Telangana districts for 2003-2004, was 1.36 lakh hectares and it further fell to 1.16 lakh hectares in 2004-2005.
- Under "Jalayagnam" launched by Late Y.S.R. (an ambitious irrigation scheme to tap every drop of river water) 26 irrigation projects were conceived to irrigate 60 lakh hectares of which 46 lakh hectares is in Andhra region and 16 lakh hectares in Telangana. Moreover the projects being taken up in Telangana are lift irrigation schemes under which only drip and sprinkler irrigation is possible or permitted. The argument is Telangana is neglected and discriminated in its share of river waters though river Godavari and Krishna are flowing from Telangana to Andhra area.

This according to the protagonists of Telangana resulted in poor economic development of the area and therefore injustice to the people of the area.

It is in this background of Agreements and Constitutional Guarantees (Art. 371 D), and their lopsided implementation by Government or some time Court decision as in the case of Hyderabad City having been declared a free zone for public employment that gave rise for the birth of TRS in 2002 and the current fast unto death by K. Chandra Sekhar Rao and the subsequent unilateral or arbitrary announcement by Union Home Minister on 09.12.2009 that the process for the separation of State has began.

Let me examine.

From out of perceived injustices to Telangana and which remain effectively unrebutted, TRS Leader K. Chandra Sekhar Rao undertook indefinite fast on 28.12.2009 for the sake of separate statehood of Telangana. In the 11 days period that ended with breaking of fast on 09.12.2009 after the announcement by Union Home Minister that the process for formation of separate state has begun; there was violence and disruption of normal life.

- Dharna (sit in protest)
- Rasta rokos, rail rokos
- Procession, burning effigies
- Burning and destroying public and private properties
- Stone pelting and injuring police
- Attacking people of Andhra area or intimidating them
- Verbal abuse and denigration
- Police lathi charge and other forms of use of force
- Suicides and heart breaks in the cause of KCR were the order of the day.

The fast of KCR and subsequent announcement of Union Home Minister that the process of separate state has begun has galvanized unity among the political parties and everybody including TDP leaders of Telangana area joined hands with congress leaders who are Ministers in Mr. Rosaiah's cabinet. These Ministers of Congress party from Telangana who till 09.12.2009 were singing paean of YSR and his son suddenly changed their stance and are more vigorous vocally etc., in the cause of separate Telangana more vocal than TRS itself. Even MPs of Telangana have suddenly changed their stance and are treating their once cherished leader Y.S. Jagan as an untouchable after he gave call for united Andhra on 12.12.2009 in Parliament. In short all MLAs, MPs, Ministers of Andhra area irrespective of party affiliation want united Andhra Pradesh while their counter parts in Telangana want separate Telangana. But Mr. K. Chandra Sekhar Rao, President Telangana Rashtra Samithi has been steadfast in the cause of separate statehood and to that extent principled.

The case of leaders of Andhra area is that the announcement made by Mr. Chidambaram is a midnight decision without any consultation or political consensus or exhausting the option of second SRC. **The decision was attacked as arbitrary, hasty and therefore unjust to their cause.**

The decision of Mr. Chidambaram that the process for separate State has begun is attacked by independent commentators as 10 Janpath inspired which had covert understanding and prior knowledge about KCR's fast. The fast itself is now attacked as a farce. It is as short as 10 days and where intravenous fluids were given to KCR.

It is said that interests of Congress party (though misplaced) were upper most in carving out a separate state than the interests of Andhra Pradesh State.

It is said that the move for a separate statehood envisaged by Central Govt. has twin hidden objectives. One is to break the hold of upper castes in state politics (Rajyadhikaram) and at the same time transfer "Rajyadhikaram" to the downtrodden castes which have been hitherto considered as castes providing various services to upper castes. It is aimed to give **political justice** to the downtrodden and depressed castes. The same view was expressed by the intellectuals from among the BC, ST, SC castes (Times of India, dt. 17.12.2009). **This transference of "Rajyadhikaram" is in addition to the political reservation which they enjoy from Parliament to Panchayat as well as reservation in Public employment, state financial support**

to students and such support for individual entrepreneurship. The posts of District Collector, Superintendent of Police, Minister accrued through legal reservations by themselves confer Rajyadhikaram. As the Republic entered its 60th year, this can be considered a crowning success to the hitherto deprived sections of Hindu society in India towards **socio-political justice**. But one has to wait and watch whether these political experiments will remove poverty, hunger and sickness etc., of the common man amongst depressed classes or throws up more Madhu Khodas.

It is now the turn of events in Andhra region which cause concern. It is a reaction to the announcement of Sri Chidambaram on 09.12.2009 that the process for formation of separate Telangana has begun. Similar strategy of fast, agitation by students, suicides, sporadic outbreak of violence is reenacted as it happened in Telangana prior to 09.12.2009. In addition all MLAs, some MPs irrespective of party affiliation resigned their posts creating a Constitutional crisis. Just as the statement of Mr. Chidambaram is attacked as hasty and arbitrary where there were no consultations and political consensus of all the stakeholders, the reaction in Andhra region is also considered hasty where the political leadership instead of guiding the students and public are guided by them or even a step ahead. **One point can be mentioned**. There is no formal decision taken by Union Cabinet for the formation of separate State pursuant to Mr. Chidambaram's statement. Therefore political leadership being led by people at this point of time is unfortunate. **If the political leadership considers that agitation and violence is a weapon for their electoral and political gains, it is unjust.** The student community needs to be educated as to whether the sacrifices they make are commensurate to the cause on hand and how the employment prospects get affected? **Students need to fight for higher ideal of good politics vis-à-vis bad politics.** Let politicians shoulder responsibility for their omissions and commissions. It is here that we need to have public debates in in Electronic Media and written articles in print Media by intellectuals and well meaning group in politics, civil society to discuss and analyse the merits and demerits of separate State inorder to douse the flames of hatred, resentment and violent acts. **Students are becoming pawns in political games.** These "public debates" to the best of my understanding are synonymous with the phrase "public reasoning" employed by Mr. Amartya Sen in his book "The idea of Justice". **Intellectuals need to elevate (not degrade) political, social cultural and at times religious life.**

Meanwhile L. Raj Gopal, M.P. left the hospital at Vijayawada where he was fasting secretly and landed at NIMS Hospital at Hyderabad on 21.12.2009, continued the fast and broke it on 22.12.2009. There was a press meet subsequently. Mr. Raj Gopal admitted that on 19.12.2009 at Vijayawada Hospital, he had intravenous fluids administered. He was self critical that his and KCR's fast are mock fasts of modern day which have no similarities with those of Gandhiji. **Fasts undertaken with the administration of saline or intravenous fluids are no fasts at all according to him**. Mr. Raj Gopal obviously had a dig at KCR's fast. Mr. Raj Gopal had a similar dig at Media which so far failed to draw a difference in these fasts. He also faulted police leadership on several courts. In this episode of secretly leaving Vijayawada and arriving at Hyderabad, by Mr. Raj Gopal without being noticed and stopped by police, there is a new twist. The Commissioner of Police and half a dozen subordinates were suspended from service for irresponsibility and neglect of duty. It happened in 24 hours without a Preliminary Enquiry and report it took the police and impartial observers by surprise. Apart from not adhering to procedure of prior enquiry report before suspending senior officers, there is more substantive question viz., that Mr. Raj Gopal was not in police or judicial custody to hold police responsible for the act of Mr. Raj Gopal secretly leaving the hospital. **All this reflect knee jerk reaction.** Even not permitting Raj Gopal to make Hyderabad as venue of his mock fast, is not right police approach as lamented by him in the press meet. **It looks that Andhra Pradesh is becoming a theatre of the absurd** where thoughtless decisions are taken at each stage leading the State from one crisis to another. Mr.

Rosaiah often stated that he will implement what ever decision the Centre takes which gives the impression that he is accountable to Congress Parry Central leadership and not to the people of Andhra Pradesh or the Legislative Assembly. **It is unfortunate that Mr. Rosaiah, though I respect him for seniority became a pawn in the political chess board of Congress High Command plunging the State into political turmoil and violence.**

On 23.12.2009 Mr. Chidambaram almost did a U-turn that in view of the changed political equations, he needs time to evolve political consesus. With this, violence in Telangana area in less than 24 hours after the statement, is back with a bang. Resignation drama of Ministers, MLAs etc., began plunging the State into political crisis. All this politics by the National and State political parties was described by Senior Journalist Mr. Sreenivasa Reddy as demonic politics.

Constitutional Scheme for Creation of New States

Art. 3 Formation of new States and alteration of areas, boundaries or names of existing States. - Parliament may by law, -

(a) form a new State by separation of territory from any State or by uniting two or more States or parts of States or by uniting any territory to a part of any State;

(b) increase the area of any State;

(c) diminish the area of any State;

(d) alter the boundaries of any State;

(e) alter the name of any State :

Provided that no Bill for the purpose shall be introduced in either House of Parliament **except on the recommendation of the President** and unless, where the proposal contained in the Bill affects the area, boundaries or name of any of the States the Bill has been referred by the President to the Legislature of that State **for expressing its views** thereon within such period as may be specified in the reference or within such further period as the President may allow and the period so specified or allowed has expired.

Explanation I – In this article, in clauses (a) to (e), "State" includes a Union territory, but in the proviso, "State" does not include a Union territory.

Explanation II – The power conferred on Parliament by clause (a) includes the power to form a new State or Union territory by uniting a part of any State or Union territory to any other State or Union territory.

Art. 189 Voting in Houses, Power of Houses to act notwithstanding Vacancies and Quorum

1. Save as otherwise provided in this Constitution, all questions at any sitting of a House of the Legislature of a State shall be determined by a majority of votes of the members present and voting, other than the Speaker or Chairman, or person acting as such.

   The Speaker or Chairman, or person acting as such, shall not vote in the first instance, but shall have and exercise a casting vote in the case of an equality of votes.
2. A House of the Legislature of a State shall have power to act notwithstanding any vacancy in the membership thereof, and any proceedings in the Legislature of a State shall be valid notwithstanding, that it is discovered subsequently that some person who was not entitled so to do sat or voted or otherwise took part in the proceedings.
3. Until the Legislature of the State by law otherwise provides, the quorum to constitute a meeting of a House of the Legislature of a State **shall be ten members or one-tenth of the total number of members of the House, whichever is greater**.
4. If at any time during a meeting of the Legislative Assembly or the Legislative Council of a State there is no quorum, it shall be the duty of the Speaker or Chairman, or person acting as such, either to adjourn the House or to suspend the meeting until there is a quorum.

Art. 3 When Analysed, takes the following form

- The Central Govt. first takes a formal decision to carve out a separate state.

- Such decision is to be communicated to the President of the Republic.
- Approval of the President needs to be obtained.
- Thereafter the decision of Central Govt. along with President's approval, needs to be communicated to State Legislature for expression of its views. **The view of State Legislature is recommendatory but not mandatory**.
- After this the bill will be introduced in Parliament and when passed it becomes a law.

True, Art. 3 is not federal in spirit. It is unitary in character where State Legislature's views can be disregarded. In respect of a decision of Central Govt. in carving out separate Telangana on the strength of agitation and fast launched by its President Mr. K.C.R., the aforesaid Article becomes totally undemocratic. **Several of the Constitutional provisions as pointed out by me in my writings are undemocratic.**

- In the 2004 General Election Telangana Rashtra Samithi won 26 Assembly seats out of a total 119 or so in Telangana.
- In 2009 General Elections it won 10 seats that too in alliance with various political parties.
- In the Greater Hyderabad Municipal Elections it did not contest at all.

How does this reflect the popular sentiment for separate statehood? TRS which has only one agenda of separate statehood stood rejected in successive elections. So invocation of Art. 3 under the above circumstances is arbitrary. When a decision is non-arbitrary it becomes democratic. And I go to the extent of stating that the Article itself is undemocratic and needs certain amendments after careful debates or we need to evolve the mechanism of a **referendum** in the Constitution to test popular will in the region desiring separation. The issue of separate states became a National one with several States like Harit Pradesh, Poorvanchal, Vidarbha, Goorkhaland making such a demand. Unless we have sound Constitutional provisions, political instability, social unrest and violence cannot be averted by police and police leadership.

The present political crisis and violence is largely built on:

- Whipping up emotions on perceived neglect and injustices to Telangana.
- Irresponsible accusations, challenges and counter challenges by politicians.
- Provocative public statements that offend and stoke regional feelings.
- Hasty and unilateral announcement of Union Home Minister on 09.12.2009.
- Hidden political agenda of certain National and State political leaders.

Emotions on both sides need to be replaced with "public reasoning". Debates, discussions and writeups in print and electronic media by well informed and well meaning citizens, intellectuals will help to dispel misgivings, misunderstandings, wrong views held and spread on neglect and injustices with reference to facts and figures in order to arrive at comparative merits and demerits of the view of protagonists of separate State and its opponents. In such a scenario remaining united or parting will not lead to bitterness and hatred between the people of the two regions.

Index